Contents

List of Figures and Tables ix

Foreword, by Thomas H. Davenport xi

Acknowledgments xiii

Introduction 1
Mary Lee Kennedy
- Why the Intranet? 1
- Information Professionals 3
- The Challenges Information Professionals Face 4
- Conclusion 13

CHAPTER 1
Current State Considerations and Future Direction of Intranets 15
Mary Lee Kennedy, Ian Littlejohn, and Cory Costanzo
- Intranets Defined 15
- Current State 17
- Potential Drivers of Future Intranets 23
- Conclusion 30

CHAPTER 2
Roles Information Professionals Play 31
Mary Lee Kennedy and Angela Abell
- The Marketplace 31
- Drivers of New Roles 35
- Intranet Trends 38
- A Framework of Roles 41
- Putting a Team Together 46
- Ongoing Professional Development 49
- Conclusion 52

CHAPTER 3
Implementing an Intranet that Makes Sense ... 55
Mary Lee Kennedy
Step One: Start with the End in Mind ... 56
Step Two: Set the Scene that Supports the End ... 60
Step Three: Break It Down ... 62
Step Four: Define the Interdependencies ... 64
Step Five: Prioritize the Work ... 65
Step Six: Put a Program in Place ... 67
Step Seven: End with the Beginning in Mind ... 68
Step Eight: Begin a Continuous Loop ... 69
Conclusion ... 69

CHAPTER 4
Governance Roles and Responsibilities ... 73
Mary Lee Kennedy
What Is Governance and Why Does It Matter for an Intranet? ... 73
Considerations in Initiating a Governance Structure ... 74
Governance Scope, Relationships, and Timing ... 78
Governance with Partners, Allies, and Customers: How to Decide ... 79
When to Initiate a Governance Effort ... 81
The Forms of Governance ... 84
Organizational Culture and Governance ... 86
Governance Roles and Responsibilities ... 92
Conclusion ... 95

CHAPTER 5
Collaboration and Communities ... 97
Debra Wallace
Collaboration Is Not an Adjective ... 98
Elements of Collaboration ... 99
Sidebar: Addressing Inappropriate Collaboration at the University of Manitoba ... 100
Critical Success Factors of Effective Collaboration ... 102
Sidebar: Increasing Capabilities for Effective Collaboration at the IDRC ... 103

Intranets for Info Pros

Information Today, Inc.
Medford, New Jersey

First printing, 2007

Intranets for Info Pros

Library of Congress Cataloging-in-Publication Data

Intranets for info pros / edited by Mary Lee Kennedy and Jane Dysart.
p. cm.
Includes bibliographical references and index.
ISBN 978-1-57387-309-3
1. Intranets (Computer networks) 2. Information storage and retrieval systems. I. Kennedy, Mary Lee, 1958- II. Dysart, Jane, 1950-
HD30.385.158 2007
004.6'82--dc22

2007035572

President and CEO: Thomas H. Hogan, Sr.
Editor-in-Chief and Publisher: John B. Bryans
Managing Editor: Amy M. Reeve
VP Graphics and Production: M. Heide Dengler
Book Designer: Kara Mia Jalkowski
Cover Designer: Lisa Boccadutre
Copyeditor: Barbara Brynko
Proofreader: Dorothy Pike
Indexer: Sharon Hughes

Levels of Collaboration 104
Potential of Collaboration 106
Sidebar: Chuck Close and the Art of Collaboration 107
Defining Communities of Practice 107
Characteristics of Communities 109
Sidebar: Front and Center—CompanyCommand Builds Leadership Capacity in the U.S. Army 111
Sidebar: Building Capacity with Professional Learning Communities: York Region District School Board 114
Learning from Experience 117
Sidebar: Communispace—Taking Communities to the Customer 117
Conclusion 121
Recommended Resources 122

CHAPTER 6
Content Management for Intranets 125
Craig St. Clair
Why Do We Need to Manage Intranet Content? 126
Enter Content and Information Asset Management 129
Gaining Intellectual Control Over Existing Content 129
Taking the Lay of the Land: User Interviews and Surveys 130
Taking the Lay of the Land: Content Inventories and Audits 134
Putting It Together: Enterprise-Wide Views and Content Life Cycles 138
Three Models of Intranet Asset Management 139
Conclusion 146
Recommended Web Sites 148

CHAPTER 7
Writing for Intranets 149
Cynthia Ross Pedersen
Simple Communication 149
Sidebar: Top Lessons Learned 151
User-Centric Writing 151
Intranets Differ from Public Web Sites 152
Online Content 153

Understanding Scalable Content Through Chocolate Cake 154
Size and Tone 156
Choosing Content Formats 157
Tools for Intranet Content 158
Solving Common Content Issues 159
Sidebar: Skills and Competencies for Web Writers 160
Sidebar: Tailoring Procedures for Call Center Use Online 163
Legal and Compliance Content 166
Recommended Web Sites 166

CHAPTER 8
Corporate Portals and Intranets 169
Craig St. Clair and Jose Claudio Terra
The Concept of a Portal and a Corporate Portal 170
Assessing Corporate Portals: Four Perspectives 171
Standardization and Enterprise Suites 180
Looking into the Future 181
Conclusion 181
Recommended Web Sites 182

CHAPTER 9
Information Architecture 183
Mike Crandall
History 184
How Does Information Architecture Fit into an Intranet? 185
Key Components in IA 189
The IA Process 192
IA for Web Sites vs. Intranets 193
Current Developments in Information Architecture 194
Future Developments 195
Managing and Staffing for IA 198
Checklist for Success 202
Conclusion 202
Examples and Lessons Learned 203
Recommended Resources 205

CHAPTER 10
Intranet Search **207**
Avi Rappoport
Why Bother with Intranet Search? 207
The ROI of Search 207
Defining the Requirements for Intranet Search 208
Technical and Organizational Aspects of Search Implementation 209
Conclusion 225
Recommended Web Sites 226

CHAPTER 11
Designing the Ultimate End-User Experience: Separating Presentation and Content **227**
Eric Hards
Is Intranet Design Different from Internet Design? 228
The Design 230
Starting the Design 231
Sidebar: The Web Designer as Technologist 232
Conclusion 249

Afterword, by Mary Lee Kennedy **251**

Bibliography **255**

About the Contributors **263**

About the Editors **267**

Index **269**

List of Figures and Tables

Figure 1.1	Conceptual Framework of an Intranet	18
Figure 1.2	Understanding Product Requirements	21
Figure 2.1	The Role of Information Professionals as Translator	42
Figure 2.2	Categories of Organizational Knowledge	43
Figure 2.3	The Role of Information Professionals	48
Figure 2.4	Routes to Development	51
Figure 3.1	Typical High-Level Project Management Process	67
Figure 4.1	Common Governance Triggers	75
Figure 4.2	Intranet Adoption Curve	82
Figure 6.1	Beginning State: Multiple Disconnected Intranets	127
Figure 6.2	Centralized Repository	140
Figure 6.3	Hybrid Version	144
Figure 7.1	Sizing It Right	156
Figure 8.1	Four Perspectives on Corporate Portals	172
Figure 9.1	Features of the Three Generations of Information Architecture	186
Figure 9.2	The Interrelationship Between the Conceptual and Physical Design of the Library Web Site	187
Figure 9.3	The Elements of User Experience	188
Figure 9.4	Example of Information Architecture Organization for Intranet Portal	199
Figure 9.5	MSWeb External Relations	200
Figure 9.6	Information Architect Requirements	201
Figure 9.7	Information Architecture for Web Sites Checklist	203
Figure 9.8	Checkpoints for Enterprise IA Projects	204
Figure 10.1	Parts of the Search Process	209
Figure 10.2	Stanford University's Search Page	219
Figure 10.3	Bertelsmann's Search Page	220
Figure 10.4	Harvard University's Search Page	221
Figure 10.5	Query Frequency Distribution	225
Figure 11.1	Moving Information to the Home Page	233

Figure 11.2	Using Visual Design to Facilitate Scanning	235
Figure 11.3	Outlining the Home Page	237
Figure 11.4	Initial Sketch	240
Figure 11.5	MiamiDade.gov Home Page Before	241
Figure 11.6	MiamiDade.gov Home Page After	242
Figure 11.7	One Font Only	245
Figure 11.8	Color Chart Showing How Other Colors That Are Used to Separate Information Are Not Adversely Affected by Use of White	246
Figure 11.9	A Few Colors Are Sufficient to Separate Information	247
Figure 11.10	High Saturation Colors in the Web-Safe Color Palette	248

Table 2.1	Stakeholders in Information Management	47
Table 3.1	Variables in Understanding Customer Requirements	57
Table 3.2	Function and Feature Tracking	62
Table 3.3	Categories, and Exemplars Within Each, to Consider in Delivering on Required Functionality	63
Table 4.1	Differentiating Partners, Allies, and Customers	80
Table 4.2	Example Governance Elements by Intranet Adoption Stage	84
Table 4.3	Organizational Cultural Paradigms	87
Table 4.4	Organizational Motivators	92
Table 5.1	Community Linkages—Choices and Decisions	105

Foreword

If you're interested in intranets and in this book, you're probably coming at the subject from one of two different perspectives: You are likely to have either a background in IT or in library/information science. This book is at the intersection of those two domains, so from either perspective you'll have something to learn.

Information technology professionals typically know a lot about technology, and not very much about information. Knowing about technology in today's world is very useful, but knowing about information is important too. There are many intranets and other IT applications that perform perfectly well from a technological sense, but they don't contain useful information or they organize the information poorly, and as a result don't get used by anyone. If you already have expertise in technology, you'll benefit from the advice in this book about how information in intranets can be captured, organized, distributed, and—most importantly—used.

The other likely readers of this book come from a library or information professional background. Although I'm not an information professional, I feel a strong kinship with them. I have both the positive and negative attributes of many information professionals. On the positive side, I love books and libraries—always have, always will. I have always felt that the best information environments are a mix of computers, networks, and people with expertise. I believe that if you're going to do a good job of managing information, you need to know something about how it's categorized, indexed, and otherwise organized. I could be a card-carrying member of the Special Libraries Association (SLA).

I share some of the less positive traits of some information professionals too. I have occasionally been accused of preferring to spend time with books instead of people. I struggle with the fact that people don't seem to like to read books and newspapers much anymore, and I occasionally rant about the move to newer media. I think the Internet is incredible, but I want to hold on to reading rooms, stacks, and even card catalogues. I even hold a stubborn attraction to cushy corporate library facilities, even though I know they are rarely used.

So I can understand why some traditional information professionals may not fully or quickly embrace intranets and other aspects of modern information life. I can sympathize with those who prefer a nice leather binding to a nice Perl script. However, I also understand that to do so is tantamount to information professional suicide. The world is clearly leaving behind the physical artifacts that many information professionals love. What's left is primarily the Internet, intranets, and the applications, content, and collaboration that ride upon them. Unfortunately, most Internet users don't seem to feel that they need much help, although they would clearly benefit from it. It's going to be hard for information professionals to make a living assisting people with the Internet. That leaves intranets and content management as the key tasks for information professionals to do in the foreseeable future. In other words, if you want a good job as an information professional, you need to know a lot about the subject of this book.

Whatever perspective you come from, if you've opened this book and read this far, you've come to the right place to learn what you need to know. You just need to keep going. Perhaps nowhere else will you find such useful content on how information and IT professionals should view and leverage intranets. Most books on intranets focus exclusively on the technical issues they involve, but this book takes a broader perspective. You'll discover where intranets are going from a technical and business function perspective, but you'll also learn about issues such as roles and governance, portals, collaboration, and so forth. The topics are tailored to the concerns of information professionals, but they are also cognizant of the fact that intranets are inherently a technical vehicle involving IT expertise. While the book is not a detailed overview of content management—the other key topic for information professionals—it does describe important CM issues in the context of intranets.

I doubt we'll still be reading this book in a decade because what constitutes an intranet is changing pretty rapidly. But as of the publication of this book, everything in the book is current and spot-on for today's organizations. Mary Lee Kennedy and the other contributors all have substantial expertise working with world-class organizations on their intranet issues. The only other advice I have is to read quickly: You need this knowledge and you need it now!

—Thomas H. Davenport
President's Distinguished Professor of
Information Technology and Management
Babson College
Wellesley, Massachusetts

Acknowledgments

Writing a book on intranets for information professionals is only possible with the input and contributions of many people. So there are many people to thank. First and foremost, I would like to thank Jane Dysart, who came to me with the book idea and helped to ensure it was completed. The authors contributed their knowledge and expertise, as well as a lot of time, in documenting their work and experience in each chapter. This work was only possible given the extensive contributions by Angela Abell, Cory Costanzo, Mike Crandall, Eric Hards, Ian Littlejohn, Avi Rappoport, Cindy Ross Pedersen, Craig St. Clair, Jose Claudio Terra, and Deb Wallace. I am especially grateful to the organizations that allowed us to include real-life work in the book. To them and the ultimate practitioners, we thank you. Several individuals helped make the book better for the reader. Thanks very much to Gosia Stergios, whose amazing research support ensured that we captured the best possible information available today in the published world, and helped to ensure the information was presented and cited correctly. Cory Costanzo and Jacqueline Dysart assisted with formatting work. We would not have completed the book without George Stergios, who ensured we met our editorial requirements. We probably could do more—and the world of the intranet is changing before our very eyes—however, we believe that with the hundred or so years of experience represented here, we can share something of value with our profession.

Ultimately, this book is for the practitioner. We hope the reader can apply the ideas and build on the applications and guidance offered in this book. It is intended for you.

—Mary Lee Kennedy

Introduction

Mary Lee Kennedy
TKG Consulting LLC

Why the Intranet?

Over the past decade, there has been a constant buzz about the Internet—perhaps the single most disruptive information technology in the last 100 years. The disruptive nature of the Internet in a vast cross-section of our world is well documented. Like other communication-based technologies (the phone, the TV, the radio), the Internet contributes to and creates an awareness of the porous nature of the world's activities and perspectives, in terms of how we interact with each other and how we interact with documented knowledge. It has had an affect on the ease with which we transcend our personal and professional lives. More than anything else, the Internet and Internet-based technologies enable an expectation of seamless and real-time movement of ideas, expertise, and information, regardless of our location or physical state. This is further defined by the devices we choose to use, as well as the format in which we contribute to or interact with information and knowledge. Our preferences for conveying and locating information and knowledge have changed dramatically in a very short time. We know that a seamless experience remains elusive, but users are expecting and demanding such an experience, a demand which increases along with ever more sophisticated expectations from solutions. For instance, Skype and other VoIP-enabled communication are enabled in intranet collaboration spaces at a low or no-fee cost to organizations. The Google Desktop toolbar provides seamless access to information for end users, along with new analytics offerings and decision-making tools for Web administrators. Fifteen years ago, this would have been science fiction and, even three years ago, completely unaffordable, let alone free.

While as individuals, we are free to choose to use these technologies to enrich our personal lives, and many of us have taken advantage of what the Internet has to offer, within organizations, there is a much more involved decision-making process that impacts the degree to which individuals can use these technologies. It is rarely an individual's choice. While users have the freedom of choice within the seemingly limitless possibilities of the Internet, there are many layers of decision-making with respect to information and knowledge sharing in an organization that removes or creates tensions between groups and between individuals within the context of the overarching organizational objectives. In the context of organizations with various expectations to consider, the job of information professionals is to enable the framework in which the best set of options are available for making choices—sometimes as decision-makers themselves or often as experts who are called to help others make the decisions. The intranet is one of the main platforms in which the decisions can be implemented.

At the simplest level, the intranet is the Internet with a firewall around it. What makes an intranet so different from the Internet has much to do with organizational dynamics. Chapter 4, Governance Roles and Responsibilities, aims to help information professionals understand the levers to engage in making decisions and implementing solutions.

It is interesting to see what the Internet was and what it has become. In a phone survey more than a decade ago, *Macworld* asked a few hundred people what they thought would be worth paying $10 per month for on the Internet. The top results included educational courses, reference books, electronic voting, and library information. The bottom results included sports statistics, role-playing games, gambling, and dating. Today, one will find that actual practice shows the inverse. Conversely, an intranet is mainly content dedicated to reference books, policies and procedures, course materials, transactional applications, and library-based information. An intranet is usually offered for free as part of tax-based systems, or at the very most, within security structures. Pay-per-view is not common on an intranet. In fact, many intranets are little more than communication vehicles or information repositories. Their potential for enabling the successful achievement of organizational objectives remains largely untapped. In fact, a survey of 101 organizations about intranet use conducted by Jane McConnell in 2006 shows that only 13 percent of those senior executives polled consider the intranet to be "business critical."

So it is no surprise that intranets are largely communication-focused (or repository gateways) rather than productivity-focused (or integrated with core organizational workflows). Integration and alignment are very difficult, particularly in complex organizations. But before we slam the door on intranets, consider that McConnell also found that the respondents believe that the full potential of intranets in decision-making has yet to be realized. This suggests an untapped opportunity for information professionals. While the Internet grows by leaps and bounds, intranets continue to find their way slowly. There is a real challenge out there for information professionals to define and demonstrate the potential of intranets. Chapter 1, Current State Considerations and Future Direction of Intranets, provides a context in which we can consider ways to achieve that potential.

Information Professionals

For the purposes of this book, an information professional is defined as any individual with training in and responsibility for facilitating the exchange of ideas, expertise, and information between people, or between people and documented knowledge. The subject of their work is the user, provider, or contributor of the information as well as the ways in which the information and its exchange is organized and made available in usable forms and formats. In this book, the landscape in which that work is done is the intranet. The experience of the information user, provider, or contributor is dependent on the interaction that the information professional creates and enables between himself or herself and the information, including the context in which the interaction takes place. Information professionals are essential to the design, implementation, and continued improvement of the experience people have when engaged with information, ideas, and expertise in making sense of a given situation, when creating new knowledge, or when making a decision. Done well, their work is taken for granted; if it is done poorly, it is ignored, or worse yet, it can get in the way.

Information professionals may be highly visible to the ultimate user, for example, reference librarians, Web interface designers, and usability testers. They may also be invisible to the ultimate user, for example, those working in content management, search engine optimization, and metadata management. Regardless, their work has become part of the ubiquitous fabric of information made possible through the development of the Internet. If the vision of Web 2.0 is realized, information and the work of information professionals have the potential to be even more widespread. Information will be available in multiple formats and in bits that are segmented according to very specific contexts. Information will be embedded in naturally occurring and secure workflows. As an information professional at a Fortune 50 company put it: "Just in time, just enough, just for me."

The ubiquitous nature of information has led to much identity-seeking that continues today without a clear resolution. Job titles, fields of study, and the very question of whether the discipline is professional in nature still remain open for discussion. It is not the intention of this work to argue for or against certification programs, or to judge the post-secondary educational degree programs that are producing many of the current practitioners. The focus here is not on the "idea" of an information professional, rather it is on what information professionals do in the context of an intranet, which has become the landscape for the exchange of ideas, expertise, and information. The book presents the practitioner's perspective, based on the work of leading practitioners and of those who study practitioner behavior. With the primary focus on the information professional, we have dedicated Chapter 2, Roles Information Professionals Play, to the practitioners' role in an electronically enabled, complex information and knowledge-sharing environment.

The Challenges Information Professionals Face

Organizational Complexity

Intranets are part of the organization that puts them in place, and, as such, they are subject to the organizational dynamics. Organizations are internally variable and work interactively with changing external environments. They have several significant moving parts that affect the ways in which information and knowledge are exchanged, including such elements as work design (physical and virtual space, reporting relationships, information networks, procedures, and regulations), human resource management (skills and competencies, reward and recognition, and learning), information management systems (IT, content management, and metadata schemas), governance, leadership, and culture (values and beliefs), and human dynamics (perceived influence, individual motivations, and individual capabilities). This complexity can be exacerbated with size, conflicting objectives, language, and cultural differences. Organizations exist in complex environments as well: Customers, partners, benefactors, economies, markets, and competitors, even entire industries can and do impact the organization in predictable and unpredictable ways. Information professionals are faced with the challenge of aligning the functionality of an intranet-based offering of products and services in the context of highly dynamic environments—in essence deciding where to start and what to do to make a significant difference.

Most intranets grew as grassroots efforts until it became impossible to find anything. Many information professionals were first asked to help find information within the unstructured information repositories. "Findability" is dependent on organizational decisions around roles and responsibilities, degrees to which individuals are held accountable for quality information, and knowledge transfer, security levels, and accessibility. In highly dynamic, flattening, and porous organizations, many information professionals are struggling with what information to manage, how much effort to focus on internal or external information sharing, and when to integrate information into natural workflows. Knowing the difference depends on determining where the greatest opportunities lie and then figuring out how best to get there. Understanding the organization is therefore key and difficult.

Effective alignment can and does help. Alignment means being embedded in the life of the organization so as to be able to adjust or instinctively change with shifts in the environment. Few information professionals are truly integrated seamlessly with the core processes of an organization. While IT is considered a strategic enabler for many organizations, the broader context of information management and knowledge sharing is less understood and not always as tangible or exciting as a new technology. Many organizations are well aware of the challenges they present in terms of change. However, the question also remains about the effort needed to formalize alignment of sharing with workflow. What is the visible difference? This book aims to show examples of work that has made a difference and to help information professionals consider how to best align themselves within their own organizational context. Chapter 3 focuses on implementing an intranet that makes sense, and Chapter 4 focuses on governance roles and responsibilities.

The Nature of Information Work and Knowledge Sharing

In the early 1990s, information-intensive activities resided in the hands of experts in financial services, professional services, defense, and transportation. In fact, there was quite a debate about how to define a knowledge worker, with a significant divide between those who created knowledge and everybody else. Today, most industries—and individuals—are information dependent. Early adopters of information-intensive work, including information workers (i.e., anyone who uses information to do their work), are found in service-based organizations such as healthcare and education, manufacturing (e.g., parts manufacturers), and energy (e.g., oil and gas companies). With the pervasiveness of information and information sharing, information workers are constantly dealing with information overload: They must balance their attention with the need to keep up with and contribute to information sharing and knowledge creation across geographies and cultures. They live with an increasing expectation that cognitively (computer-aided or not) they will make sense of large quantities of structured and unstructured data.

In the late 1990s, the emphasis was on managing structured data and on storing documents as a part of formal information-management and knowledge-capture procedures. To do this, the organization instructed its workforce to follow carefully orchestrated and managed linear processes where step (a) was expected to precede step (b). The linear, rigid process flow reflected the principles that were predominant in the Industrial Age. Today, in the knowledge economy where the collective knowledge of an organization is its greatest asset, there is a growing acceptance that most information workers live in a world of multitasking and continuous partial attention. We know their needs for information forms and formats vary and they are usually situation-specific, limitless in terms of natural boundaries such as language and physical place, and more sophisticated in terms of expectations around personalization. Coupled with this is an understanding that many current information workers—and upcoming generations of workers—still prefer to share information directly (i.e., person-to-person, with varying degrees of trust), unencumbered by process and formality, through any number of preferred communications channels, Web-based or otherwise. Past efforts demonstrated that formal requirements of information workers to document their tacit knowledge in explicit forms rarely succeeded, unless mandated by policy or regulatory requirements. Even then, there are limits to what is reasonable. Today, with the significant concerns about "lost knowledge" as a result of aging populations in countries such as the U.S., Japan, and Europe, it is impossible for organizations to explicitly capture all potentially important lost knowledge. Given this understanding of user preferences, what can information professionals do as enablers of information and knowledge exchanges? This question will be addressed throughout the book as we explore some of the information behaviors in the 21st century that the information professional will want to understand.

Information workers tend to multitask and to work in an environment of continuous partial attention. They move between tasks and between applications as they interact with a variety of roles and people at the same time, taking on different identities depending on the interaction they are having (e.g., as an individual contributor or manager, as a decision-maker or researcher). The changing nature of information work remains the subject of continued study, with recent work on continuous partial attention by Linda Stone, and the cognitive impact of multitasking by Joshua Rubenstein, David E. Meyer, and Jeffrey E. Evans. These cognitive differences are particularly important as organizations look to transfer knowledge between generations of workers, on-board individuals at different stages of their professional life, and introduce new technologies and work designs. The need to be sensitive to the nature of information work and information workers is not new, although it seems to be significantly impacted by the introduction of new technologies, the flattening of organizations, and the fluid nature of organizations' work today.

The intranet enables the work of individuals and groups of individuals. It is helpful to understand collaboration and community building in order to enable effective information and knowledge exchanges. Collaboration is becoming a critical skill and an underlying principle of the 21st-century information worker (e.g., contributions to Wikipedia, the depth of research and consulting practices focused on social networking, and the significant discussions around university and industrial labs collaboration in the applied sciences). Given the collaborative emphasis in many organizations today (either through interdisciplinary, interorganizational, cross-functional, or flattened hierarchies), one needs to take into account the social nature of information work as documented through social network analysis, communities of practice, and studies on virtual collaboration, as well as those studies that review cognitive processes and preferences that transform information into knowledge, and knowledge into decision-making.

Collaboration is made up of individuals. Individuals tend to share information iteratively and within a perceived understanding of a given context. They become cognizant of the knowledge they need or have to share, and at the same time, they are seeking to make sense of the context in which they are participating. If we put it another way, there is a commonly held principle of knowledge management: "I only know what I need to know when I need to know it." In other words, you do not know what you know until you need to know it. Individuals also bring past experiences and perceptions with them when seeking out understanding. These experiences and perceptions affect the way they act and interact when exchanging knowledge. Individuals engage in "sense-making" as they interact iteratively to understand the context in which they find themselves—seeking or gaining clarity. They seek understanding in order to make decisions. On the other hand, they may use what they understand to create new knowledge upon which others will make decisions and act.

There are, in broad terms, three schools of thought on sense-making, which the reader may want to explore for a better understanding of individual behavior in organizations. The Modernists base their work on the science models of Isaac Newton and Karl Popper. They use normative methods such as Six Sigma. The Post-Modernists base their work on the science model of Kuhn. They use methods such as appreciative inquiry, storytelling, and intense facilitation. The Naturalizers base their work on the cognitive science and the science of complexity. They use methods such as pattern recognition and emergence. Sense-making is important to the study of information use and the ability of an intranet to enable effective use and exchange, in order to explore how individuals will engage with it in making sense of their surroundings. Three recent models of sense-making are also defined here. In his book *The Knowing Organization,* Chun Wei Choo offers a model that focuses on the way information is used and how sense-making interacts with knowledge creation and decision-making. Brenda Dervin's model analyzes information seeking and use in terms of a "situation-gap-use" triangle designed to answer the following three questions:

1. What in your situation is stopping you from moving forward?
2. What questions or confusions do you have?
3. What kind of help do you hope to get?

Dave Snowden's work highlights the need we have to manage for serendipity (i.e., placing ourselves in situations where we can encounter what he calls "happy accidents") and the need to be enabled to synthesize new meaning and understanding. The very essence of innovation, organizational change, and learning requires it. He employs narrative techniques such as anecdote circles and two-stage emergence to identify knowledge objects and organizational dynamics. Narrative techniques also assist with capturing that which we do not know we do not know. In the context of sense-making, much is yet to be learned as to how an intranet can help. As an enabler, the information professional will want to consider the role that the intranet plays in decision-making and knowledge creation, and this will require an understanding of sense-making.

It will not be a surprise to the reader that the intranet has the potential to be, and often is, an enabler of learning and decision-making. Therefore, by extension, the process of designing and implementing a virtual experience, such as is possible with an intranet, requires an understanding of learning and decision-making preferences. Preferences may be represented in terms of instructor-led, self-paced, peer- or mentor-based learning, as well as content formats (video, text, slide decks, and voice) and the ways in which decisions are made (e.g., individually, through consensus, or through broad-based collaboration). However, information professionals must go beyond the obvious (form, format, and communication method) and understand the basics that affect their readiness to even participate—the essence of being part of a collaborative effort or a community, an understanding of how individuals and organizations enable sense-making for decision-making and knowledge creation. Chapter 5, Collaboration and Communities, addresses the topic of community and collaboration, predominant attributes of today's organizations and one the intranet has the potential to influence significantly.

The Nature of Information Management

The foundational work in the 1980s on data, information, and knowledge in organizations (see Davenport and Prusak, 1998) and the work on tacit and explicit information and knowledge (see Nonaka and Takeuchi, 1995; Leonard and Swap, 2005) are important to understanding the nature of information and knowledge creation and sharing. Over time, of course, the nature of information management has changed. Early on, most information professionals tried to pin information and knowledge down by structuring it in ways that deposited it in repositories. The Web changed this dramatically by enabling anyone to publish anything as unstructured material. Now there is much work to integrate structured and unstructured material, and content and data. Information professionals tried to manage it all (structured and unstructured) by adding metadata tags, but there were not enough information professionals to do the job, and there was not enough willpower in most organizations to get anyone else to spend time doing it either. In the meantime, the amount of information available for broader and broader use exponentially increased and was deposited in more and more places (such as hard drives, virtual drives, wikis, portals, shared drives, and memory sticks). Information professionals became more practical and worked with organizations to prioritize the information that needed to be codified. They created knowledge maps, information audits, workflow analysis, and two-by-two prioritization tables to make sense of what mattered most to decision-makers, innovators, and analysts. Business rules were developed to guide actions taken to improve practice, leveraging past successes and failures. Even these efforts have led to errors (most publicly in the healthcare field)—some as costly as the loss of human life. Clearly, information and knowledge are not straightforward propositions.

Because of the proliferation of structured data and the large datasets most organizations work with, the proliferation of multimedia formats (e.g., podcasts, Webinars, and videolinks) used in publishing and education, and the growth of collaborative authoring tools such as blogs and wikis, maintaining information quality on an intranet is a significant challenge. While many intranets remain publishing platforms, more are becoming collaboration spaces where the materials have the potential to change radically over time. This book seeks to assist the information professional with decisions that must be made about information quality for an intranet in Chapter 6, Content Management for Intranets, and in Chapter 7, Writing for Intranets.

The Nature of Web Technologies

In 2001, the Information Worker Productivity Council (a now-defunct industry-based research group) completed an assessment of information workers' use of various technologies within organizations to communicate, store, and share information. The survey focused on e-mail, instant messenger (IM), portals, Web sites, the phone, and personal devices (PDAs), such as BlackBerrys. Today, this list would be even more varied, with the addition of VoIP technologies, RSS feeds, wikis, blogs, podcasts, and Webinars. Information professionals must be savvy about the advantages and disadvantages of each instrument as well as variations in software functionality within any one type. The purpose and relative strength of the medium is as important as the quality of the exchange or information within it.

Three shifts related to the Web and Web technologies are important to consider today: Web 2.0, the Long Tail, and Agile Computing. They stand out because of their impact on information use and the exchange of knowledge. From a purely technological perspective, Web 2.0 is software, database, and Web service rolled into one. This is particularly appealing to organizations as the need to upgrade legacy systems (an extremely expensive proposition) may be reduced and therefore may be less of a distraction to their efforts. With portals becoming a mainstay of many organizations, the reader will want to review Chapter 8 on portals and intranets, particularly with a view on how Web 2.0 changes user expectations of portals.

Ideally, a Web 2.0-based platform improves as more people use and contribute to it. In fact, Web 2.0 is designed to create the capability to take advantage of the organizations' collective intelligence. Information architecture, particularly those elements related to the use and management of metadata and the design and implementation of "wayfinding" tools, plays an important role. Chapter 9, Information Architecture, seeks to assist information professionals in understanding the opportunity and requirements of implementing information architecture.

The "Long Tail" is a name popularized by Chris Anderson's 2004 article in *Wired Magazine* about the opportunity for Internet-based businesses to increase sales by focusing on the information sought at the long end of the tail. It is based on a long-known feature of statistical distributions (Zipf, Power laws, Pareto distributions, and/or general Lévy distributions). In these distributions, a high-frequency or high-amplitude population is followed by a low-frequency or low-amplitude population that gradually "tails off." Imagine a large hump on the left-hand side of the screen with a long tail extending to the right. In terms of the intranet, there is an opportunity to surface the information in the long end of the tail, which may represent a greater proportion of the knowledge created and shared than that represented in the shorter end. Chapter 10, Intranet Search, focuses on search and seeks to support information professionals' work in designing and implementing search services that meet their organization's needs, including those characterized by the Long Tail.

The Web has always been dynamic. While early work adopted formal, often protracted, application development processes (e.g., waterfall techniques), today the Web is benefiting from the principles inherent in Agile Computing—an iterative design methodology that engages a direct dialog between the customer and the development team. Agile Computing gets the product out the door faster, with compelling user acceptance. Information professionals with an understanding of user behavior, organizational priorities, and technical and business parameters will improve the outcome of their products and services. Chapter 11, Designing the Ultimate End-User Experience: Separating Presentation and Content, provides the information professional with design principles and practices for intranet-based products.

The nature of information technologies, and particularly Web-based technologies, is that it is not always easy to predict what will happen next. Ten years ago, we did not have Flickr, Wikipedia, or folksonomies. Recent changes are just as dramatic. Consider the recent growth and popularity of rule-based software for decision-making (Cognos), the transmission of holographic images that transport people to engage in conference-type discussions (see Kurzweil Technologies), the ability to use patterning software to make sense of large sets of unstructured data or text-based information (see Cognitive Edge), as well as the much-discussed semantic Web. Information professionals both contribute to and benefit from the innovative forces in high technology enabled by new developments, such as the proliferation of services offered by Google and content made accessible through Open Source efforts.

What will come next? The Afterword provides a context in which information professionals might consider their contribution to the intranet (e.g., making it a more useful platform for information and knowledge exchange).

Conclusion

Information professionals exist and function within a complex environment that is highly dynamic internally and as part of a larger ecosystem. It is not always possible or even desirable to understand all the forces that lead to changes within the context of the intranet. However, it is our responsibility to ensure our work enables the information and knowledge exchanges that may lead to relevant and valuable information-based work, whether it is through sense-making, knowledge creation, or decision-making, and whether the person is a receiver of, contributor to, or participant in an exchange. The intranet is one of the landscapes in which information work occurs. It is a strategic, but largely untapped, landscape that is influenced significantly by the Internet and other new technology developments that affect our personal lives. This book aims to provide the reader with an understanding of its potential, with practical guidance about the fundamentals that can be employed to add value to an organization.

CHAPTER 1

Current State Considerations and Future Direction of Intranets

Mary Lee Kennedy
TKG Consulting LLC

Ian Littlejohn
ICP Consulting

Cory Costanzo
ABT Associates

Intranets Defined

Intranets are key enablers of the information and knowledge-sharing experience created between people within organizations. They represent part of a larger ecosystem that includes information technology platforms such as productivity tools (e.g., word processing, presentation software, Web-conferencing), Internet sites, extranets, IT applications, and even older forms of organizational information (e.g., online catalogs and paper-filing cabinets). By itself, the introduction of an IT platform, a filing cabinet, or an enterprise information platform will not ensure successful adoption of information and knowledge-sharing. Over time, it has become clear that there is a holistic view that needs to be understood in order to bring about successful adoption and an ongoing exchange of ideas, expertise, and information. The ecosystem is made up of people, processes, content, and technology.

The opportunities offered by the very existence of an intranet have evolved over the past 10 to 15 years. Originally, intranets were a series of static HTML pages. Today, they are dynamic and complex. They may host applications that access information from a variety of information stores (e.g., files, databases, and dialogue among people, e-mail, and documents). Intranets access these information stores through a variety of applications, including portals, collaboration sites, and line-of-business applications (such as performance management or procurement). These applications leverage search metaphors that access content management systems and search engines, are protected by security protocols, and are guided by metrics. Intranets are used for real-time conferencing, for expertise location and real-time conversations, as well as for team collaboration. Today, companies conduct global meetings on intranets. The idea that an author can create a page and place it in the public domain is really encapsulated today in the form of blogs and wikis. While some intranets are still viable as static HTML pages, the ability to manage massive amounts of information in dynamic workplaces means that intranets have had to become more dynamic and complicated themselves.

Just as intranets embrace both static and dynamic information, they are more than just silos for content; they are becoming communities themselves. Intranets, as enablers of a connected enterprise, bring together individual, team, unit, and organization-wide virtual spaces. Today, they reflect the multidisciplinary, cross-cultural, and cross-boundary nature of work. The global nature of all sectors in today's working environment complicates matters further by requiring an understanding of culture and the ability to support local needs. Culture, though, is not unique to geography, language, or ethnic origin. Culture can vary from one subsection of an organization to another, and language varies between disciplines, sometimes yielding situations where the same word can have very different meanings. This creates the need for information professionals to understand how work gets done from the user's perspective. In fact, there has been a resurgence of business process analysis, something that emerged in the 1980s under the guise of business process reengineering. In many circles, intranets are being viewed in terms of meeting business requirements and are understood in the context of business process alignment.

Successful intranets come in various shapes and sizes. In considering the future value of the intranet, this chapter focuses on current trends, long-term bets, and critical takeaways for information professionals involved in intranet design, implementation, and management.

Current State

Simply put, the intranet is an Internet with a firewall around it. This description requires additional explanation about what happens behind a firewall. The intranet is many things; a one-word description does not do justice to the complexities inherent to the intranet world. However, Figure 1.1 outlines a perspective on the more common components found in an intranet environment. These are the nuts and bolts or, if you like, functional components. They do not represent either the technology choices or the organizational design requirements that make an intranet useful within a given context.

Figure 1.1 suggests areas that need to be considered when reviewing an intranet, starting with an understanding of how the user wants and needs to interface with the medium, and considering some ways in which the end-users are able to interact with personalized content and customized displays, to communicate and collaborate, to receive alerts, to know when a colleague is present, and to understand how to use the most important parts for their work. Information professionals also need to consider the work it takes to integrate resources that have been organized through structured methods such as taxonomy and classification tools, and through processes (either automated or human-intensive). The intranet must provide metrics and support security, privacy, authentication, informed decision-making with respect to governance, content management, and "findability." Ideally, an intranet is designed with little need for user education, but in all likelihood, there will need to be an education and user-assistance component. Figure 1.1 provides a conceptual framework in which to understand the basic elements of the intranet.

Essentially, the intranet has the potential of being whatever it can and should be, given the resource restrictions and organizational boundaries surrounding it. There are an enormous number of technology choices to be made when looking at intranet applications, and custom-built applications continue to be a popular choice for many organizations. These choices can fluctuate depending on resident expertise, strength of senior sponsorship, technology integration costs, sophistication of user expectations, and (of course) available budget.

As discussed previously, intranets were initially made up of static pages intended for communicating work previously covered in print or for providing access to documents such as policies and procedures

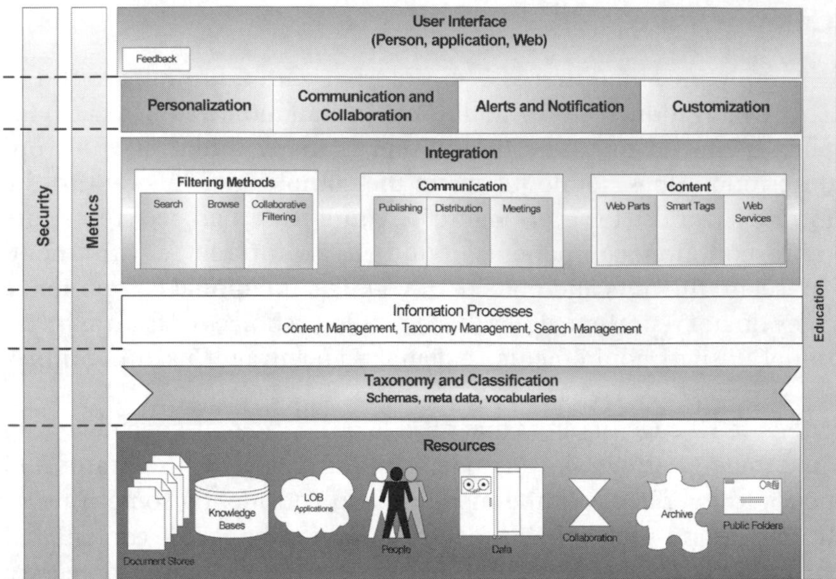

Figure 1.1 Conceptual Framework of an Intranet

that could be located through Web technologies. It was the electronic copycat of print publications. Today, intranets still can do this, but they are also used to enable a variety of activities including, but not limited to, interactive communication such as presence management, collaboration, e-learning, project management, market intelligence, and performance reviews. While text was originally the primary form, an intranet now provides access to a multitude of media forms. The intranet was once a one-size-fits-all solution in the early days, but it has moved on to personalized context. Gone are the debates regarding customization; the focus is now geared toward personalization, collaborative filtering, and even intranets-on-the-go, as accessed through mobile devices. In fact, an intranet has the potential to enable almost anything an organization needs to do. Nielsen Norman Group's report, "Intranet Design Annual 2006," highlighted some of the best intranets and demonstrated applications ranging from individual productivity to group collaboration and from one-way communication to interactive communication. Examples included intranets that enable the following:

- Internal communications
- Administrative tasks

- Procurement
- Searching and collaborative filtering
- Training and e-learning
- Team collaboration
- Messaging

A significant challenge for intranets has been deciding what needs to be managed and what does not. A Web site is the product of a scientific effort with highly managed content, studied and calculated audience targeting, and dependencies on relationships with services such as Google, Yahoo!, and other Internet aggregation mechanisms that expose sites and their related content. Certainly, the individual empowerment afforded by the Internet remains, creating an environment where a business of one has the potential to compete with a business of thousands, or where the voice of one has the potential of connecting with the voice of thousands. In fact, it has been fairly common practice among intranet practitioners to review developments on the Internet and think about what might make sense in the intranet world.

While the Internet can be a good predictor of what will be successful on an intranet, a significant difference is emerging: The intranet is focused more and more on individual and group productivity, whether through deliberate top-down direction (such as increasing employee understanding of organizational direction, supporting talent management, and decision-making) or through team choices (such as project sites). While there certainly are collaborative filtering elements on an Internet, it remains focused on information sharing through "publishing," including blogs and wikis, as well as leveraging significant commercial platforms for transactions such as online banking and monetary exchanges. Both intranets and the Internet share common elements in search, navigation, and the need to deliver a predictable experience. Still, intranets remain a less-orchestrated experience, often tied together through some minimal amount of branding, templates, and information architecture standards. The Internet is a heavily studied, monitored, and resourced experience. An intranet is usually a mosaic that is organized, at best, by an information architecture and governance structure and, at worst, not at all. Intranets continue to struggle with the natural tension between grassroots authoring and collaboration, and top-down direction and the need to lead.

While technology continues to be a strong focal point when developing an intranet, more organizations realize that a deep understanding of information-user behavior and organizational priority setting needs to drive decision-making. Intranet users can be very sophisticated, particularly those for whom the Internet is a part of their daily lives. Users expect a significant degree of relevance and alignment but rarely understand why this does not occur. Given user interaction on the Internet with presence management, electronic shopping, context-sensitive search results, collaboration with strangers and best friends, multimedia forms of information delivery, and the highly interactive nature of authoring, role playing, and gaming, users have an expectation that these options are possible in an organization as well. Intranets are simply an extension of their lives—one more place where they can work with each other and find what they need. These users expect to move seamlessly from one virtual environment to the other. But this is rarely the case. Organizations still tend to dismiss functionality, such as instant messaging (IM), that may be considered a distraction. Security worries can also be a concern. Given that intranets are only just beginning to integrate applications, there is not always a solid understanding of their benefit to worker productivity as individuals, between individuals, or between functions.

Alan Cooper's work in the late 1990s on the value of the user perspective on software development expanded to the Web. The development of personas as a reflection of user requirements has had a significant impact on Internet and intranet user design, whether the design is for a Web site or a Web-based application. Work done by TKG Consulting expanded this concept by taking into consideration the user experience as recounted by the users themselves—not as opinion or desire, but as an articulation of the actual experience or experiences. Traditionally, personas have been built based on observations made by information designers through methods such as contextual inquiry or workplace ethnography. This is then complemented by market analysis and by formal usability studies. The addition of experience as narrated by the users themselves adds the perception that drives their user behavior. Figure 1.2 expands Cooper's original work to include collective experience as a significant factor in informing user requirements. The major components in establishing a product design (including functionality, features,

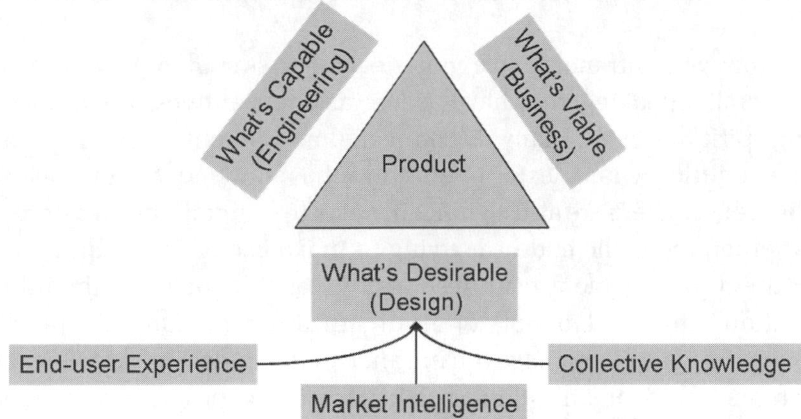

Figure 1.2 Understanding Product Requirements (Source: Cooper, Alan. *The Inmates Are Running the Asylum: Why High Tech Products Drive Us Crazy and How to Restore the Sanity*. Indianapolis: Sams Publishing, 1999: 73)

and content) in such a process are depicted in Figure 1.2. Desirability and tolerance for price or user cost need to be balanced against more traditional issues such as reliability and desired functionality. Figure 1.2 outlines the important considerations information professionals need to be aware of in understanding product requirements.

Desirability is defined by the following:

- End-user experience studies such as contextual inquiry and usability
- An assessment of market behavior based on market research on peers, leaders, or potential disruptive innovations
- A review of collective experience as expressed through patterns that emerge from shared user experiences

Capability focuses on skills and competencies that can be brought to bear on product development. This is usually done through a capability assessment review. Viability focuses on organizations' boundaries in terms of willingness to commit resources (people and money) to develop and manage a product. Ultimately, a decision will be made, but the decision usually comes down to what the organization believes it can get for what it can afford as prioritized against its objectives.

However, intranets have not developed in an organized way. Generally speaking, they have been grassroots entities. The pioneering spirit has led to many disconnected and potentially very expensive entities where experimentation has not led to any visible difference. There are also significant costs to maintaining an intranet, whether one is the end-user trying to make use of the medium, the content management team responsible for the quality of the information being used (or not), or the organization that funds the people to do the work. To manage the intranet so that it delivers a visible difference, many organizations, particularly in the past five years, have initiated governance processes. The governance process provides a setting for the decision-making framework. Ultimately, what is created on an intranet will be a combination of what any given individual chooses to do on it and the framework that the organization chooses to put in place to empower the individual and groups within the organization. Governance, communication, education, and even performance management will influence the usefulness of an intranet. However, understanding the governance structure (either formal or informal) that makes most sense at any given point in time in the life cycle of an intranet is critical. Building communication channels that will create affinity groups that learn together, and managers who will have a clear understanding of the skills needed, including the significant interdisciplinary skills to provide the capability to leverage information and knowledge sharing, can be facilitated through a decision-making framework that brings all interested parties together.

As we mentioned before, an intranet can be many things. Knowing what an intranet should be for a given organization requires a studied approach—an approach that not all organizations have the expertise or time to undertake. However, more organizations have intranets and are faced with a series of challenging questions, such as the following:

1. What can an intranet do in terms of making our organization more successful?
2. What skills and competencies do we need to have to make an intranet successful?

3. How does an intranet relate to the other information technology plans we have?
4. Who owns the intranet?
5. How will we know if we are doing the right things?
6. What have other organizations done that worked or did not work?

Chapter 2 of this book helps answer some of these tough questions. Cases are cited throughout the book to apply learning from other organizations.

Potential Drivers of Future Intranets

Intranets are underexploited in many organizations. More opportunities are appearing to integrate them. Exactly what this should look like depends on the organization, and, if the past is any predictor of the future, will likely be driven significantly by expectations based on the Internet. In other words, as organizational and individual needs change with respect to information, ideas, and expertise sharing, so too will their work environments continue to evolve. While technology is likely to continue to enable increasingly sophisticated choices, managing expectations and ensuring intranets are relevant, reliable, and accurate, it will rely on an intersection of technology, organizational need, and the capacity of the organization to meet the needs and to identify and prioritize them appropriately. Individuals may—or may not—choose to leverage the intranet to share knowledge with others, whether informally or formally. With increased activity in social networks, information professionals face the challenge of enabling strong and useful bonds between the external world and the internal organization. In fact, there is a merging of the Internet and the intranet—what was once called the extranet. The firewall moves depending on who we let into our circle. In other words, technology is now integral to the way organizations work, which is taken for granted, as is the ability to work across boundaries and within different groups regardless of whether they are part of our organization. What this really means is that intranets are now part of the very complexity inherent in human interaction, and information professionals must be ready to address topics such as privacy, social networks, learning styles, decision-making styles, and user behavior such as multitasking and continuous partial attention, as well as traditional areas such as content management, taxonomy, and skills more suited to information management rather than tacit knowledge exchanges.

One can argue that, within any organization, the degree to which individual and group productivity increases, or the degree to which an organization takes advantage of what it knows, is significantly impacted by the ability of the organization to exchange ideas, expertise, and information. Certainly studies on innovation (see Clayton Christensen) or new management challenges on attracting and keeping talent (see the Oct. 6, 2006 issue of *The Economist*) reflect this principle. Anyone in an organization concerned about the aging workforce knows well how critical the knowledge exchanges are (see Dave DeLong). The intranet has a role to play here—far beyond its roots as a communication vehicle. The context of knowledge sharing is very complex, though, and, coupled with the fact that organizations and individuals are ready at different times to adopt technologies to assist in this, intranet-based collaboration becomes challenging. For some organizations, pressure to do so will originate with an external impetus. Other organizations will be more interested in identifying opportunities for themselves and then trying them out. To understand how to work with these very different tolerances for risk, or even seekers of change, information professionals may want to read Geoffrey Moore's (1999) work on technology adoption and the work of Clayton Christiansen on technology disruption. The Internet was certainly a disruptive technology, and probably not the last one in our lifetimes. Even so, the intranet has not seen the same intensity in uptake as the Internet. Are there technologies out there that will impact the intranet? Are there human behaviors (i.e., organizational drivers) that will impact the usefulness of the intranet? Most certainly, but to what degree remains uncertain.

The future is dependent on organizations' adoption preferences, and these are tied to organizational culture as well as the perceived value proposition of an intranet. Information professionals are accountable for helping to bring on new improvements, even if they are not disruptive ones, in a meaningful context, in accountable ways.

In 2002, Yochai Benkler projected a future that envisions "groups of individuals successfully collaborating on large-scale projects following a diverse cluster of motivational drives and social signals, rather than either market prices or managerial commands." This flattening of the organization is enabled by connecting individuals through technology-based enablers such as an intranet. According to the Forrester Group, the information workplace of the future will incorporate contextual, role-based information, voice, documents, rich media, process models, business intelligence, and real-time analytics. We will benefit from just-in-time learning and work collaboratively. Due to the nature of service-oriented architectures, we will benefit from presence management, information rights, and personalization in both online and offline scenarios across a multitude of devices. Many organizations are creating such an information workplace, though much work remains to be done, especially in establishing the mechanisms that enable context-sensitivity.

We have currently identified the following trends:

1. Intranets will become more populated with actionable information. People are drowning in information, and many senior executives, as exemplified by surveys such as those from the Economist Intelligence Unit in 2005, need their organizations to make decisions quickly based on accurate information. Intranets can be helpful in capturing quality information from inside and outside an organization and in presenting that information in meaningful ways through business and decision-making tools. Locating that information will be easy, since it will be findable regardless of the device or where the individual starts looking for it.

2. Intranets will be used more often to aid executive decisions by providing visualizations of cross-departmental data and cross-unit performance measurements. Dashboards are popular again, and so is the next generation of executive information systems (for those of you who were also part of that effort in the late 1980s and early 1990s). Web-based technologies and new standards such as SOAP (Simple Object Access Protocol or Service Oriented Architecture Protocol) have made it easier (not easy, but easier) to integrate Web applications in a single user interface and harness information from across organizations. Visualization tools make it possible for people to process large amounts of information quickly. As large-scale analytical packages make it possible to

crunch and mine both numbers and text, these visualization tools will be integral to executive decision-making.

3. Intranets will become even more important when acting as an employee forum for inter-unit strategic linkages and leadership communication. This will occur in an increasing number of globally diversified companies since the current page-per-department model is contradictory to an enterprise-wide knowledge sharing culture. IBM's intranet, also known as "w3 On Demand Workplace," is described by its CIO as "a powerful productivity and collaboration tool for 329,000 IBM employees in 75 countries" (Market Wire, 2006). While not every organization will need to showcase its own technology (Microsoft could say the same thing, for instance), intranets will need to stop existing simply as a reflection of organizational hierarchy and start providing insight into the work being done. As organizations depend more and more on interdisciplinary teams to meet their objectives, the organizational chart becomes only one avenue by which to access and search for information, and collaboration becomes an increasingly important way of getting work done.

4. Context is going to be a big driver moving forward. Employees will want to work in a digital environment that is configured toward their own requirements. This goes way beyond the ability to personalize content or customize screen configurations. Rather, this will mean the ability to tag and retrieve content according to specific contextual needs. As a person builds more tags, the systems will begin to monitor patterns that reflect user behavior, making relevant content suggestions that can be pushed to the user. This can be achieved not only through tagging but also through usage statistics and reporting: What type of data is being accessed and how often is certain data being accessed?

5. Intranet localization will be more prominent, yielding an intranet that is available to all cultures and languages represented in the workforce. Internet technologies make it possible to communicate across time, distance,

and technology incompatibilities. Interestingly, good intentions do not always lead to cross-boundary information sharing. As reported by Sue Newell, Harry Scarborough, and Jacky Swan of the University of London (2001), internal "electronic fences" emerged as an outcome of intranet development in one case study. However, with the increasing recognition of the need for knowledge as an imperative for a globally aware world, information will need to be available across natural boundaries such as language, time, and expertise in ways that enable both a breadth and depth of understanding. While educational institutions are rarely leaders in adopting new technologies and work design, e-learning may be one application where broad cultural and linguistic localization occurs.

6. The future of intranet design will strive further for the right balance between rigid usability standards and format control (e.g., through taxonomies) and flexible creativity (e.g., blogs and wikis). Neither technology nor human willpower will bring the information stores together in meaningful ways. Information architecture will need to find the level where taxonomies, controlled vocabularies, and metadata standards are meaningful in information retrieval and browsing. Usability studies will find a balance between a managed experience and one that does enough to get the user from "A-to-Z" and back to "D" again, as well as minimizing the amount of learning required simply to "drive" the intranet. Growth will depend on the ability to support new ways of sharing knowledge and information, and organizations are likely to continue to struggle with adoption based on their tolerance for risk. This conversation will move from the backroom to one between the users, decision-makers, and professionals responsible for intranet health.

7. Information overload will continue and new types of search will continue for the quest for relevancy. Google's innovative search technologies set the standard today for dealing with information overload. Regardless, the plethora of search engines out there and new inventions

occur regularly, such as the developments in faceted taxonomies, visualization, and collaborative filtering. Search will shortly become common across all information stores (e-mail, the Web, file-shares, etc.). While the debate will continue about the semantic Web, the value of a metadata framework, and the promise of artificial intelligence, search is likely to continue to frustrate most of us.

8. Organizational requirements will ensure that intranet professionals partner rather than compete. With the increasingly sophisticated environment that an intranet presents, the interdependencies of skill sets will require the ability to work with others who speak a different language, approach the intranet from different perspectives, and appear as a professional team in the eyes of the organization. The unifying factor will be the organizational need, and those organizations that design from the user perspective will be the most successful. Traditional boundary spanners between core disciplines involved will continue to bring successful intranets into existence. It will take very mature partnering skills, workflow analysis, and user experience-based skills to do this well.
9. There will be an increased need to reign in the confusion. Governance plays a major role in large intranet systems. Different organizational units often have their own tools and create their own sites. Search tools are not always able to find and retrieve content across the different environments without the use of a multitude of connectors that can link intranet sites and their associated content. This often requires a standardization of tools, navigation, look and feel, and content management processes. Organizational units will want to develop editorial committees to make sure that content and communication is relevant, appropriate, and updated. A content management community will be encouraged to meet monthly to discuss topics such as standards, lessons learned, and new functionality.
10. A major challenge is going to be the management of growing volumes of content. As more decentralized

behavior emerges on the intranet, infrastructure (i.e., team spaces and project collaboration spaces) and the amount of duplication and redundant content will grow exponentially. Management and archiving practices will need to be able to determine duplication and to sort the relevant from the irrelevant. Regulatory controls will also have a fundamental effect on managing and archiving of content. More and more companies will need to be able to find all content or data to support regulatory requirements.

11. There will be a move toward using rich Internet applications through intranet environments. This will see a move toward more client-side processing of fat-client applications rather than the traditional server-based processing of thin-client applications. Rich Internet applications combine the ease of Web technologies with the power of desktop applications, and solutions can be rolled out using the intranet infrastructure. Services will be moved into Web services that can then be maintained in one central place and accessed by multiple different services as required. Companies will move toward open standards to ensure they are not locked into any particular proprietary technology. Companies are concerned about how quickly the technology is changing and about selecting a particular vendor only to find that the vendor is not in business a few years later or has been acquired by a competitor.

12. Another big challenge is the continuous integration of new tools, services, and infrastructure into the existing intranet. Certain tools and services will need to be capable of supporting the entire enterprise. In essence, everybody in the organization will use these capabilities. In other instances, specific tools and services will need to support specific divisions or departments. The services or tools will need to support specific value-adding or strategic requirements that will merit their inclusion over and above those standards provided in the organization.

13. Business cases and financial-based assessments will continue to be a challenge for intranet initiatives. Return on investment (ROI), productivity measures, and impact will continue to be assessed alongside qualitative data and anecdotal material.

Conclusion

The intranet, in many instances, grew out of grassroots initiatives with little thought to connecting the intellectual assets of the enterprise. The primary purpose has been to communicate with employees and to share broad-based policy documents. Going forward, there are several opportunities centered on collaboration and leveraging ideas. Some of the challenges that intranets will help address are the following:

- Identifying and mapping intangible assets
- Recognizing the information and knowledge exchanges that occur in organizations
- Accelerating learning
- Enabling a platform for innovation
- Supporting programs for employee engagement
- Creating ways to enable a performance-oriented culture
- Highlighting priority knowledge

Other challenges will surely emerge, and information professionals will need to be ready to address them as they occur.

CHAPTER 2

Roles Information Professionals Play

Mary Lee Kennedy
TKG Consulting LLC

Angela Abell
TFPL Ltd.

Information professionals with intranet-based responsibilities are interested in knowing what work is emerging in the marketplace, what they need to know to do their best work, and what opportunities are available to them for ongoing professional development. With the incredible speed of change in information technology, the increasing levels of sophistication of the user base, and the ubiquitous nature of information, keeping pace with, let alone leading the intranet experience, is a challenge.

The Marketplace

One way to look at the marketplace is to consider the types of positions posted in job advertisements. While there are drawbacks to this methodology, namely that all jobs are not necessarily posted, it does provide a publicly available dataset for considering emerging job positions. For example, in September 2006, a quick search for "content management or content manager or information manager or information management or knowledge manager or knowledge management or information architect or information architecture or intranet or user experience or user research" through Monster.com's listing of all geographic areas led to about 500 results. Typical job titles included Intranet Content Manager/Webmaster, Knowledge Manager, Business Analyst, Information Architect/Interaction

Designer, Portals and Enterprise Content Manager. An analysis of the results led to the following four broad conclusions:

1. Information visualization is gaining importance and not just in the area of Information Architecture, but especially in the display of large sets of qualitative data. Traditional information skills (finding, analyzing, and synthesizing information) are becoming less of a competitive advantage unless they are presented in ways that cut through the noise and depict insights for decision-making, sense-making, or knowledge creation.

2. Information skills are being further shaped by the alignment with organizational objectives and core processes, especially in competitive intelligence, strategy, competitive advantage, and value measurement. Information skills do not reside in a vacuum and individuals must be able to articulate how they contribute to organizational desired outcomes.

3. Information professionals have become more akin to knowledge managers, seeing and acting on entire organizational knowledge maps and flows; their roles are closer to an information advisor, connector, trainer, publisher, boundary spanner, etc. Knowledge of organizational practices and process alignment are critical.

4. Given the convergence of information-related services, information professionals need to have additional skills more typical of user anthropologists, smart marketers, workflow analysts, and publishers.

TFPL, an established information and knowledge management company based in the U.K., recently conducted an in-depth research study of the corporate, government, and academic market. The methodology included a review of advertised positions, the analysis of positions managed through TFPL's recruiting and job placement services, an extensive Web-based survey of practitioners, internal brainstorming with TFPL consultants and recruiters, plus individual interviews and focus groups with practitioners. The analysis of the e-survey concluded that the highest proportion of newly created jobs were related to the management of staff who collaborate in online environments, information governance, the promotion and exploitation of electronic content, and information analysis. The firm also found that a significant proportion of the new jobs focused on project management, information architecture, and supporting end-users. Roles carrying the primary function of information analysis, project management, and information architecture appeared to represent the greatest growth areas in the e-information job market. In the context of the study, an "e-information role" was "one that is directly related to the development and application of those processes which facilitate the creation, acquisition, capture, organization, security, flow, and sharing of electronic information, and has a significant element (more than 50 percent) of information or knowledge management in its responsibility." The interviews and focus groups indicated a complex picture of roles relating to the management of electronic information with some labeled as information or knowledge roles but with a significant number with very different job titles.

The idea that information roles change is not new. Changes in the marketplace can be understood in the context of new developments in professional associations and in the growth of new disciplines and collaboration between peer practitioners. In 2003, the Special Libraries Association (SLA) issued a revised edition of the *Competencies for Information Professionals of the 21st Century*. The previous edition was published in 1997 with the same title. The 2003 edition cites the "astounding growth of the Internet and the rise of electronic communications and storage media" as transforming the work of information professionals. The document identifies two major types of competencies: professional and personal. The four major professional competencies include managing information organizations, managing information resources, managing information services, and applying information tools and technologies. The description of the latter highlights the ability to assess, select, and apply current and emerging information tools and to create information access and delivery solutions—all essential to the effective use of an intranet.

In the early 1990s, Knowledge Management (KM) emerged as a concept that was expected to have a significant impact on organizational working practices and raise the profile of information roles. KM and information management (IM) are different disciplines. KM concerns the development and exchange of tacit knowledge through the interaction between people. IM concerns the creation, sharing, use, and organization of explicit knowledge in multiple information formats and artifacts. In some organizations, the two disciplines have become integrated, and information professionals have become knowledge managers, part of KM teams, or managers of the KM function. In other cases, the IM and KM functions are kept very separate although there are obviously blurred lines between the two, and their respective effectiveness is totally interdependent. However, as earlier TFPL research found, whatever the corporate response, the KM concept has done a great deal to broaden the view of the competencies required by information professionals in these environments (see TFPL Ltd., 1999, 2001; Abels, 2003; Abell, 2005).

Recently, the Massachusetts Institute of Technology and the University of Southampton announced a new research program titled "Web Science." Web Science has social and engineering dimensions. According to the researchers, it extends well beyond traditional computer science to include the emerging research in social networks and the social sciences, in essence, studying how people behave on the Web. It shifts the focus from the computer to the decentralized Web systems. While the initial step is to fund a research program, the goal is to offer graduate and undergraduate programs in Web Science. Tim Berners-Lee, the inventor of the basic Internet software, will lead the program. Web Science is related to another emerging new interdisciplinary field called "Services Science." Services Science is the study of using computing, collaborative networks, and knowledge in disciplines ranging from economics to anthropology to lift productivity and develop new products in the services sector.

Volunteer-based professional organizations such as the Information Architecture Institute (see iainstitute.org/pg/about_us.php) have emerged in the past few years. The Information Architecture Institute (IAI), which was founded in 2003, already has more than 1,000 members representing 60 countries. The institute defines Information Architecture as:

1. The structural design of shared information environments
2. The art and science of organizing and labeling Web sites, intranets, online communities, and software to support usability and findability
3. An emerging community of practice focused on bringing principles of design and architecture to the digital landscape

Another newly established volunteer-based organization is CMPros (www.cmprofessionals.org). Founded in 2004, CMPros represents more than 850 members from around the globe. Recently, CMPros posted a draft set of content management skills that focus on four categories: analysis/recommendation, project management, information architecture/design, and technology awareness.

As these five examples demonstrate, whether the reader comes from a traditional field (such as library or computer science) or from an emerging one (such as information architecture or content management), clearly the marketplace is requiring new skills and competencies, with others certainly to follow.

Drivers of New Roles

Occasionally, individuals look around at the jobs available in the marketplace and are excited, amazed, or panicked by the disparity between what they know how to do and what the market is looking for in a recruit. They may even find that it is harder and harder to find a job that reflects their current position or hard skills. On the other hand, those individuals who seek to explore new ways of organizing information, managing resources, and creating the ultimate user experience will likely find many opportunities. One way to avoid surprises and to capitalize on opportunities is to understand what is driving the emergence of new roles for information professionals. TFPL did just this. It is probably not a shock to anyone to find out that the study suggests that the key driver of shifting roles is the organization's adoption of new information and communications technologies. This adoption changes the way organizations work, sometimes radically, affecting key business processes and working practices, how organizations engage with the marketplace, and how they define business drivers. These information and communication technology (ICT) driven changes have led to a greater understanding of the impact information has on the organization and to a reassessment of information roles and responsibilities. There are clearly differences in focus in the public and private sectors, but they also have drivers in common that are clearly information-led.

Business Drivers

Expectations of Employees and Clients

The Google generation is now very much evident in the workforce. Employees expect to have reliable information at their fingertips, continual connection to people wherever they are, and equipment that fits into a top pocket. Clients want to compare services and products, expect speed and quality, and demand that their views and requirements are considered. People expect the digital world to work for them.

Organizational Models and Productivity

Organizations are increasingly networked with their business relationships and operations reflecting the connectivity made possible by ICT. These networks provide flexibility and enable diverse collaborations, partnerships, and outsourcing arrangements. However, they rely on good interpersonal relationships and effective information flows. The drive to realize a return on investment in information, people, and technology is compelling all organizations to focus on IM and KM tools and processes, and on managing and organizing their information resources.

Explosion of Information

Although the concept of information overload is not new, the continued growth of ICT has increased its perceived impact on individuals and organizations. Structured and unstructured information is created and pushed and pulled in numerous ways for diverse audiences and for different purposes. Ensuring that information can be collected and deployed for effective use is a key challenge. For example, information about clients and citizens needs to be consolidated from a range of sources, but both private and public sector organizations find that this is not a simple task.

Public Sector Drivers—Connection and Collaboration

The public sector's agenda in the developed world is clearly about the use of ICT for connection and collaboration: connection between the service providers themselves (the institutions and agencies that provide public services), collaboration between public and private sector partners, and communication between the service providers and the citizen. The U.K. government has set out its vision for using ICT to facilitate the delivery of more effective and efficient services through improved infrastructure and practices in two papers, "Connecting the U.K.: The Digital Strategy" and "Transformational Government: Enabled by Technology." Similar initiatives to maximize information benefits through electronic environments are evident in many countries. For examples, see "An Information Management and Technology Blueprint for the NSW: A Well-Connected Future" for Australia's New South Wales; "Implementing the Federal Enterprise Architecture at EPA" for the environmental agency of the U.S.; and

"Information Assets in the Government of Alberta: A Management Framework" for Alberta, Canada.

Private Sector—Globalization and Risk

In the private sector, an increasingly global marketplace presents a complex mix of challenges. Financial performance is still the key indicator of success, but organizations face many other issues that affect their ability to meet targets and sustain their competitive advantage. The market is increasingly fickle. It changes allegiances and suppliers as new competition, often exploiting technology in novel ways, emerges. Market agility and innovation, fueled by information, are vital.

According to the AON Biennial Survey of 1995, the top risks for companies were perceived to be in health and safety, fire, flood, and terrorism. By 2005, these risks were still high on the corporate agenda, but they had been joined by new risks such as loss of reputation, failure to meet the impact of regulation, and corporate governance. As risk and reputation management becomes a serious issue, corporations have to be increasingly vigilant to minimize the risk of litigation and bad press. In global companies, e-risk, including information leakage and misuse, is extremely high and requires excellent information governance.

Information Drivers

Software and Technology Tools

Software and technology tools influence the way information is collected, analyzed, and distributed. Intelligent agents, search engines, and automated tools have encouraged expectations of information "untouched by human hand." Operational tools such as customer relationship management systems (CRMS) and electronic document and records management systems (EDRMS) seem to offer a means of collating and making information available from disparate sources. Intranets, extranets, and portals enable access to a range of sources; Web 2.0 appears to bring together many of the strands of information management in a Web environment; and developments in communications, such as wireless technology, mean that employees can plug into information systems from airports, cafes, and client sites. However, the implementation of these tools has exposed the highly complex processes involved in managing document and information life cycles, thereby contributing to the current focus on enterprise content management as a business process.

Social Computing and Collaboration

Exploiting the opportunities offered by social computing and associated collaborative software is one of the most visible current information and ICT challenges. Interpersonal communication has become an integral part of creating knowledge and information, hence the value placed on communities and networks. Working in virtual teams requires tools that enable the exchange of documents and information, plus collaborative authoring and analysis. Wikis and blogs have taken relatively little time to become part of the suite of tools used for discussion and collaborative writing. At the same time, new media publishing is opening up ways for organizations and individuals to handle and distribute information. Information specialists are faced with facilitating this interaction while devising ways to manage the resulting information assets.

Content

New tools have stimulated new sources, which content integrators seek to incorporate in their offerings. For example, Factiva has entered a partnership with Intelliseek to incorporate quality blog content. At a practitioner level, we are seeing an explosion of information sources produced by organizations and professions. Some are freely available; others are fee-based. One example in the U.K. is Dr Foster Intelligence, a partnership between the Information Centre for Health and Social Care and Dr Foster Holdings LLP. It provides a mix of information, research, and toolkits for the healthcare sector and clearly exploits technology to provide niche information products to its target audience.

Intranet Trends

In Chapter 1, we articulated some of the overarching trends we see in the development of intranets. In looking at each of these, information professionals will want to consider whether they have the skills and competencies, and indeed the organizational position, to assist in addressing such changes, or in influencing organizational adoption of more appropriate developments. Let's consider three of the trends covered in Chapter 1.

Trend 1. *Intranets will become more populated with actionable information.* What will information professionals need to know for information workers to do something useful quickly with the information they find? Certainly the ability to display information in meaningful ways (visualization, large data and text-based synthesis, personalization, and contextualization) will be important. There is quite a lot to do still. For example, a Forrester survey (Morris, 2005) reports that less than half of respondents found it easy to find what they needed on an intranet while conversely in a Pew Internet and American Life project (Fallows, 2005), 87 percent of Internet searchers reported successful search experiences.

Trend 6. *The future of intranet design will strive further for the right balance between rigid usability standards and format control (e.g., through taxonomies) and flexible creativity (e.g., blogs and wikis).* We suggest that usability and information architecture will help to do this by serving as a mediator between organizational hierarchy and emerging information technologies that enable more grassroots efforts. Information professionals will want to consider their abilities to represent information workers' needs in the context of their work and their interaction with interfaces, to mediate organizational dynamics and systems of influence and power, and to organize the information itself.

Trend 10. *A major challenge is going to be the management of growing volumes of content. As more decentralized behavior emerges on intranets, infrastructure (i.e., team spaces and project collaboration spaces) and the amount of duplication and redundant content will grow exponentially.* Early work in digital libraries highlighted the need to manage collections of digitized materials mainly from research libraries or large public institutions such as the Library of Congress. As electronic records became the norm for most organizations, records managers struggled with managing the lifecycle of organizational documents, particularly business critical records or those that ensured the privacy of citizens. Efforts such as the one originating with Gordon Bell in which he digitizes all his life and creates the means to access it are not commonplace yet (see the MyLifeBits Project Web site).

Technologies developed for the Internet are generally believed to impact the suite of tools considered in enabling an intranet. However, in reviewing secondary sources in terms of the potential impact the Internet has on the intranet, the authors came up with very few references. We believe this is due to their significant purposes: Intranets are focused on enabling information workers to do their best work; the Internet has broader social and commercial purposes. Both may leverage similar technologies, but the adoption of those technologies is largely driven by a perceived recognition of their immediate value. Some academics, including Andrew McAfee (2006), have called for the emergence of a collaboration-based enterprise enabled by wikis, blogs, and group-messaging software that reflects "the way work really gets done." McAfee calls these intranet-focused technologies "Enterprise 2.0 Technologies." Their focus is on "those platforms that companies can buy or build in order to make visible the practices and outputs of their knowledge workers" (p. 23). The biggest challenges, though, remain the same as those that information professionals have struggled with for as long as there have been networked information processes:

1. That knowledge workers won't use them because they simply do not help them do their jobs
2. That early adoption is by information professionals themselves who may taint adoption through their own bias
3. That managers will not support knowledge workers in providing the time or motivation to use them
4. That interfaces are cumbersome and disconnected
5. That the intranet platform may not lead to the behavior management wants and that the natural reaction is to shut it down

Thomas Davenport (2006) responded to Enterprise 2.0 with an important note on the role of the organizations' dynamics, articulating the significant impact that organizational hierarchies have in the adoption of information technologies:

> *Let's face it. The world is a hierarchical place. Some people have more power than others, and they don't want their judgments questioned by lower-level individuals who own a keyboard. ... We can wish that power and capability were more evenly distributed, but a set of technologies isn't going to make it so. Looks like we're still in Enterprise 1.0 after all.*

If the Internet is a predictor of intranet information technology adoption, then the summary of findings from Debra Fallows's study for the Pew Internet and American Life Project (2005) titled "The Future of the Internet II" will interest readers. Pew surveyed technology thinkers and stakeholders, asking them to assess the future social, political, and economic impact of the Internet. Their findings included the following points:

- A global, low-cost network will thrive in 2020 and will be available to most people around the world.
- Humans will remain in charge of technology.
- People will wittingly or unwittingly share more about themselves with some benefits but also some loss of privacy.
- Some people will remain unconnected due to economic circumstances or as a matter of choice.
- Those people who are online will spend more time connected to "sophisticated, compelling, networked synthetic worlds."
- English will remain the world's lingua franca.
- The investment priorities for the Internet are to build network capacity and to spread knowledge about technology to help people of all nations.

A Framework of Roles

Intranets exist within the dynamics of organizations, and, given their various uses, enabling roles will have a broad range of responsibilities, which include the following:

- Supporting top-down and interdepartment communications
- Supporting project team work
- Searching for tacit and explicit information from within and outside the organization
- Creating the design of broad systems to enable a variety of work styles and organizational design preferences

In the broadest terms, an intranet is both a reflection of the governance model (see Chapter 4) and of the ways in which users actually do their work, as well as a reflection of the work of information professionals. Therefore, while the core skills of information professionals will enable the systems in place to meet user and organizational requirements, those skills must also be able to interact with organizational partners such as Human Resources and Finance. One might think of the information professional role as the translator between two broad organizational tensions (see Figure 2.1). Note that the information professional will need to be cognizant of the external pressures affecting the decision-making of organizational/management decision-makers as well as the behavior of users and non-users (which will include members of organizational/management decision-makers). This tension means that, in some measure, information professionals (or a part of a team of information professionals) must be able to translate user behavior, information management, and knowledge-exchange principles and practices, as well as take on the organizational perspective of senior decision-makers.

Within any given organization, the role of an information professional will be focused on enabling the creation and exchange of knowledge as evidenced in tacit and explicit information. Popadiuk and Choo present a summary of approaches to knowledge classification that articulates the topics that information professionals

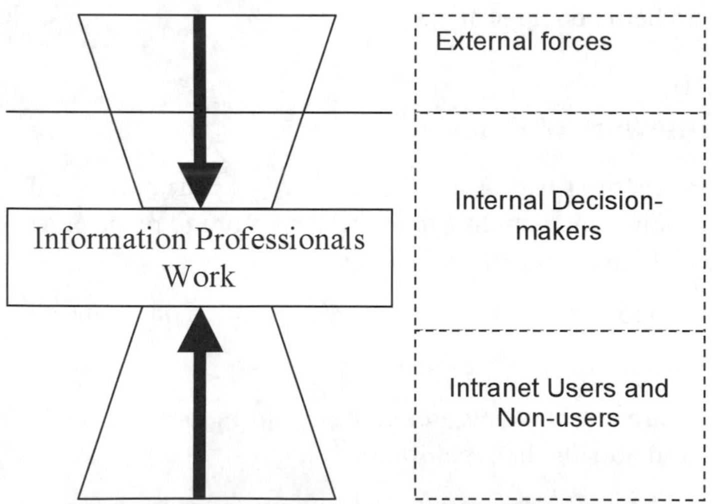

Figure 2.1 The Role of Information Professionals as Translator

need to understand in order to effectively carry out their role (see Figure 2.2).

For instance, in order to enable individual knowledge creation or collective knowledge creation, information professionals will study individual and group information behavior. Given the influence culture has on individual and collective knowledge sharing and information use, information professionals will want to understand the dynamics within their organizations and be able to assist others in making sense of complex issues involving beliefs and values. Information may be centered solely between individuals or teams within the organization, but much of that information may seed what is eventually presented externally to customers, partners, and even competitors. Information professionals must therefore understand information lifecycles. The nature of information itself is highly fragmented with individual and group preferences for using different repositories, different applications, and even in the various categorization schemes individuals and groups feel comfortable using to tag their knowledge. Information professionals must therefore understand the complex nature of information itself.

In studying roles associated with the management of electronic resources, TFPL identified six clusters of responsibilities. These are

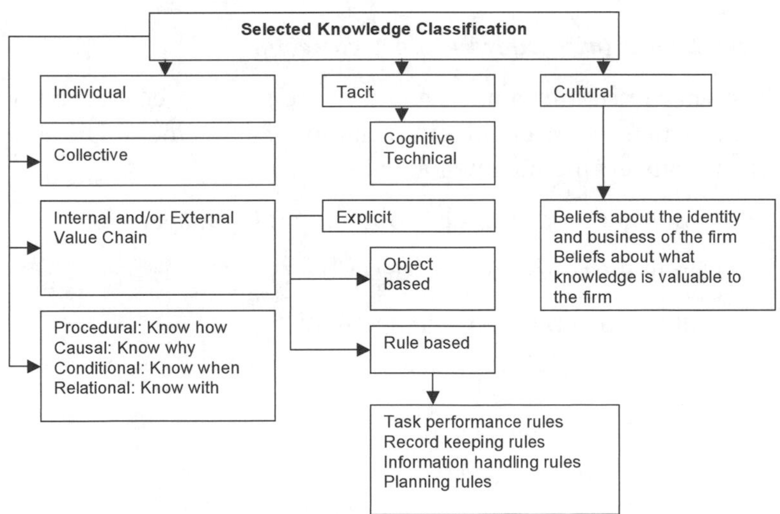

Figure 2.2 Categories of Organizational Knowledge (Source: Popadiuk, Silvio and Chum Wei Choo. "Innovation and Knowledge Creation: How Are These Concepts Related." *International Journal of Information Management* 26 (2006): 302–312)

not organizational clusters, and while they do reflect a set of responsibilities, they are not intended to be job descriptions. Their value is in articulating the work that needs to be done and serves as an excellent starting place for identifying the breadth and depth of the work to do in managing e-resources on an intranet. Associated functions such as organizational design, marketing, and finance are not included.

Cluster 1: Information Strategy

The information strategy group is focused on those activities associated with determining strategies and policies that set the direction of information management. The cluster can be further divided into four sub-clusters:

- Strategic planning
- Business/operational planning
- Process design
- People and team development

Example roles include Chief Knowledge Officer, Business Process Analyst, Strategy Manager, and Head of Information.

Cluster 2: Enterprise Information Architecture

The enterprise information architecture group is concerned with the infrastructure that enables information management. The associated sub-clusters include the following:

- Information systems development and management
- Configure/constitute and describe
- Collection/repository management
- Content management
- Data management
- Presentation

Example roles include Enterprise Information Architect, Head of Knowledge and Information Systems, Content Manager, Database Analyst, Taxonomy Specialist, DIP Ontology Engineer, and Corporate Data Process and Policy Manager.

Cluster 3: Information Governance

The information governance group is called upon to ensure good information governance, and is composed of four sub-clusters:

- Information risk analysis
- Information security
- Curation and disposal
- Compliance with legislation, regulation, and corporate standards

Example roles include Director of Information Governance, Information Lifecycle Manager, Records Manager, and Privacy Officer.

Cluster 4: Content Creation and Acquisition

The content creation and acquisition group supports the creation of information or the acquisition of external or internal information resources. The six sub-clusters include the following:

- Writing and editing
- Records creation and collection
- Knowledge management
- Supporting collaborative and virtual working
- Sourcing internal information
- Acquisition/procurement (external information)

Example roles include Head of Digital Communications, Internal Communications Officer, Knowledge Broker, and Acquisitions Lead.

Cluster 5: Communication and Publication

The communication and publication group identifies internal and external markets, including information product development, and the development and management of challenges for publishing and communication. The four sub-clusters include the following:

- Publishing channels
- Communication channels

- Information packaging and re-purposing
- Business development/marketing

Example roles include Head of Internet and E-communications, Web Services and Content Manager, Intranet Content Advisor, Publisher, Editor, and Information Product Designer.

Cluster 6: Information Exploitation and Use

The information exploitation and use group focuses on the use or support of the use of information. The eight sub-clusters are the following:

- Competitive intelligence
- Decision support
- User support
- Client/product support
- Supporting e-business
- Supporting e-learning
- Search/research
- Analysis and informatics

Example roles include Competitive Intelligence Officer, Head of E-Learning Support, Business Analyst, Statistician, Data Miner, Information Literacy Coach, and Usability Support.

Putting a Team Together

Information professionals work within the context of an organization. Given this, their need to participate on cross-functional and cross-departmental teams, as well as to lead teams of multidisciplinary members, is an obvious one. Putting together a team is an important consideration.

An effective intranet team will reflect the complex range of stakeholders in the information environment. All those people who contribute to the information scene, who rely on access and use of reliable information, and who have an interest in the organization meeting its objectives and corporate responsibilities are potential stakeholders. They are the intranet clients and contributors. There are few business areas and functions that do not rely on information to support their work, and an increasing number of functions and disciplines acknowledge their role in information creation, management, and use. A number of functions are often very visible stakeholders (Library and Information Services, Information Technology and Management Departments, Human Resources, and Communication) but both TFPL research and marketplace intelligence suggest that the picture is more complex than this. Table 2.1 provides an indication of the scope of information stakeholders, although this picture is almost certainly incomplete.

We are witnessing a merging of information professional disciplines (Library and Information Services, Knowledge Management, Information Management, Records Management, Web, and IT) and the integration of new disciplines into the arena, plus the creation of new information roles. While everyone has an information responsibility in his or her daily work, the identification and allocation of

Table 2.1 Stakeholders in Information Management

'Visible' IM Stakeholders	IM Stakeholders—Facilitators	IM Stakeholders—Users and Contributors
Communications	Change Management	Business Development
Information Technology	Customer & Service Departments	Corporate Affairs
IM and IT Groups	Customer Relationship Managers	Corporate Performance
Human Resources	Knowledge & Information Analysts	Corporate Secretariat
Knowledge Management	Publishing	Directors & Leadership
Library and Information Services	Records Management & Archives	Finance
	Professional Support	Front Line Staff
	Lawyers	Marketing & Sales
	Program & Project Managers	Operational Research
	Solutions Architects	Organizational Development & Learning
	Statisticians	Planners
	Technical support	Policy Staff
	Web Teams	Research & Evaluation
		Team Managers
		Value for Money Team

explicit IM responsibilities is increasingly becoming essential to the development of robust information management capability. Information and intranet teams need an identifiable core of professional information competence complimented by experience and skills from a number of disciplines, functions, and business lines.

Work undertaken by TFPL in 2001 for the U.K.'s Information Services National Training Organization (ISNTO) suggests that future corporate knowledge and information teams will focus on infrastructure (the infostructure team) and/or on creation and exploitation (the exploitation/application team) (see Figure 2.3).

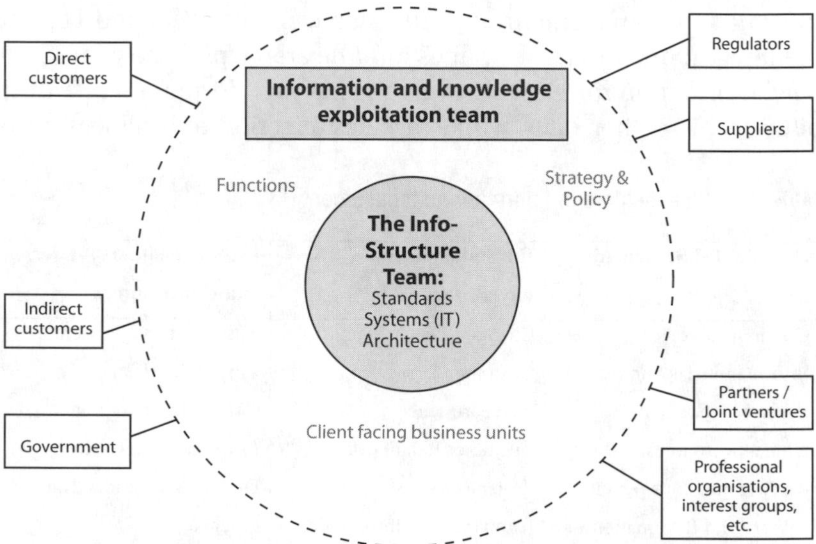

Figure 2.3 The Role of Information Professionals (Source: TFPL Ltd. "Scenarios for the Knowledge Economy: Strategic Information Skills." TFPL Ltd. for the ISNTO. 2001)

The infostructure team will focus on principles, tools, and systems such as the following:

- Information architecture
- The acquisition of information resources (internal and external)
- Information governance issues including systems and standards

- Content, collection, and records management

The creation/exploitation team will be client-focused and facilitate:

- The creation of content
- The capture of information
- The delivery in appropriate formats for the audience
- The use and analysis of information

The essence of these teams is that they are multidisciplinary. The infostructure team requires input from IT, HR, organizational development, the legal department, communications, and the various business units. The creation/exploitation team includes information professionals, "superusers" (experts in their field using specific information sources), journalists, editors, product managers, etc. Not everyone on the team is likely to be a fulltime member but their combined expertise and experience make up the team profile.

We are observing this team model emerging in many organizations albeit with diverse approaches. These are invariably small, fulltime teams, often virtual ones, working with colleagues across different functions and business units and whose time allocation to information work ranges from 100 percent to very occasional. The role of the core team is very much that of "producer," persuading (without any direct authority or power) people to work towards a common goal, in consistent ways, and to allocate time and resources.

The effective intranet team needs exactly the same understanding. It requires a core infrastructure, yet equally important are the client-facing roles: the people who ensure that relevant and usable content is developed, edited, maintained, and used. However good their information or management skills, or how thorough their understanding of the power of technology, what makes them effective is their ability to win hearts and minds. They need to demonstrate value and impact, and to be able to influence and negotiate. Core information competence is a given, but a healthy injection of political, business, and communication skills is necessary to design and implement an effective intranet.

Ongoing Professional Development

New opportunities and challenges emerge as ICT developments continue to facilitate innovative ways of working and as information becomes recognized as a critical corporate resource. As one participant in the TFPL information responsibilities project said, "Convergence of information sharing, security, assurance, risk management and corporate governance functions will lead to new roles/responsibilities for IM, KM and ICT program/project managers."

Some emerging opportunities build on traditional information skills and functions, while others build on the skills of other disciplines and business experience. These challenges are increasing the need for both a breadth of skills and depth of expertise in the following areas:

- Integrating internal and external information in multimedia formats
- Becoming active in the content creation phase of the information life cycle
- Delivering reliable and usable information through a variety of publication and communication channels

Many information responsibilities call for a range of skills that are unlikely to be found in any one discipline. The key to career development is to understand an organization's business objectives and the critical information processes that underpin them, and to be able to work in productive partnerships to develop and deliver information services and processes that support the achievement of those objectives. Individuals and team managers need to build personal development plans that ensure that skills and experience are continually renewed and refreshed. Life-long learning has to be a reality.

Professional development can and should take a number of routes, as illustrated by the model based on that suggested by Amin Rajan and individuals and team managers (see Figure 2.4).

Taught learning is often the first route that comes to mind. The acquisition of additional qualifications enables individuals to either deepen or broaden their range of knowledge. In-house programs enable skills valued by the currently employed to be developed, while professional bodies encourage the development of core professional and transferable skills.

There are many guides to academic courses and details of library and information professional bodies such as the American Library Association (ALA) and the Special Libraries Association (SLA) in the U.S., and the Chartered Institute of Library and Information

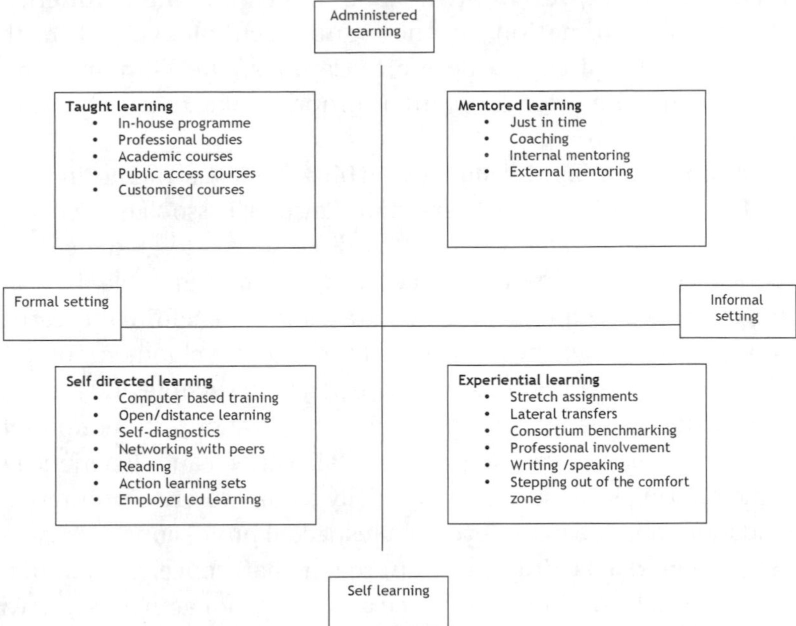

Figure 2.4 Routes to Development (Source: Rajan, Amin and Penny van Eupen. *Leading People*. 2nd ed. Centre for Research and Technology in Europe, 1996)

Professionals (CILIP) in the U.K. There are also other relevant professional bodies, some IT-focused (the British Computer Society in the U.K.), some focused on training and development (the Chartered Institute for Personal Development in the U.K.), and some business-related organizations.

Self-directed learning describes an approach to learning (rather than a methodology) and reflects current thinking that puts the responsibility for professional development on the individual as well as the employer. Computer-based and distance learning grants the learner flexibility to decide when and where to learn, while self-assessment helps individuals understand their own development needs and interests. Networking, action learning sets, and employer learning networks all provide the support that people may need when managing their own development, and provides them with access to a broad range of experience.

Professional associations and industry conferences and online communities facilitate networking and access to self-directed courses, including KMWorld (Asia, Europe, the U.S.), American Society for Information Science and Technology(ASIST), the Information Architecture Summit, Campos, the Gilman Group (gilbane.com), Knowledge Board (Europe) (www.knowledgeboard.com), and KM Europe.

Mentored learning, including coaching, personal mentoring, and "just in time tools" (such as After Action Reviews, Lesson Learned databases, etc.), provides individuals with direct access to guidance from experienced people. These approaches require considerable time and input from other people and also require commitment from the learner, but they are proving to be popular and powerful development routes.

Professional organizations are active in helping people find mentors and coaches, as are many commercial organizations. It is important that individuals look carefully at the qualifications and experience of people offering such services, especially in the absence of a recommendation from their employer or a respected professional body.

Experiential learning is an approach that actively encourages individuals to learn from experience and to look for activities that will contribute to their professional and personal development. Of the activities suggested in Figure 2.4, stretch assignments, lateral transfers, and consortium benchmarking require the cooperation of the employer, manager, or other organizations, and must be carefully managed if individuals are to have positive learning experiences. Participation in professional organization work, writing, and speaking are all steps that individuals can take on their own. "Stepping out of the comfort zone" can be taken to mean involving individuals on activities such as community work or outward-bound courses, "exposing them to uncommon experience which enhances their physical and emotional stamina" (Rajan). It can equally mean taking the decision to do something that is new and challenging in order to extend your experience and abilities.

There is good advice and ideas relating to experiential learning (including consideration of individual learning styles) in the literature. A good place to start is with "David Kolb on Experiential Learning" (www.infed.org/biblio/b-explrn.htm).

Conclusion

Two things are certain. First, ICT will continue to impact fundamentally the business drivers of organizations and the way they manage their information. Opportunities for information specialists will broaden, but realizing these opportunities will demand an ability to adapt and re-skill.

Second, many disciplines contribute to an effective electronic information environment, and the boundaries between these disciplines will continue to blur. The information teams of tomorrow will have knowledge and information expertise, ICT understanding and skills, excellent project and change management skills, process design and business skills, and facilitation and negotiation skills.

A new breed of information professional is already evident, one that has the ability to work in multi-disciplinary teams and is willing to learn from other disciplines. This new breed will possess these capacities:

- To understand, engage with, and feel driven by the business imperatives of the organization
- To keep abreast of technological and organizational developments
- To understand the mix of skills and expertise that contributes to IM capability
- A solid foundation of core information management skills
- A real understanding of, and ability to articulate, the value that they bring to their organization and to the daily work of their colleagues

It is clear from the marketplace that information is increasingly "everyone's responsibility," but information professional roles, both traditional and nontraditional, are essential to meeting IM challenges. Some of the key challenges will be the following:

- Information and data security in an environment where collaboration and sharing underpins business models
- Information risk mitigation and the need for good information governance
- The development of information and enterprise architectures that ensure return on investment in information, people, and technology
- Information design and the development of information products that enable the effective use of information

- Convergence of content and suppliers making managing supply chains more complicated and difficult
- Transformation of information into organizational intelligence

The extended need for information competence throughout the organization is driving the development of roles concerned with the transfer of information skills. Intranet and information teams need not only to develop their own skills but will increasingly need to be able to develop information skills across their organization.

CHAPTER 3

Implementing an Intranet that Makes Sense

Mary Lee Kennedy
TKG Consulting LLC

An intranet is a technology-enabled environment that an organization and its individuals use to meet specific objectives. In and of itself, it has little to no value. Very few organizations would establish an intranet without a reason. Done poorly, an intranet contributes to conditions that bog down organizations, such as information overload, poor communication, missed opportunities, and duplication of effort. When developed and managed in support of objectives, an intranet can play a significant role in providing access to relevant information, connecting people, delivering information at the point of need, building common understanding, helping people learn new skills and competencies, and enabling collaborative project work. There are innumerable objectives that an intranet can support. The key is to align the objectives with user and organizational needs and to establish a workable framework to ensure ongoing value.

This chapter focuses on providing practitioners with a framework in which to align the intranet in the context of the organization's objectives and to decide what makes sense in terms of functionality, processes, human resources, and change management.

Alignment is an ongoing process that is broken down into eight critical steps. Regardless of how big (e.g., enterprise search or e-learning effort) or how small (e.g., communications column or addition of an RSS feed), some semblance of these eight steps needs to be addressed for initial and ongoing success. The eight steps are the following:

1. Start with the end in mind

2. Set the scene that supports the end
3. Break it down
4. Define the interdependencies
5. Prioritize the work
6. Put a program in place
7. End with the beginning in mind
8. Begin a continuous loop

Step One: Start with the End in Mind

What will be visibly different and for whom? As when reading any well-constructed story, the audience needs to understand the setting, the characters, the issues and problems that are being resolved, the behaviors and actions involved, the plot that leads to change, and a belief that there is a credible outcome that is measurable. Most importantly, it needs to address the most obvious question—why do this?

Essentially, this step turns the work of defining user requirements into a vision of depicting what the user experience would be like if the user requirements were met—a subtle but important difference. The audience, sometimes referred to as stakeholders and which includes decision-making constituents, needs to understand what is being proposed and why it matters.

In a sense, intranets are like any large organizing space, be it a city, a business, or a public park: There are many, many choices to be made. Intranets are amorphous and often get confused with their component technology parts: portal applications, search, navigation, Web sites, team sites, presence management, e-learning, Web-conferencing, etc. Assessing the work in terms of the experience helps ensure that whatever is put in place enables the experience to come to life.

The first and most important decision is to understand what the target audience needs in terms of decision-making and use. This is a view from the customer's perspective. Table 3.1 outlines some of the variables to consider in prompting customers to understand their requirements.

Table 3.1 Variables in Understanding Customer Requirements

Need Defined By ...	Need Expressed In Terms Of ...	Target Audience Defined As ...
• Senior champion • Unit or group of users (could be split out by function, by cross-disciplinary team, by goal, etc.) • Information professionals (could be split out by function or team or goal etc.)	• Individual productivity • Group productivity • Collaboration • Information sharing • Information finding • Communication • Learning	• Individuals • A group • A unit • Intra-organizational • Across an entire organization • Between organizations (an extranet) • Outside the organization (the Internet)

The next important step is to consider the needs in the context of organizational priorities. At this point, the key is to understand whether there are natural ties to the realization of organizational objectives or known pain points. Depending on the organizational culture, some representation of senior stakeholders may need to be understood. For large-scale undertakings, senior stakeholder involvement will be critical. A vetting of the work in terms of perceived value will help focus on what is likely to move forward successfully.

Now it is time to begin managing stakeholder expectations. Many projects flounder because of differing expectations, which can often stem from language barriers and experience gaps. It is extremely important that the expectations be clear up front:

1. What is the need?
2. How does the stakeholder see success?
3. How will he or she measure success?
4. How many resources does the stakeholder think it will take to address the need?
5. To what extent is the stakeholder wanting to or needing to involve others in the decision-making process?

6. What role does the stakeholder want to take?
7. What role does the stakeholder expect you to take?
8. How does the stakeholder want to communicate with you and how often?

Senior stakeholders rarely take on a problem that they want to "fail" at, so as the expert, it will be essential to understand up front all the scoping, communication, and decision-making questions. Paraphrasing cannot be underestimated in ensuring both the information professional and the senior stakeholders operate using the same definition of success.

Information professionals, units, and groups commonly identify needs. The main challenge will be getting a shared understanding of what success will look like and to clarify what work roles are involved. Often, intranets are a meeting ground of individual, group, and organizational workflows. This can lead to significant confusion about expectations and roles. Defining success will require understanding of what the group and individuals within the group want to do, what they want to do differently, what their needs and wants are, and how to establish the benefit to the organization. In some cases, changes initiated without a senior stakeholder can be realized, although the changes will require stakeholder support in most cases.

Success, as defined in Step One, will depend on agreement of the following:

- The expected outcomes, especially clarity around measurable differences
- Who (functions, specific individuals, or groups) will behave differently as a result of the work involving the intranet, what the changes will look like, and why they matter; this needs to include all the potential roles, such as users, decision-makers, and information professionals
- An initial understanding of the parameters within which success is expected to occur (i.e., time, money, and staff)

While a senior stakeholder, a group, or information professional may be the initial starting place for an intranet project, in order to complete the description of the desired end-state, there will need to be a significant understanding of user requirements. Most stakeholders will want to know that the proposal has been researched and understood. In data-intensive organizations, the research required may take an upfront investment of time and money. Homework will be required to inform Step Two and may be required to understand the following:

- Desired use of the intranet as measured by methods such as focus groups, anecdote circles, online surveys, and individual interviews
- Current use as measured by methods such as usability, contextual inquiry, workplace ethnography, and narrative capture
- Benchmark use as measured through comparisons with like organizations and leading practitioners
- Industry, adoption, and practice trends as evidenced through primary or secondary market and industry research

At the end of this step, the organization needs to agree on a clear vision statement that describes the desired end-state. The following is an example of a clear vision statement that articulates the desired end-state:

> *Employees can find and be informed about the people and information required to do their jobs, trust that the results are relevant, and be presented with consistent results that are in context and presented in ways they can make use of.*
>
> *As an employee, I can:*

1. *Find quality information to help me do my job*
2. *Determine information relevance based on my own knowledge and expertise*
3. *Trust and believe in the reliability and credibility of the information and knowledge*
4. *Find out who else has knowledge, find out what they know, and, if they are willing, engage them in a dialogue*

5. *Find the same information, knowledge, and people from any starting point in the information system (portal, team site, application, information store)*
6. *Learn about new resources relevant to me as they become available*

There also needs to be agreement on how the vision speaks to an agreed set of problem statements. Examples of problem statements include the following:

- Difficulty in finding and retrieving the right information
- Challenges in locating people and understanding what they know
- Inability to organize the intranet as a navigable space and create a comfortable sense of place

With a set of problem statements, it is important that the vision addresses the primary set of objectives that the project is expected to address. This leads to establishing a set of measures. For instance, with the problem statements just noted, the objectives would be the following:

- Improve the ability to find and retrieve the right information
- Improve the ability to find people and what they know
- Organize the intranet and create a sense of place

These three items (vision, problem statement, and objectives) serve as anchors for managing expectations throughout the remainder of the work.

Step Two: Set the Scene that Supports the End

What does the intranet need to offer in order to deliver on the desired end-state and project objectives as articulated in Step One? Before jumping to a solution (which is very typical but also almost always of limited value as it often leads to a discussion about technology pros and cons as opposed to how the target audience needs to function), it is critical that the characters play out their roles. A studied approach to all the moving parts covered in the vision description is essential.

Triggers that create an opportunity for change commonly include the following:

- Technology
- Breakdowns in communication
- Lost business opportunities
- Loss of human life
- Diminishing quality standards

Given the increased capabilities that technology offers, technology may be the first suggested solution. Over the past decade, many examples of technology-led intranet efforts were offered. In fact, the majority of intranet solutions have been technology-led. Failed efforts are often due to the lack of attention to process alignment. In other words, they failed because they did not involve the end-users in their design. Step Two is designed to avoid this type of failure.

In setting the scene, intranets need to be understood in the context of their environment, taking into account culture, goals and objectives, workflows, personalities, schedules, and technology. The intranet impacts—and is impacted by—the environment in which it operates. To complicate the situation more, an intranet can have many moving parts, such as portals, Web sites, search engines, navigation schemes, content management systems, document repositories, VoIP, presence management, Web services, Web conferencing, and platforms. They can also serve many masters, including internal communications, senior management, human resources, product teams, information providers, and learning teams. While this is—and will continue to be—a dynamic and complex reflection of human behavior, it is worth evaluating how each part will be required to meet the objectives and the end-state, preparing both the team tasked with meeting the objectives and those who will benefit from the work. In fact, history shows that it is absolutely critical that those who will be impacted by the changes be involved in the design.

Setting the scene requires a process description, functional understanding at each point in the process, and an articulation of the skills and competencies required by the end-users and functionality enablers. Experts in business process or workflow analysis may initiate this step by first understanding the current process and then documenting the changes that need to be made. It is our recommendation that you start by understanding how the work needs to be done. By focusing on the desired process, the focus will be on those things that can be changed as opposed to focusing on those things that are broken. A gap analysis can follow to assess how big or how small the changes need to be.

Once the process is documented, a list of functional elements needs to be identified and mapped. Table 3.2 provides an example of a list that can be used to track functional elements over time and to use in prioritizing them throughout the product development process. This same list will include any notes that must be documented for those who are responsible for establishing a specification, implementing functions, features, or content elements, and administering training and education of end-users.

Table 3.2 Function and Feature Tracking

Function Element Identifier	Function	Feature Identifier	Feature	Associated Content	Priority	Comments
Number	Name/ description	Number	Name/ description	Source/ location	Number	

Verify both the process and the functional elements with the intended audiences: users, decision-makers, and information professionals. It may be worthwhile putting together wireframes or paper copies so the audiences can critique and recommend changes to the environment. Iterative discussions and trials will ensure that expectations remain clear and trade-offs are made within an agreed framework.

Step Three: Break It Down

What will it take to deliver the scenario(s) defined in Step Two? Specifically, how will the functionality be enabled? There are four main categories of enablers to consider: people, content, design, and technology. Table 3.3 provides exemplars in each category to consider when understanding what capabilities are needed to deliver functionality requirements. Further exploration of each is detailed in subsequent chapters in the book.

For each step in the process, clear roles and responsibilities need to be assigned, such as the following:

Table 3.3 Categories, and Exemplars Within Each, to Consider in Delivering on Required Functionality

People: Roles and Responsibilities	Content: Information and Communication	Design: Information Architecture, Content Management, and Graphics	Technology
• Decision-making rights • Skills and competencies • Change management processes • Information sharing responsibilities • Web writing skills	• Metadata standards and practices • Content licensing requirements • Editorial program	• Navigation schemes • Publishing templates • Search results display	• Search engine • Presence management • Single sign-on • Security

- Establishment of roles and decision-making rights
- Determination of the escalation path in decision-making
- Change of management responsibilities
- Identification of skills and competencies required by end-users and enablers
- Expectations of the organization in terms of contributing to and using the intranet

A gap analysis needs to be completed, and a plan needs to be put in place that outlines the resources required and the governance structure required; other items, such as goals and objectives, need to be determined and put in place to ensure that the people who manage the intranet are adequately prepared. Conversations will be needed to clarify what is desired and realistic with stakeholders including management, target audiences, teams, partners, allies, and champions.

All significant information sources that support the work must be identified in order to clarify any potential gaps in sources and in access to sources. Information sources need to be reviewed in terms of update frequency, quality, the form and format in which the information needs to be made available, and, increasingly, access rights and security.

The information architects, content managers, and graphic designers must determine the best way to manage and present the intranet information and interface to the users in order to create the desired experience as described in the vision statement. They will need to test their assumptions against the primary objectives to make sure they support the expected outcomes. This team of experts usually works as part of a multidisciplinary group that includes the organization's technologists. Their presence is key given the significant interdependencies common in the intranet as Web applications become the norm.

The output of this work is an understanding of who is responsible for what, what information is required, how it needs to be organized, what processes need to be in place to support the vision, what the interface will require in terms of resources, and what the supporting technology will need to do. With human resource requirements, information requirements, and technical requirements defined, a specification document can be established and referred to as tradeoffs are made later on. At this point, any assumptions about technology can be double-checked, and the list of technology options can be shortened. Assumptions about people, information, and design can be reviewed and updated.

Step Four: Define the Interdependencies

How do all the parts work together? An intranet creates a set of connections, whether it is between individuals, between teams, or across an entire organization. The connections exist in several ways:

- Between the interface and the people
- Between people and the way they work
- Between information sources and the interface
- Between information sources
- Between applications and Web technologies

- Between applications and information
- Between applications and the interface

It can become rather complicated.

Some connections are critical to understand, and others will emerge over time. The critical interdependencies must be addressed at the outset, ensuring that the roles and responsibilities are clear at various stages of deployment, the end-user can easily move from one part of the intranet to the other once changes have been instituted, and the physical connections occur in meaningful ways. Which connections are critical will depend on the outcomes of Steps Two and Three (i.e., what functionality needs to exist and what details—people, information, design, and technology—will enable the functionality). Thus, this step focuses on confirming the interdependencies found in Steps Two and Three, checking for any others that will likely emerge when verifying the known dependencies. Ideally, a multidisciplinary team representing the various stakeholders (decision-makers, users, information professionals) would walk through the known dependencies and probe for others that will assist in the successful deployment and ongoing usefulness of the intranet project.

Step Five: Prioritize the Work

What matters most and in what order? Prioritization may actually occur earlier in the process. However, it must occur by Step Five at the latest. In fact, prioritization often occurs in defining the desired workflow, in establishing the functionality, and at the point in time when the people, information, design, and technical requirements are documented. Even so, there will always be too many things to do and not enough time to do them. It is quite likely that stalemates and analyses will become difficult to discern in terms of appropriate next steps. At this point, the choices need to be presented before a decision-making body—either an individual or a group of individuals. The whole picture of what it will take to realize the vision needs to be explained in a way and in a language that the decision-makers can understand. Depending on the culture, it may be a steering committee, a single meeting with an executive sponsor, a democratic vote, or some other variation. The format in which it is presented will depend on the communication and decision-making preferences (see Chapter 4 for more on governance).

Several ways exist in which to facilitate prioritization. Given that expectations are continuously managed throughout the process, the starting point will be the confirmed agreement on the primary objectives. Prioritization can then be outlined based on an agreed set of variables, including, but not limited to the following:

- Cost (time and money)
- Feasibility
- Impact to the organization
- Magnitude of organizational change
- Risk
- Technical alignment
- Urgency

A framework may involve weighting each variable and then scoring each feature, functionality, or content source against it. Or it may take place in a group discussion that evaluates the features, functionality, and content sources based on relative importance in a simple two-by-two matrix. Pick a prioritization tool that is commonly used in your organization.

For projects that affect only one function in one department or unit, prioritization may be more straightforward than those projects that affect multiple functions or multiple units. The iterative nature of projects today will ensure that work progresses with stakeholder engagement, but it is critical to get the priority buckets selected. For example, prioritization may occur in the context of personas that have been developed. In this case, features and functionality have already been prioritized. Each feature and function can be reviewed against agreed variables that will affect the decision to engage organizational resources. At some point, the resources will run out. At that point, the features and functionality will be set. Urgency is another example of a unit to use in the prioritization process. The features and functionality that will address the most urgent needs will receive the first batch of resources.

Once the priorities are set, it will be important to verify the expectations regarding resource expenditures, set a schedule that meets stakeholder requirements and recognizes the effort needed for successful delivery, establish a clear communication plan to all relevant parties addressing the priority-based decisions that have been made, and outline the communication plan to inform all those who will be impacted by the planned changes. If the key participants have been regularly involved, the work going forward will be focused on getting things done rather than trying to understand the priorities. It will be worth keeping the work that was developed regarding the features, functionality, and content choices that are not prioritized. Often, those items that were not considered priorities may turn out to be priorities as the work progresses, or they may be questioned at another time, and it will be important to clearly articulate the reason behind the decision of whether to make them a priority.

The outcome of this step will be a set of prioritized features, functionality, and content (as appropriate) with a clear understanding of the resources required to enable them, the commitment of the organization behind them, and verification of expectations around decision-making and communication requirements.

Step Six: Put a Program in Place

How will the work get done and, of equal importance, how will it be managed on an ongoing basis? Project management skills will be required to manage the resources that have been approved to create the changes in terms of people, technology, content, schedules, and communication. This is a significant role that requires an understanding of resource management, change management, workflow design, and technology. In essence, this individual or team of individuals will be responsible for ensuring that the connections are made, that each element works as defined in the specifications, and within a bounded set of time and resources. Figure 3.1 outlines a typical high-level project management process. With the growing popularity of Agile Computing, these elements remain in place with a highly interactive development phase involving customers in decision-making as development takes place.

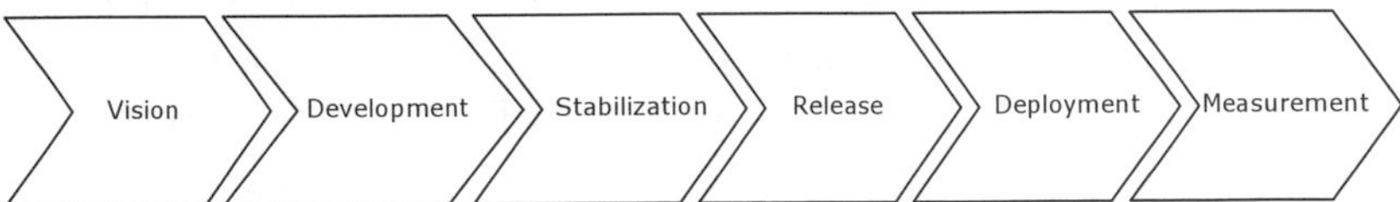

Figure 3.1 Typical High-Level Project Management Process

While it is not the intention of this section to define the project management process, some lessons learned may be useful to the practitioner, such as the following:

- Communicate consistently and frequently with all stakeholders
- Ensure that the human resources involved in delivering the scheduled activities are involved in putting the schedule together and are rewarded and recognized for staying on schedule and working together
- Hold regular and predictable team meetings
- Under-promise and over-deliver
- Remember it is better to over-schedule and give time back than to under-schedule and constantly be asking for more time
- Plan for the implementation and ongoing work—make sure the two parts include the transition of resources and workflow from project implementation to regular, ongoing intranet maintenance
- Make sure the implementation meets specifications, particularly the ability to show the measurable results defined in Step One
- Keep the process iterative: Over-designed projects rarely keep up with the users' expectations and can be obsolete the moment they are implemented

The outcome of this step is the successful implementation of the project, including user education and stabilized operations.

Step Seven: End with the Beginning in Mind

How will the organization know that the right things are being done? Multiple stakeholders are usually involved in most intranet projects. Small projects may have a reduced number of stakeholders. Regardless of the numbers, there will be stakeholders from the target user base, the experts who work on the project, and those responsible for ongoing management. They will need to be engaged at the time of deployment.

To finalize a project in a way that ensures ongoing credibility, it is important to ensure that stakeholder expectations have been met. If they have not been met, then it is important that this is not a surprise. A successful project ends with no unpleasant surprises. When wrapping up the project, ensure that a communication plan is tailored to each target stakeholder group. Deliver training where required and documentation to support ongoing operations. Ensure that a support framework has been created for the transition period. Complete the work with a checklist that highlights how the work delivers on the objectives, including the implementation of a measurement program (e.g., scorecard, written monthly report, or dashboard) that demonstrates today's impact and a way to measure impact in the future.

Step Eight: Begin a Continuous Loop

The potential of the intranet is vast. Organizations have to set priorities in the contexts in which they find themselves. Resources are almost certainly scarce, the environment is constantly in flux, and change continues to be disruptive to most people. New initiatives that are perceived as distractions will hardly be prioritized. Therefore, it is important that intranet work becomes part of the organization's natural workflow and that needs are captured throughout the process. Continuous improvement can be sorted into small projects, medium projects, and large projects with organizational agreement about the changes that can take place without investing in a significant project management effort. Some changes need to be done quickly; some merit discussion before action; some require homework like that discussed in Step One. The degree to which the line is drawn is very contextual to the organization. When a change is requested that goes beyond the quick fix, then it will be time to return to Step One.

Conclusion

Information professionals may want to leverage the lessons learned in more than 20 years of working on internal systems and intranet projects associated with executive information systems, market and competitive intelligence, intellectual asset management, information management, content integration, expertise location, collaboration, search, and internal communications. In implementing a suite of products and services on an intranet, our experience suggests considering the following:

Begin with a stakeholder that is a natural starting point, whether that is the most senior member or the most junior member of a team. Work your way up to the level in the decision hierarchy where resources can be assigned and the work of Step One can be carried out.

It is easier to manage expectations if you begin with a pilot project. Large-scale projects have less chance of success.

Communication is absolutely critical all the way through the effort. Communication needs to ensure a consistent understanding of requirements and expectations; even if they change, as they likely will, as the project is scoped. The vision and the objectives are the anchor, and they should be referred to in all communications.

Use the language of the stakeholders, and always double-check to make sure that the meaning is understood.

Involve as many stakeholders in the design as possible. They can choose to opt out, but it is important that they feel they have been included. Stakeholders who actually will use the intranet project in their daily lives must be committed and must be permanent members of the project team. Otherwise, the project runs a significant risk of failure.

It takes a multidisciplinary team to bring an intranet project to life. The ability to manage such a team is critical. Objective project management styles will ensure that everyone buys into the project; otherwise, biases and silos will emerge.

Use the objectives to develop a measurable impact on meeting the organizational need. How that measurement is done and reported to stakeholders is best understood within the common practice of the organization. There are many perspectives on how to measure. Find what works best for those stakeholders who control resources and make decisions. Get them to agree on the measures before you do too much work!

The transition between project implementation and operations has to occur early on—not when the project is already finished.

Intranets are largely driven by changes in technology or organizations that are becoming more aware of what technology can help them do. Understand the levels of tolerance in the organization for technology change. Some organizations look for very stable environments that have been proven over time; others prefer to test new waters. Often this depends on the scope of work. Know what makes most sense in your organization.

While successful projects are expected to require little if any training and education, reality dictates that this is not the case. Deploy with education: Train beforehand. If expectations are clear all along, there should not be any unfortunate surprises.

CHAPTER 4

Governance Roles and Responsibilities

Mary Lee Kennedy
TKG Consulting LLC

What Is Governance and Why Does It Matter for an Intranet?

Governance is a term used to describe a system of policies, procedures, standards, and guidelines. It establishes a framework for defining (1) who is responsible for what and (2) how decisions are made. It is the means by which a government or organization operates. In the information industry, it is also used to describe the processes that need to be adhered to in conducting project work and managing the ongoing work of a department or team. In terms of information and knowledge management, the role of governance is to ensure the delivery of a predictable environment. The predictability is established by the articulation of roles and responsibilities, the creation of a system of intertwined and understood accountability, and especially the clarification of how decisions are made. Governance provides the framework for managing the current environment as well as future change and growth.

For the purposes of this book, we separate governance into two parts:

1. Project Governance

Intranets are regularly the subject of project work, either in regard to first implementations or to ongoing improvements. Like most technology-enabled products and services, their rate of change has the potential to outpace the ability for all stakeholders to stay connected with a project's purpose and outcomes. Project governance has the primary purpose of ensuring that the project delivers on its promises and that decision-making occurs as agreed by the stakeholder community. Specifically, project governance is responsible for the following:

- Outlining the relationships between all internal and external project groups
- Establishing who is responsible for what and how project decisions are made
- Articulating the required flow of project information between the stakeholders
- Defining the processes and standards used for moving from one stage of a project to another

2. Ongoing Intranet Management Governance

The governance structure for ongoing intranet management has the following objectives:

- Setting and defining the rules and procedures for making decisions related to an intranet
- Providing the organizational structure through which objectives and measurable outcomes are set
- Providing the means of achieving the set objectives
- Monitoring and reporting on performance against the set objectives

Rarely are the two sets of governance without some overlap. Often, a part of the group will be responsible for the ongoing project management responsibilities as well. In fact, a link is critical for consistency between one project phase and the next. The key difference between the two is the degree to which the group is responsible for setting the scope of the work. In an ongoing governance structure, it is assumed that the stakeholders buy-in to a set of objectives that will require their support in terms of time, money, and human resources. Often in project work, the team is given an objective or is led by someone who has made a business case for a specific objective.

Considerations in Initiating a Governance Structure

Any governance review and implementation is a change management process. As such, it is important to identify the trigger (or "burning bridge," as it is often referred to in change management training). Once the common cause and urgency is determined, it is important to understand the scope of the governance model, address organizational readiness, and ensure that governance is clear on three fundamental relationships: customers, allies, and partners.

Governance Triggers

There are internal, industry, and societal triggers for governance. By identifying the trigger (whether it is largely reactive or proactive), an information professional can determine who the stakeholders are; what their primary interests are in terms of the intranet; what the priorities are for policies, standards, guidelines, and procedures; and what roles and responsibilities need to be defined and resourced. Figure 4.1 depicts common internal and external triggers of governance efforts.

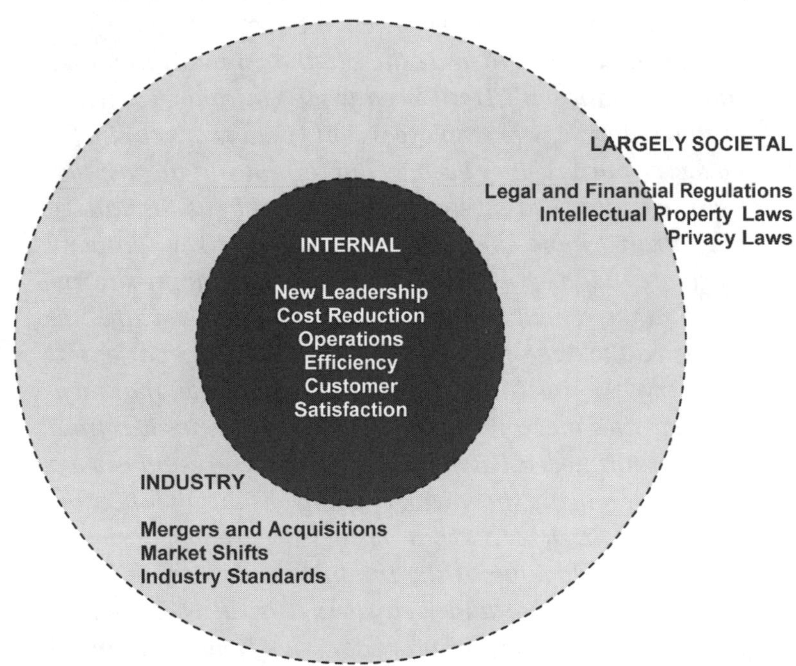

Figure 4.1 Common Governance Triggers

Internal Triggers

Like the Internet, many early generation intranets grew organically from the auspices of innovative experts who were early adopters. Over time, it was not unusual to discover new internal Web sites, duplicate applications and efforts, many pockets of expertise, conflicts in information sources and published documents, and innovative projects that were not widely publicized.

Organizations that adopted intranets at a later stage have been able to learn from their early adopter counterparts: Start small, establish user requirements up front, set a vision, take small steps rather than large leaps, and be clear about roles and responsibilities. Even larger organizations with thousands of Web sites (such as Microsoft and HP) have focused on structuring intranets, bringing together disparate stakeholders, and simplifying the user experience. In the words of Barbara Williams, a vice president at Hewlett Packard:

> *The intranet is really a tool for the employees of the company. It enables them to easily share information with others, to find information they need in order to do their jobs, and it enables them to find others in the company that they can collaborate with. Until recently, HP's intranet was wide-open territory, where employees could deploy a Web site for whatever purpose they deemed appropriate. In the last two years, we launched several efforts to enable us to manage our intranet more effectively, just like other key company assets are managed. We took an inventory of all the sites on the intranet, retired those that were no longer relevant, and registered the remaining sites and their owners in a central directory. We instituted processes to validate that new intranet sites met a business need and had approval from the appropriate level of management. We also established a process for retiring sites on an ongoing basis as they became outdated or irrelevant to our business. As we look forward, we are really looking at the intranet as something larger than just hardware and Web sites; it is an ecosystem of information, people, and processes (all of which are interdependent) and a fundamental support structure for our business.*

Usually, but not always, internal triggers relate to operational efficiencies (e.g., reduction of duplication in effort and reduction of noise in information flows), a need to improve or increase customer relationships (e.g., present one organization to the customer and understand what resources exist within the organization in order to address customer needs), or a need to focus on the leader's vision or strategic objectives (e.g., new markets, new products, and process improvements).

Industry Triggers

Shifts in industry standards (e.g., XML) may lead to revisiting the way work is done. Moving from one standard base (e.g., HTML) to another requires a significant investment in new skills, as well as a review of processes that are associated with the change. Governance assumes that the "go ahead" decision has been made. Clearly, any decision will require an assessment of operating costs and the initial investment required to make and sustain the changes.

If two organizations are joined, a common vision will require rethinking old ways of getting work done. This will necessitate a review of cultural alignment, how decisions are made, and who needs to be involved in the decision-making. In a merger-and-acquisition situation, the intranet can play a key role in enabling employee access to information and collaboration. Like any communication tool, it must be reviewed in terms of the culture (e.g., whether communication is done face-to-face, in small groups, announced to all employees via streaming media, interactive through blogs or weekly publications, or all of the above). As an information collection tool, the intranet will be critical in terms of learning about the organization, who is leading it, what projects are on the go, what the company's values and beliefs are, and how employees share information (including how much need-to-know information is actually available via the intranet). As a result, intranet users will make judgments about how open or closed the organization is in sharing information.

Shifts in industries can be either reactive or proactive. For an intranet, the origin itself is not as important as ensuring it is clear as to what needs to change—is it the medium itself, the way of doing work, the relationship between two organizations, or something else such as the ability to reach each employee with a consistent message?

Societal Triggers

With the advent of questions regarding corporate governance and individual privacy, significant rulings have been passed that include Sarbanes-Oxley (U.S.), the Freedom of Information Act (U.K.), and HIPAA (U.S.). These rulings require information to be collected, managed, and accessed under new government regulations. Processes need to be reviewed; security norms need to be assessed and adjusted where relevant; decisions need to be made about where information will be kept, which version is the master version, and who maintains what responsibilities during the information life cycle.

In January 2005, the British government officially adopted the Freedom of Information Act (FOIA). Changes across all government ministries were required to ensure that an individual's data is protected and yet easily accessible to the individuals. This change required governance decisions in the Parliament, within each department, and between departments. The public needed to be educated about what would and would not be available to them as individuals. Work processes were revised, information management altered, and information sharing within and outside of departments reviewed and adapted. Technology investments, especially those related to content management, were revisited, and investments were made in addressing workflow analysis, taxonomy construction, and authoring templates. Data accessibility standards and rules were reviewed and reset.

Societal changes are often reactive. It is important for those who are responsible for all or part of an intranet to note the scope of responsibility, the relationships intertwined with the scope, and the appropriate timing of various governance elements.

Governance Scope, Relationships, and Timing

Triggers help identify the scope of responsibility in terms of policies, standards, guidelines, and procedures. An individual must understand whether the governance needs to address a trigger's impact between organizations, within an organization as a whole, between organizational units, or within units or departments. This is not as obvious as it may first appear. The Sarbanes-Oxley ruling outlines significant changes that must occur, but it does not impact every process, role, and organizational unit; it is particularly focused on financial and accounting practices. XML has the potential to impact every information process, but given the costs involved, it is likely to be adopted and implemented in stages. Seemingly simpler changes, such as the need to reduce duplicated efforts between functions, incur much broader stakeholder involvement. It is necessary to frame the scope and gather stakeholder feedback to ensure that the scope is a shared one.

Actual governance depends on the direct sphere of influence one has in regards to department-level, unit-level, intra-organization, or inter-organization, and how an individual chooses to engage with others who have a common goal. Obtaining clarity in the type of relationship that exists is essential to establishing key roles and responsibilities. Table 4.1 outlines some key considerations when mapping stakeholder relationships.

Governance with Partners, Allies, or Customers: How to Decide

There is often confusion about governance because information professionals have an unclear understanding of the type of relationship they have with another organization or individual. Table 4.1 seeks to clarify the differences between them. The first point in each column highlights the primary difference in terms of what is shared between two entities.

Governance between partners requires agreement on the structure. By sharing a common goal, the governance framework must ensure joint accountability. The following quote from 1997 (U.S. Army Material Command, *Partnering for Success Guide*, 2007) summarizes a great analogy to consider when establishing a governance structure with a partner:

> *The Partnering Philosophy is not unique. It is similar to picking a partner at the office picnic and entering the three-legged race. The partners have their legs tied together and know that to win the race they must reach the finish line; however, if they run in different directions, do not start at the same time and on the same leg, or do not hold each other up and keep each other out of potholes on the path to the finish line, neither will finish successfully.*

Table 4.1 Differentiating Partners, Allies, and Customers

Partners	Allies	Customers
• Share goals • Set and agree to roles and responsibilities with respect to action items and deliverables to and from both groups • Measure and achieve success jointly • Acknowledge expertise and credibility from both groups • Agree at a high enough level so that resources are dedicated as needed • Integrate and reciprocate work where applicable to further both group's goals	• Share values and beliefs • Agree to be visibly active and counted in each other's "camp" • Measure success in terms of ongoing trust and demonstrated commitment • Acknowledge a common set of values and beliefs, and mutual respect • Agree informally (usually) to support each other as needed • Engage when there is a need to support each group's goals … rarely involves resource commitment	• Establish a service level agreement • Finalize defined action items and deliverables • Measure success as a customer value creation • "Buy" expertise in a service or product offering • May only need to escalate when service-level agreement is unmet • Use the service or product to further their own goals

Governance between allies is less formal and can be considered in terms of input rather than joint decision-making. Allies are like a support group or a set of functions that are not directly impacted by results but rather hold common values, beliefs, or expertise that can assist in achieving the overall objective.

Customers, on the other hand, directly impact—and are impacted by—the governance structure. Customers are the target audience for the product and service, and as end-users of the intranet, they must be considered key stakeholders, particularly in the definition of detailed strategic and tactical requirements. Many intranet efforts have failed by ignoring this critical audience. For example, one key finding of an information and knowledge-sharing study conducted in several large U.S. hospital systems in 2004 by Tom Davenport and the present author was that any change in process that ignored the end-user resulted in wasted time, wasted effort, and even the cancellation of multimillion dollar implementations.

At a minimum, a governance structure needs to involve the following stakeholders:

- Customers/end-users whose input defines the requirements for intranet use.
- Partners whose input defines the degree of impact on policies, standards, and procedures, together with guidelines that fit into the scope of a governance trigger (i.e., the objective or "burning bridge" for which the governance need exists).
- Allies who inform, champion, and offer guidance to the governance process as objective bystanders.
- An overall sponsor (or sponsors) directly impacted by the governance structure. These need to be individuals who play senior roles (as senior as possible) or individuals who can address a strategic change request and who represent the entire scope of the exercise (department-level, unit-level, inter-organization, or intra-organization). These individuals act as champions for the initiative at the senior decision-making table.

When to Initiate a Governance Effort

Timing is a critical consideration when implementing a governance structure. At different stages of an intranet implementation, different governance elements are necessary. Consider Jan Damsgaard and Rens Scheeper's intranet adoption curve as depicted in Figure 4.2.

Essentially, Damsgaard and Scheepers show a significant drop in intranet adoption when significant events occur, specifically when there are events that require actions related to governance. Consider the following:

At the Initiation stage, sponsorship is key. Governance requires identifying a sponsor or sponsors that will champion the initiative in the context of the primary triggers. This does not need to occur at the onset of the intranet initiative. However, to ensure ongoing funding, the establishment of a clear purpose, and the organization of information and knowledge assets that are accessible via the intranet, a

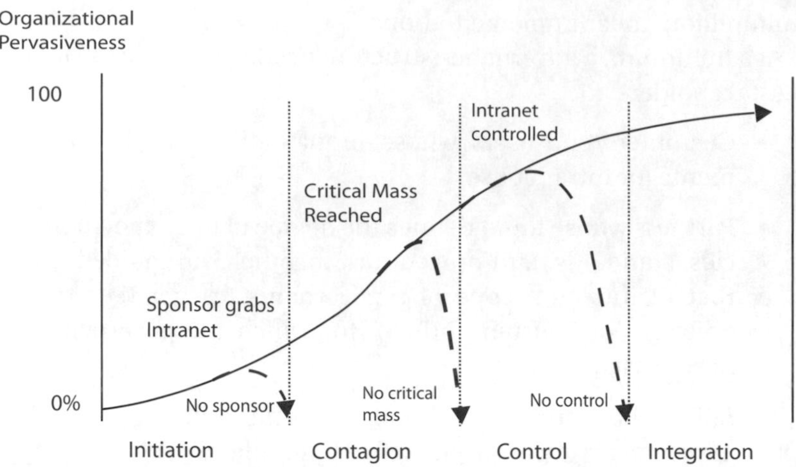

Figure 4.2 Intranet Adoption Curve (Source: Damsgaard, Jan and Rens Scheepers. "Managing the Crises in Intranet Implementation: A Stage Model." *Information Systems Journal* 10.2 (2000): 131–150)

senior sponsor is required who represents the business case in planning and resource allocation discussions.

Assuming that sponsorship exists (either formally or informally) to ensure the day-to-day operations of the intranet, the justification for further intranet development lies in using the medium by a critical mass of the organization's employees. Damsgaard and Scheepers call this "contagion." End-user requirements must be met, and contagion will not occur without including the customer or end-user requirements in the decision-making processes. Intranet initiatives that spend time trying to find users to make use of the system are rarely successful. End-users and customers may not always reside in the same groups. Customers can be other departments that use intranet services for their end-users (i.e., a central service group is the service provider to a channel and the channel owns the end-user). Both groups need to agree on end-user needs for the future development of products and services.

As Steve Lovitt, an information analyst for the Grant County Public Utility Department, states:

> *The most important thing we have done is make an intranet that allows each department or area to have its own uniqueness, but still be able to use a standard template and keep all*

parts of the intranet functionally the same using the same standards. This means that wherever any user goes on the site, it remains familiar. Second, we always interview the area employees who place the request for any new intranet development. Understanding what they need and desire, and then educating them on what we all can do and offer, helps us make a successful product for the end-user. With all the sites operating the same, we cannot only tell them, but we can also demonstrate how their sites may look and function, so they have a better understanding.

Given that the purpose of governance, in terms of information and knowledge management, is to ensure delivery of a predictable environment, governance must address the operations that will provide an accepted level of control. How this actually occurs, and the form that it takes, depends on culture (see the following section).

Control is gained by establishing functional responsibilities. Teams and individuals are accountable for the various intranet components (portal, Web sites, overall architecture, content management, search, taxonomy, design, navigation, information life cycle management, etc.). With clarity around roles and responsibilities in the context of defined organizational triggers and customer and end-user requirements, a predictable experience is possible.

The intranet is only truly integrated into the organizational environment once it plays a role in the everyday working experience of the employee. This is in contrast to having the intranet simply as an extension or benefit of the day-to-day working environment. While content integration software is certainly one of the potential extensions of the traditional portal, this is not the intent we are addressing here. Integration is considered in the following aspects:

- Perception (intranet is part of the work being done)
- Practice (intranet resources are used in completing work tasks)
- Technology (standards and platforms exist so information can be embedded within the intranet-based applications or on the devices that a process depends on)

Table 4.2 provides example governance elements to consider at each stage of intranet adoption.

Table 4.2 Example Governance Elements by Intranet Adoption Stage

Adoption Stage	Initiation	Contagion	Control	Integration
Sample Governance Elements	• Sponsor defined and identified • Owner or owners defined and identified • Project governance (short-term)	• Initiation plus: End-user or organizational representation • Functional governance begins (e.g., information architecture) including key guidelines and standards • Project manager	• Contagion plus: Steering Committee • Formal boards • Policies	• Institutionalized operating and capital budget • Component of organizational planning • Component of organizational measurement

Early Governance → **Mature Governance**

The Forms of Governance

Governance takes on many forms. It has formal instantiations such as boards, committees, task forces, audit processes, change control hierarchies, and documented policies, standards, and guidelines. Informal aspects of governance include implicit gestures such as a nod of the head by a senior manager, ad hoc peer reviews, and even handshakes. Many cultural considerations will inform a decision in terms of how formal or informal the governance structure needs to be and what the best choices are for ensuring success in decision-making processes (see the next section, Organizational Culture and Governance).

For the reader with less experience in differentiating among boards, committees, task forces, policies, standards, guidelines, and procedures, definitions, distinctive elements, and examples follow.

Boards almost always exist as advisory groups that are called in to provide guidance on strategy. Organizations typically have a board of directors to guide the senior team responsible for delivering on a strategic plan. For the intranet, boards are most often assembled using senior representatives from inside or outside the company. The board's primary function is to ensure that the strategy makes sense, is realistic, and is executable given the resources available to the organization.

Committees and their sub-committees are focused on the operational oversight involved in executing strategy. They may be a coordinating unit, but they rarely are involved in the day-to-day management of intranet-related work. Rather, they tend to focus on ensuring that all perspectives are considered when delivering work. Committees are generally composed of representatives from the ownership base.

Task forces are typically ad hoc in nature and are established for a specific period. They are given a mandate by the board or a committee and are expected to adhere to a tightly scoped objective. Generally, task forces are led by the most senior expert in the organization or, alternatively, a highly objective leader who facilitates a group of subject experts. The group's collective expertise is then applied to addressing the task outlined in the mandate.

Policies are usually documented to comply with legal and financial requirements. There are usually significant financial or legal implications for not adhering to the policy. They are established to protect an organization and its individuals or audiences that have a relationship with the organization and its employees. Policies are essential to the ongoing viability of an organization. Due to the serious consequences of policy infringement, policies are broadly communicated and often referred to using footnotes in documents and, as such, are brought to the attention of all members engaged with the organization. Examples of policies related to the intranet include information security, privacy, copyright, and information and records retention.

Standards are widely accepted conventions that contributors and administrators are expected to follow to ensure that the intranet meets its goals. They are usually written down and agreed upon by a body of experts who understand the implications of adopting them. External standards may be adopted, such as W3C, Dublin Core, or Newsxml. Such specific standards may be further designed for the organization by an internal group or by external experts in the field. Internal standards are often instituted in response to a lack of industry consensus or to address unique considerations (e.g., product names). Even in the most hierarchical organizations, standards designed without a perceived need are likely to be avoided. This is particularly true because the implementation of standards often requires some compromise. In general, standards exist to ensure a specific level of quality or a level of agreement among the various parties responsible for its realization. Examples of intranet standards include metadata standards, navigation standards, accessibility standards, and content authoring standards.

Guidelines are recommendations or "good practices" that increase the predictability of the intranet when they are followed. Guidelines are not mandatory. They are generally developed based on experience attained within the organization or on observations and formal benchmarking regarding the experiences of other organizations. Guidelines affect the "final touches" of the intranet—those things that will definitely make a difference but are not considered critical to achieving the objective. In many organizations, there is an expectation that any good practitioner will follow the guidelines and, even more importantly, will contribute to improvements over time. A major compliment paid to any employee is when his or her personal guideline is formally documented as an exemplar guideline for others to follow. Examples of guidelines include design guidelines, guidelines for authoring intranet content, and guidelines for conducting content audits.

It may be questionable as to whether *procedures* are a form of governance or simply an instructional tool. It is not the purpose of this text to debate whether procedures are a form of governance or not. For the everyday practitioner, procedures are step-by-step "how-to" items usually written for a specific function or level of expertise. They are used to ensure that specific tasks are completed in adherence to standards and guidelines. Mostly, they exist to allow for good work to be duplicated. Not all organizations have written procedures; this leads to significant intranet quality challenges over time. Examples of procedures include conducting usability testing, conducting end-user needs assessments, managing taxonomy change control, and implementing indexing practices.

Organizational Culture and Governance

Culture is the most fundamental element of any work setting. It is especially evident in any activity related to establishing and running a governance structure. Agreement on the most useful forms of intranet governance (which includes timing, roles, and responsibilities) requires sensitivity to values, beliefs, norms, and formal and informal rules. Any change in the intranet has the potential to change the culture (just ask a group whose access to the Internet was or was not denied). An intranet also has the capability to be used as a tool in cultural change (for example, choosing to make all project plans available to a broad group of employees).

In their chapter on cultural change in the multivolume work titled *Organizational Studies,* Debra Meyerson and Joanne Martin (2001) provide three different paradigms in cultural focus: integration, differentiation, or ambiguity. While it is not the intent of this text to define culture, it is worthwhile to present these three paradigms, allowing us to consider each in terms of ways in which to establish governance frameworks that will work best for a given organization. A summary of the cultural paradigms is outlined in Table 4.3.

Table 4.3 Organizational Cultural Paradigms

Paradigm Name	**Integration**	**Differentiation**	**Ambiguity**
Degree of consistency among cultural manifestations	*Consistency*	Inconsistency and consistency	Lack of clarity (neither clearly inconsistent nor clearly consistent) and irreconcilable inconsistencies
Degree of consensus among members of culture	Organization-wide	*Within, not between, subcultures*	Issue specific consensus, dissensus, and confusion among individuals
Reaction to ambiguity	Denial	Channeling	*Acceptance*
Metaphor for paradigm	Hologram; clearing in the jungle	Islands of clarity in sea of ambiguity	Web; jungle

Source: Meyerson, Debra, and Joanne Martin. “Cultural Change” in *Organizational Studies*, vol. I, ed. Warwick Organizational Behavior Staff. Florence, Kentucky: Routledge (2001): 330–335.

In Paradigm 1 (Integration), culture is defined as that which is shared by and/or unique to a given organization or group. Culture, according to this definition, is an integration mechanism, the social or normative glue that holds together a potentially diverse group of organizational members. An intranet governance model in Paradigm 1 would reflect the unity, is driven by a commonly held vision and mission, and could likely be managed by a central team.

In Paradigm 2 (Differentiation), culture is characterized by differentiation and diversity. The subunits are important, including groups and individuals. Culture is formed by influences both inside and outside of the organization. There is no single, monolithic dominant culture. An intranet governance model in Paradigm 2 would bring together those elements that benefit all the subunits, with substantial independence for unique unit capabilities. A central services unit may serve the needs of the whole, but much of the work and responsibility is likely distributed to the units.

The main cultural differentiator between Paradigm 3 (Ambiguity) and Paradigms 1 or 2 is the degree that ambiguity is accepted. In Paradigm 3, complexity and the lack of clarity is made legitimate and becomes a primary focus of attention. From a Paradigm 3 perspective, irreconcilable interpretations are simultaneously entertained and paradoxes are embraced. There are no shared, integrated values other than the awareness of ambiguity itself. An intranet governance model in Paradigm 3 would be based on shared practices, exchanges of ideas, and focused on very specific common needs such as search, with no requirement to ensure that everything is uniform. At the same time, ease of information access might become a strategic driver for change if the organization needs to address customer satisfaction or market interruptions as a goal.

Knowing which form is most appropriate for your organization's culture is critical. It can mean the difference between successful implementation or failure. For example, take these two cases (their identities are left blind on purpose).

Case One: Type 2 Paradigm Culture

Setting: Organization A is a highly decentralized global organization with subunits that are fairly independent and accountable for their profit-and-loss statements. The organization's intranet is globally available, almost any type of technology can be used, and every employee is a potential author and publisher. Web sites are developed and managed locally. The result is a proliferation of information and Web sites, and very little infrastructure is available to organize the intranet for a seamless user experience.

Drivers for change: The end-user experience is inconsistent, and the ability for the intranet to return quality information to its end-users is consistently unreliable. This results in lost revenue, mistakes that incur unplanned expenses, and dissatisfied employees and customers. The need for independence no longer outweighs the need to find required information.

Governance approach: The first attempt was unsuccessful to bring the various portal owners together to agree on a set of common practices for taxonomy management. In this highly competitive environment where every portal owner's reputation matters, finding common ground is tough. The need to innovate is both a must and a challenge in creating a successful intranet. Information governance methods are used to gain internal customers by helping each portal owner become successful. After several years of successfully proving the value of centralized services (portal owner by portal owner), a formal governance structure is implemented with clear roles and responsibilities. Stakeholder engagement is broad and focused on critical elements, such as taxonomy, privacy, navigation, and design. There are no policies beyond those that are legally required. Standards and guidelines are self-policed with a few resources held centrally responsible for project management, central services, and monitoring progress toward shared goals. Progress is slow.

Case Two: Type 1 Paradigm Culture

Setting: Organization B is moderately centralized, and its subunits rely on centralized operational units to act as the glue for functional support. Subunits are accountable for specific products or customers. Functional expertise is the organizing unit. All resources not considered core to a product or customer, such as IT, content purchases, Web production, and design, are managed centrally. The organization's intranet is available globally. To date, it has been managed as a technology platform that extends the enterprise and is in the process of being reviewed in terms of the user experience in sharing ideas, expertise, and information.

Drivers for change: There is a widely held belief by the executive committee that knowledge is being lost, productivity gains are possible, and duplicated costs are increasing expenses. The exact nature of the opportunity remains undefined. The ease with which information can be exchanged via the Internet, e-mail, BlackBerrys, and phones has created a perception that much more is possible within the organization's own firewall.

Governance approach: From the beginning, a triumvirate is established between the "information management" organization, the information technology (IT) organization, and the marketing and communications organization. Some tension exists in the alliance as exact roles and responsibilities must be worked out. Together, this central services team makes a recommendation to senior management to add structure to the intranet. Clear roles and responsibilities are outlined and formal sign-off is given. A communication plan for the alliance and for key stakeholders is established to ensure all-around accountability. Business units are engaged one-by-one to identify user experience requirements. Policies are reviewed, with new ones being established in areas such as privacy, intellectual property rights, and security. Standards and guidelines are established for the three central services and for anyone with an author or publisher role. Formal training occurs. Policing is carried out by the central service units that are accountable for instituting change in the broader organization. Infractions are brought to the attention of a key contact in each subject discipline.

It is important to note the different organizational approaches to governance:

- Organization A (a Paradigm 2 culture) needs to bring its intranet together in increments. Given the focus on differentiation, decision-making resides within the subunits, and the central group remains small, earning the organization's respect over time. Little organizational formality exists since the units are accountable to themselves. Changes occur formally and informally and require broad stakeholder engagement. Where there are common elements of interest, there is a significant amount of investment, with little investment being funneled to unique subunit needs. The small central services team leads by managing commonly required services.
- Organization B (a Paradigm 1 culture) needs to establish a partnership or alliance up front to create a center for

intranet initiatives. With approval by the senior management team, the group establishes a list of action items and proposes policies, standards, and guidelines required to deliver the desired end-user experience. The central team is responsible for thought leadership, program management, delivery of services, and training.

Governance outcomes depend on the ability to make decisions that are then acted upon. Decision-making styles and follow-up are influenced by organizational behavior. Table 4.4, which is based on the work of Geoffrey Moore (2002), can be used to determine how to motivate members within an organization to adopt a governance framework, how to engage, and what to consider in terms of the scope of inclusion in the decision-making process.

On an individual basis, governance structures must consider whether key stakeholders (particularly senior executives and partners) can make decisions based on consensus, broad-based collaboration, trusted-few collaboration, or independent reasoning.

It is worth outlining a decision-making process that is transparent. Steps to include the following:

1. Frame the decision
2. Gather information
3. Identify all feasible alternatives
4. Identify criteria for evaluating alternatives
5. Apply criteria to the alternatives
6. Make the decision
7. Take action
8. Learn from the experience

Governance Roles and Responsibilities

At the end of the day, governance comes down to individuals who are responsible for accomplishing their assigned tasks. Many projects have failed or ended up less than successful due to role confusion or a lack of sufficiently explicit tasks, expected outcomes, and assignments.

There are critical roles to consider in initiating and steering an intranet through to integration. Perhaps the best way to look at roles

Table 4.4 Organizational Motivators

Culture	Competence	Control	Collaboration	Cultivation
Cherishes	Achievement	Power and security	Affiliation	Self-realization
Celebrates	Superior individual	Meeting the plan	Power of teamwork	Creative expression
Prioritizes	The work	The system	The people	The idea
Asks	How?	What?	Who?	Why?
Leads by	Expertise	Authority	Role	Charisma
Organizes as	Work projects	Hierarchy	Persistent teams	As little as possible
Recruits for	Competitiveness	Reliability	Cooperativeness	Brilliance

Source: Moore, Geoffrey A. *Living on the Fault Line: Managing for Shareholder Value in Any Economy.* rev. ed. NY: Harper Collins, 2002.

is in terms of timing. Throughout an intranet initiative, the owner(s) and the sponsor(s) persist. These two roles are critical throughout the entire process.

Initiation Primary Roles and Responsibilities

In the critical Initiation stage, the owner or owners are accountable for the following:

- Identifying quick wins
- Demonstrating organizational value to potential sponsors
- Engaging a sponsor
- Communicating the intranet's use and utility to the broader community
- Getting the work done

The sponsor or sponsors are expected to do the following:

- Engage senior members of the organization
- Champion resource allocations, policies, and standards
- Represent and provide insight into the organization's priorities and direction

- Provide senior input into strategies, plans, and projects

Contagion Primary Roles and Responsibilities

In the Contagion stage, the owner or owners would be encouraged to add the following to their duties:

- Aligning intranet priorities with organizational or unit objectives
- Engaging and meeting customer and end-user requirements
- Forming the team required to run the operation and complete the projects
- Developing and driving the adoption of standards and guidelines, particularly functional standards and guidelines
- Reporting on work and progress against objectives
- Identifying opportunities for improvement

The sponsor or sponsors should consider including the following:

- Championing resource allocations, policies, and standards
- Representing and providing insight into the organization's priorities and direction
- Providing senior input into strategies, plans, and projects

A project manager would be accountable for the following:

- Engaging cross-organizational teams in functional improvements
- Completing projects tasked by the sponsor and other senior champions
- Establishing procedures

Control Primary Roles and Responsibilities

In the Control stage, the owner or owners must ensure that functions are formed with clear roles and responsibilities.

The sponsor or sponsors are expected to continue in the following activities:

- Engaging senior members of the organization, encouraging their groups to participate
- Championing resource allocations, policies, and standards
- Representing and providing insight into the organization's priorities and direction
- Providing senior input into strategies, plans, and projects

Functions are formed in units or in central groups tasked with the following:

- Understanding and prioritizing user requirements
- Developing, managing, and supporting the information environment in areas of expertise such as
    - Information and systems architecture
    - Content selection
    - Content management
    - User interface design
    - Editorial programs
- Change control
- Quality management
- Monitoring and measuring progress against objectives
- Identifying opportunities for improvement

Formal entities such as a steering committee and boards are formed to do the following:

- Provide feedback on strategic alignment
- Recommend policy development

Committees, subcommittees, and task forces may be engaged to work on specific intranet areas such as the following:

- Taxonomy
- Findability

- Collaboration
- Business process alignment (including the development of specific standards, guidelines, and practices that will improve predictability)

Integration Primary Roles and Responsibilities

Essentially, a fully integrated intranet requires an ownership that is accountable for the operating budget; unit budget; developing and enforcing policies, standards, and guidelines; and assigning resources to align work with strategic objectives.

The sponsor(s) will be required to champion the needs of the organization, and represent those needs in senior-level discussions and funding processes.

Governing units (boards, steering committees, functions, and project management) will focus on ensuring that the strategy is correct and the work done meets stakeholder expectations.

Conclusion

This chapter has focused on considerations in governing an intranet. Key takeaways include the following:

1. Develop governance in conjunction with those responsible for its adoption. Close association and ongoing interaction with those who will be using the intranet will ensure that it is actively used.
2. Education plays a major role in successful governance. Ensure that everyone understands why, how, and when.
3. It is important to leave ownership in the hands of those who are best able to complete the work. For example, content should reside with the organizational units, IT infrastructure should reside with the IT group, and the user interface should reside with the design team. While tougher to manage, this approach leads to superior outputs.
4. Understand what really needs to be governed. It is not necessary to govern everything. Given the grassroots nature of many intranet initiatives, it is worth defining

how organizations will integrate. This will help ensure that effective information and knowledge transfer occurs. It may not be necessary to govern integration down to the last detail of the last Web-based page. Intra-organizational standards are often easier to implement, and they tend to generate positive results that are readily apparent to the broader organization.

5. Governance exists at many levels and functions within an organization. One should design accordingly and redesign infrequently to avoid confusion.
6. There are five primary roles that have emerged in association with intranet development and use: technology champion, organizational sponsor, intranet coordinator, intranet developer, and content provider.
7. Where would the intranet be without content? Ensure that the governance model makes quality content easy to contribute and easy to deliver.
8. Governance needs to be consistent with predictable outcomes. Governance requires compliance and the ability to ensure that conditions for a successful intranet are met.

CHAPTER 5

Collaboration and Communities

Debra Wallace
TKG Consulting LLC

A single-word search of "collaboration" using Google Scholar resulted in a mountainous list of papers ranging from "Dijet Production by Color Singlet Exchange at the Fermilab Tevatron" to "Measurement of the Beam-Spin Azimuthal Asymmetry Associated with Deeply-Virtual Compton Scattering." The citations encompassed an unusual array of subjects with absolutely no mention of collaboration in the titles. What these papers have in common, other than perhaps not being a casual dinner topic in the average household, is that they are all the result of collaboration.

Like many current management approaches, collaboration is hardly new. People have been working together in formal and informal ways since that proverbial "dawn of time." Most of our scientific discoveries, works of art, and inventions are in fact the result of some level of collaboration—not the sole brainchild of one individual's effort. What is different today and worthy of our attention are the new ways that these collaborative efforts are enabled by information and computer technologies (ICTs). Intranets are challenging Allen's 50-Foot Rule of co-locating for effective collaboration (Lipnack and Stamp, 2000, p. 20), providing opportunities for people to work together 24/7 around the globe through synchronous and asynchronous channels.

However, intranets and a wide-range of new ICTs are only two pieces of the collaboration puzzle. Technology does not drive collaboration—people and purpose drive it. Effective collaboration relies on more than an intranet portal and tools for collaborative software—a lesson some knowledge management practitioners are learning as significant numbers of their technology-focused approaches are falling short of expectations.

In this chapter, we will take a look at the fundamentals of collaboration—the elements that work in concert to create an environment for effective collaboration. We will also explore one of the more successful structures for supporting collaboration: communities of practice. As a forum for innovation based on a climate of trust, communities of practice are generating value for organizations, individuals, and professions in ways that researchers and practitioners never dreamed of when they first identified their potential.

Collaboration Is Not an Adjective

We begin with a definition of collaboration because like many ideas touted as silver bullets to solve management challenges or the next killer app to outperform the competition, collaboration is currently enjoying center stage, often without a thorough understanding of what is involved. We have seen a wide range of understanding about the meaning of collaboration. Some organizations have articulated a comprehensive definition; others misunderstand the complexities and nuances and unceremoniously lump any form of group or teamwork into the mix; and still others do not have a clue what it means to truly collaborate—often the term does not even enter the corporate lexicon. For the organizations that get it, collaboration is leveraged as a generative capability that's integral to their success in the emerging networked economy.

The verb "to collaborate" was introduced into the English language in the late 19th century. It comes from the Latin *collaborare*, which literally means "to work together" (e.g., co-labor or toil). The Oxford English Dictionary Online defines it as "the act of working in conjunction with another or others, to co-operate."

Incorporating Aristotle's notion that "the whole is greater than the sum of its parts," Bruner (1991) defines collaboration as:

> *A process to reach goals that cannot be achieved acting singly (or at a minimum, cannot be reached efficiently) ... it includes: jointly developing and agreeing to a set of common goals and directions; sharing responsibility for obtaining those goals; and working together to achieve those goals, using the expertise of each collaborator.* (p. 6)

This definition highlights the value-added nature of collaboration and outlines key elements of a collaborative effort. It stands as the working definition of collaboration for this chapter.

The nature of collaboration varies depending on the purpose and approaches that define the collaborative effort. The process can range from a low level where work is divided up, people go off and complete their section or sections, and then come back and contribute their work as segments of a final product, to the highest level where a continuous, iterative exchange of ideas and infusion of tacit knowledge creates an outcome based on a synthesis of thought and the experience of the contributors.

But collaboration also has a dark side. Webster's Online Dictionary provides a comprehensive overview of the term, including a quote from Boulle's screenplay for *The Bridge on the River Kwai*: "The fact is, what we're doing could be construed as—forgive me, sir—collaboration with the enemy." Collaboration is not always desirable as in the case of the University of Manitoba's stand on inappropriate collaboration, for example (see the sidebar on page 100).

Collaboration sits squarely on the long list of "C-words" found in the discourse of the knowledge and learning field as well in information technology (e.g., cooperate, communicate, connect, contribute, commit, converse)—capabilities that ready organizations to meet the changing demands of their clients and stakeholders.

Elements of Collaboration

Among the thousands of references to collaboration on the Internet, only a relatively small number of resources refer specifically to the process of collaboration itself. A study of collaboration in the intelligence community (Hall, 1999) identified 10 elements, based on a review of academic research on and industry experience with effective collaboration. These elements are discussed in terms of implementing tools to support collaboration, but they can be more broadly applied to any collaborative effort:

- *Culture of sharing*. The culture supports an organization-wide sharing of knowledge and information. Senior management emphasizes the importance of collaboration as a strategic capability, and the organization's structure and business processes enable it.

Addressing Inappropriate Collaboration at the University of Manitoba

While the academic community is largely based on collaboration and relies heavily on peer review, student grades are based on individual work, unless otherwise specified. To help students understand what constitutes "inappropriate collaboration," the University of Manitoba has clearly articulated definitions, outlined student responsibilities, and identified a process for addressing unethical behavior.

Most universities have stated codes of conduct or behavior, processes for addressing infractions, and assistance to resolve conflicts. When inappropriate collaboration is equated with cheating, the university's integrity is damaged and the consequences are severe. In an environment where collaboration may not be a default approach, knowing boundaries, clarifying intentions, and verifying actions is the student's responsibility. Effective collaboration relies on knowing the ground rules, including when collaboration is inappropriate. (See University of Manitoba: Student Advocacy Web site at www.cc.umanitoba.ca/student/resource/student_advocacy/inappropriate_collaborate.shtml.)

- *Common goal.* The focus and motivation to participate are based on a common purpose or goal. Measuring the group's progress toward achieving the goal helps clarify direction and make explicit the value-add that collaboration brings to the effort.
- *Process and workflow.* The collaboration process and how it integrates with existing workflows is identified, including the processes and flows, types of information to be shared, and application of tools.
- *Trust.* The information shared is accurate and reliable and is managed in an agreed upon manner. A trusting relationship

exists based on a social network where participants have confidence in one another and in their working relationships.

- *Rules of engagement.* Procedures, protocols, and regulations are identified to guide the process of collaboration, especially the standard approaches to communicating and decision-making.
- *Mutual benefit.* An equitable distribution of effort and benefit is articulated.
- *Management support.* All levels of management engage in visible, active communication of the benefits of collaboration, commit needed resources, demonstrate involvement, and acknowledge successes.
- *Team rewards.* Knowledge sharing is promoted and recognized in alignment with the organization's evaluation and reward systems. A balance between recognition for individual and team efforts is clearly articulated and understood.
- *Training.* Effective collaboration skills are developed in conjunction with the effective use of tools integrated with established work processes and routines.
- *Critical mass.* An appropriate number of active participants are engaged to make the systems that support collaboration viable in enabling the effort.

What is clear with this list of elements is that technology alone does not drive collaboration. Rather, culture continues to hold the pole position—to be the trump card in any effort, no matter the type of organization. As enablers, information and computer technologies have provided opportunities for effective collaboration to a greater extent than perhaps any other resource or tool, barring communication devices such as the telephone and medieval guild wagons. But technology (e.g., e-mail, Web conferencing, portals, online workspaces, and instant messaging [IM] identified as the top tools that support collaboration by Alice Dragoon) is doomed for failure if a collaborative culture is not in place—a fact that is reinforced throughout the literature, yet not heeded by the people making technology decisions.

Because of the prominent role that culture plays and the tendency to focus on technology alone to enable collaborative workspaces, identifying the elements of collaboration within any given organization should be the first step in building the capacity to collaborate. Mapping the process from instances of effective collaboration within an organization will provide a more accurate picture. Then, benchmarking against other industry examples highlights the gaps and suggests areas for improvement. We have found this approach to be more successful than adopting a synthesis of elements from the literature, or worse yet, employing the lowest common denominator as a "cookie-cutter" approach. By using an appreciative inquiry methodology and identifying what the components of effective collaboration are within a specific context, organizations are further ahead because they can build on a foundation already in place, which is aligned with cultural norms, rather than starting from scratch.

Critical Success Factors of Effective Collaboration

All collaborative efforts rely heavily on the participants' capability to dialogue. As Groff and Jones point out, "collaboration is not about debate or discussion—it is about dialogue" (2003, p. 57). Through the exchange of ideas, where varying viewpoints and perspectives are considered, dialogue encourages people to expand their current thinking and consider new possibilities—the heart of learning and innovation.

Groff and Jones suggest that the following six success factors are critical and need to be in place to achieve effective collaboration (pp. 57–63):

1. *Dialogue.* As previously noted, central to the process of collaboration is the ability to engage in an exchange of ideas where participants respect a diversity of perspectives.

2. *Trust.* Frank, honest dialogue requires a high degree of trust that the opinions and experiences expressed will be received with an open mind by everyone engaged in the dialogue.

Increasing Capabilities for Effective Collaboration at the IDRC

The International Development Research Centre (IDRC, a 35-year-old Canadian public corporation) is committed to increasing research capacity in developing countries—focusing on projects that create knowledge at the local level for building healthier, more equitable, and more prosperous societies. Long considered a model of knowledge sharing, much of IDRC's success in stretching the reach of its funding relies on collaboration as a core capability for creating and maintaining its many external partnerships, networks, secretariats, and communities of practice.

With regional offices and individual field offices around the world and a global, transdisciplinary collaborative research approach, IDRC staff rely on collaboration to complete most aspects of their work. Since the staff didn't want to become "shoemaker's children," an internal collaboration study was undertaken to assess current practice and identify gaps. Researchers found that high value was universally placed on effective collaboration, but no systematic approach for developing and sustaining the capabilities needed to enable the process was in place.

Raising awareness with key stakeholders about the need for IDRC to focus more on collaboration as a core capability led to identifying a framework for collaboration, highlighting examples of best practice, and leveraging existing tools and resources. This was a reminder that core capabilities need to be constantly nurtured and improved. (See the IDRC Web site at www.idrc.ca and the Bellanet: Supporting Collaboration in the Development Community Web site at www.bellanet.org.)

3. *Common goals.* Although a variety of agendas and assumptions may be "on the table," the group must agree

early in the process on a direction for the work—the goal or goals that unite everyone in their work together.

4. *Empathy*. Finding common ground with people whose perspectives or views are at odds with the rest of the group requires that all participants must be able to identify and understand opposing viewpoints and work toward win-win resolutions.

5. *Openness*. Assumptions must be brought out into the open to avoid misunderstandings and errors.

6. *Collaboration skills*. Effective communication, especially active listening, and conflict resolution are key collaboration skills required by all group members.

Levels of Collaboration

All collaborations are not created equal. To understand the expectations, possibilities, types of resources required, and extent to which processes and policies should be developed, the nature of the collaboration needs to be defined.

The National Network for Collaboration has outlined a framework for facilitating collaboration between universities and communities. The organization suggests that at the start of any collaboration, the parties need to define the relationship as a means of providing focus and clarity. Table 5.1 borrows Hogue's matrix of five levels of relationships with the corresponding characteristics grouped by purpose, structure, and processes.

Although this framework is specific to a particular model of collaboration (i.e., community/university), it provides a useful diagnostic. Just as organizations need to identify the elements of effective collaboration within that organization's context, there is value in understanding the levels of collaboration that exist both internally and externally. Creating a maturity model that characterizes informal, lower-order collaborative efforts through to highly structured and complex forms of collaboration can be used to manage expectations and balance resource needs.

Table 5.1 Community Linkages—Choices and Decisions

Levels	Purpose	Structure	Process
Networking	• Dialog and common understanding • Clearinghouse for information • Create base of support	• Loose/flexible link • Roles loosely defined • Community action is primary link among members	• Low-key leadership • Minimal decision-making • Little conflict • Informal communication
Cooperation or Alliance	• Match needs and provide coordination • Limit duplication of services • Ensure tasks are done	• Central body of people as communication hub • Semiformal links • Roles somewhat defined • Links are advisory • Group leverages/raises money	• Facilitative leaders • Complex decision-making • Some conflict • Formal communications within the central group
Coordination or Partnership	• Share resources to address common issues • Merge resource base to create something new	• Central body of people consists of decision-makers • Roles defined • Links formalized • Group develops new resources and joint budget	• Autonomous leadership but focus in on issue • Group decision-making in central and subgroups • Communication is frequent and clear
Coalition	• Share ideas and be willing to pull resources from existing systems • Develop commitment for a minimum of three years	• All members involved in decision-making • Roles and time defined • Links formal with written agreement • Group develops new resources and joint budget	• Shared leadership • Decision-making formal with all members • Communication is common and prioritized
Collaboration	• Accomplish shared vision and impact benchmarks • Build interdependent system to address issues and opportunities	• Consensus used in shared decision-making • Roles, time, and evaluation formalized • Links are formal and written in work assignments	• Leadership high, trust level high, productivity high • Ideas and decisions equally shared • Highly developed communication

Source: Hogue, Teresa. *Community Based Collaborations—Wellness Multiplied.* Oregon Center for Community Leadership, 1994. crs.uvm.edu/nnco/collab/framework.html (accessed July 20, 2007).

Potential of Collaboration

Kouzes and Posner (2002) sum up the potential of collaboration:

> *Collaboration is* the *critical competency for achieving and sustaining high performance—especially in the Internet Age. It won't be the ability to fiercely compete but the ability to lovingly cooperate that will determine success.* (p. 242)

The playing field and the rules of engagement for any organization are in flux as we transition from the traditions of the Industrial Age to the new norms of the "Whatever-it-ends-up-being-called" Age. (Ages are only defined once they are over.) Whether or not the capability to "lovingly cooperate," as previously suggested, becomes the norm in the foreseeable future is debatable. However, from the common thread seen in current management literature, we do know that in order to survive, organizations need "to be flexible, adaptive, and to continually reinvent themselves" (Skyrme, 1999, p. 3). To this list of attributes, we would add that they also need to have superior capabilities to collaborate both internally and externally with their full range of stakeholders, including their competitors and customers.

However, our experience is that organizations do not typically recognize collaboration as a distinct or core capability. Collaboration as a process needs to be enabled and enhanced as it remains under the radar of some decision-makers. For example, at the first meeting of the World Summit on the Information Society, which was held in Geneva in 2003, a global forum of representatives from governments as well as the private and public sectors outlined a vision for creating a people-centered, inclusive Information Society. The 29 key goals and related objectives contained in the action plan rely heavily on a high degree of effective collaboration to achieve the suggested partnerships and cooperation. While the plan outlines the need for learning and skill development, it does not explicitly address the need to build the capacity to collaborate. Without a foundation of collaboration-specific capabilities, it is unlikely that the link between strategy and performance is achievable.

Without the purposeful and systematic development of the capabilities needed to collaborate effectively, organizations cannot realize their full potential. Interestingly, one of the most effective ways to build this capacity resides in one of the oldest forms of learning structures—the communities of practice that exist with or without the knowledge and support of the organizations in which they thrive.

Chuck Close and the Art of Collaboration

Collaboration is at the heart of contemporary American artist Chuck Close's work. Known for his unique approach to portraits, which may be best described as a collaboration of images (e.g., smaller images or patterns of color created within a grid produce the larger image), Close also relies heavily on a collaborative process to produce his prints.

What may take up to two years to complete, the collaboration with master printmakers is a finely tuned process between the two realms of creative genius. Although Close is somewhat reluctant to give up control of his final product, he recognizes the value in collaboration versus a simple delineation of roles—a handoff of plate to printer. The exchange of ideas extends the possibilities, culminating in a final product that exceeds the talents of the individual on his or her own.

Process and *collaboration* are key words that define Close's approach to his art and create the title or a recent look at his distinguished career and significant contribution to American art. (See Terrie Sultan and Richard Shiff, *Chuck Close Prints: Process and Collaboration,* Princeton, NJ: Princeton University Press, 2003, www.chuckclose.coe.uh.edu/process/index.html.)

Defining Communities of Practice

Since the concept of communities of practice was introduced by researchers Jean Lave and Etienne Wenger (who were at the Institute for Research on Learning), communities have gained enormous attention in both the private and public sectors. Wenger has continued to study the phenomena and retains guru status on the social interaction, value proposition, mechanics, and technology enablers of communities. But practitioners from a growing number of successful community strategies implemented in every size, shape, and construct of organization have contributed significantly to both the theory and the practice of this learning and knowledge workhorse.

Community conjures up a whole range of images, from the physical place where we live (e.g., town, city, or metropolis) to the intangible sense of belonging that we feel when we are part of a group (e.g., a religious organization, service club, or self-help group). As with any new concept, agreeing upon a standard definition is a challenge, and identifying characteristics is basically a work in progress as early adopters continue to push the boundaries in search of greater understanding.

Returning to Wenger's seminal work, he and his colleagues McDermott and Snyder (2002) define communities of practice as:

> *Groups of people who share a concern, a set of problems, or a passion about a topic, and who deepen their understanding and knowledge of this area by interacting on an ongoing basis.* (p. 4)

In the context of the strategic value proposition of communities of practice for organizations, Saint-Onge and Armstrong (2004) offer another perspective on the definition:

> *Groups of self-governing people whose practice is aligned with strategic imperatives and who are challenged to create shareholder value by generating knowledge and increasing capabilities.* (p. 159)

And, looking at communities from the perspective of a professional practice, the innovators behind the development of CompanyCommand describe their professional forum for U.S. Army officers in these words:

> *Professionals sharing the wisdom of practice and creating new insights about company-level leadership.* (Dixon et al., 2005, p. vi)

This range of perspectives on a definition (multiplied by a magnitude of *x* if we include the additional definitions offered on Web sites about communities of practice) shows the incredible adaptability of the structure to any given situation. It also suggests the need to identify a continuum of community of practice types from informal, grassroots, temporary communities to highly structured, resourced, and formalized communities. Saint-Onge and Wallace (2003) provide a description of characteristics for each type of community of practice at a median point on such a continuum. They suggest that it is important to understand the nature of the community in order to manage expectations about the value proposition for the stakeholders involved in developing and sustaining a particular community.

While there is a range of form and function within the concept of communities of practice, there is the added challenge of nailing down a definition and set of characteristics in that, "Not every community is a community of practice" (Wenger et al., p. 41). The authors point out the differences between communities and business or functional units; project or operational teams; and informal networks, communities of interest, and professional associations. Again, they note that it is critical to be specific about how you define a community of practice in order to manage expectations regarding levels of participation and contribution, and to provide appropriate resources to support the community's activities. Then there is the added danger that if *everything* is considered a community, then the uniqueness of the structure and its possibilities is lost, or at the very least, greatly diminished.

Due to widespread access to inexpensive channels of communication, the concept of community has also expanded to include a virtual state. The limitations of the physical boundaries of a co-located community are not a factor of membership for online or virtual communities of practice. What can result is a community that literally never sleeps—a community member somewhere is always available to keep the conversation moving forward in real time. And while face-to-face contact tends to foster trusting relationships more quickly, virtual communities, where members have never actually met, can still be extremely effective.

Characteristics of Communities

As we saw previously in the multiple definitions of communities of practice, the same holds true for identifying the characteristics of this collaborative structure. Rumizen's romp through the field of knowledge management in the oxymoronic *The Complete Idiot's Guide to Knowledge Management* (2002) provides a starting point for the list of attributes:

- In most organizations, a community of practice is made up of volunteers. No one forces the members to belong or contribute.
- While community members learn and work together, they do not necessarily produce deliverables or operate within defined schedules and timetables.
- They are distinguished by their passion for what brings them together.
- While they may have some stated goals, they are broader and more general than the goals of work groups and teams. Their goals also may fluctuate more.
- Their members tend to be like each other, perhaps with the same types of jobs and skills or some other common interest or bond.
- They last as long as the members want them to last.

Saint-Onge and Wallace flesh out the characteristics from their experience in the private sector, where they developed communities of practice as a strategic capability aligned with business imperatives:

- *Share a common purpose.* Communities share a desire to collaborate with colleagues, a commitment to learning and generating new capabilities, and a need to find a solution to issues or problems related to their area of practice.
- *Utilize productive inquiry.* Communities of practice exist to find answers to questions that are situated in practice. Members have a high degree of "need to know" and have found that by asking questions within the community, the responses are situated in experience and directly related to the realities of work.
- *Self-manage* through governance structure, principles and conventions, the shared leadership of members, and some

Front and Center—CompanyCommand Builds Leadership Capacity in the U.S. Army

"I am currently deployed and had a soldier pass away ... I would appreciate anything you can do to assist me."

This call for help on how to best approach a unit's first casualty came from a leader on the ground in Iraq. Within minutes, links to information about handling a soldier loss were provided. However, more importantly, practical insights that could only be gained through personal experience were offered by seven CompanyCommand members who themselves had dealt with the loss of a soldier.

CompanyCommand started as a grassroots effort by a group of officers who experienced the benefit of sharing knowledge to increase individual leadership effectiveness. Growing from informal face-to-face conversations into a sophisticated electronic exchange resourced by the U.S. Military Academy, CompanyCommand supports more than 10,000 members who log more than 100,000 page views per month on its knowledge-sharing portal.

This was more than a Web site offering discrete bits of knowledge; members become engaged in a *forum* in the truest sense of the word—new knowledge emerges through a dynamic process of exchange and discovery, not from merely posting information. Leaders with experience connect with developing leaders in on-going conversations where they share and build upon one another's knowledge. This network of past, present, and future company commanders has made a significant contribution to building individual and collective leadership capacity, while furthering the profession of arms. (See CompanyCommand: Building Combat-Ready Teams Web site at companycommand.army.mil.)

form of facilitation. Communities are not just amorphous shapes that lumber along. They have purpose, direction, and a way to self-organize to meet their goals.

- *Generate knowledge* that supports the practice. Through productive inquiry, access to internal and external information, and contributions of members, new knowledge objects are created by the community that forms the content or domain of their practice.
- *Self-govern* on the basis of agreed-upon conventions. The members govern the community through norms and guidelines that have been developed through consensus within the community, not imposed by the organization.
- *Assume accountability* for supporting one another. The community exists as a resource for its members. It takes full responsibility for providing an effective and productive forum. Within this context, each member assumes the responsibility to support fellow members as required.
- *Collaborate via multiple channels.* Communities use a variety of synchronous and asynchronous forms of collaborative tools, including face-to-face meetings, to enable their discussions.
- *Receive support from the organization.* While the organizational support may not be directly given or accepted by any given community, there exists within the organization an acknowledgment of the social nature of learning and the benefits of providing opportunities for employees to collaborate and learn.

While lists of characteristics may vary depending on the example, Wenger et al. provide a basic structural model that can be used as a framework (pp. 27–40). The characteristics plus the critical success factors previously listed can easily hang off this scaffold:

- *Domain.* The common ground—the knowledgebase that defines a set of issues—creates a common identity and legitimizes the community.
- *Community.* This is a group of people who care about the domain.

- *Practice.* The shared practice is developed by the people in order to be effective in the domain.

Collaboration—The Value of Communities

People committed to learning, to harnessing the collective wisdom of a group in order to develop innovative solutions that further a practice or profession, create significant value for the stakeholders involved with the community—individuals, organizations, the practice or profession, and for the community itself. This value is both tangible and intangible as well as short and long term. The community's efforts can improve business outcomes and develop organizational capabilities, while improving the work experience and fostering professional development for individuals (Wenger et al., p. 14–18). No matter what value is created by the community, building the capability to engage in effective collaboration is constant across the many advantages that result from the collaboration that takes place in communities. The emerging knowledge-driven, networked economy is changing the way organizations do business or provide services, particularly how they work with other organizations. Value networks, strategic alliances, partnerships, business-to-business connectivity are just some of the forms of collaboration that are creating mutual benefit between and among organizations. The notion of "co-opetition" (where corporations that typically compete for business are now aligning to create solutions in collaboration with their competitors) is gaining management attention.

We know from our earlier look at collaboration that specific capabilities are needed to maximize the possibilities of a collaborative effort. A community of practice is a perfect structure for developing these capabilities. It draws on the expertise of people across the organization, often from different functional or business units, who bring varying perspectives on developing integrated solutions. Because organizations with community strategies have the capacity for internal collaboration, they have a better chance at succeeding at external collaborations. Organizations with communities of practice have the capabilities and the capacity for capitalizing on each other's strengths, engaging in productive dialogues, and developing integrated solutions for their customers (Saint-Onge and Wallace, pp. 61–63).

Building Capacity with Professional Learning Communities: York Region District School Board

To build capacity in support of large-scale change, the York Region District School Board (with more than 100,000 students in Ontario, Canada) developed a professional learning community focused on literacy—on creating a knowledge base of instructional and assessment strategies for increasing student achievement. Under a program umbrella championed by senior district administrators called The Literacy Collaborative, classroom teachers, school literacy lead teachers, school administrators, and district curriculum consultants are committed to "raising the bar and closing the gap" in a unique community of learners.

School-based literacy teams fuel the professional learning community with study groups, action research projects, job-embedded professional development, and continuous informal knowledge sharing. The literacy teams across the district come together as cohorts on a quarterly basis to explore two interconnected themes: 1) literacy and 2) leadership and change management. The first theme is facilitated by district curriculum consultants, and the second theme is facilitated by leading educators from the University of Toronto who work in partnership with the district. Community learning culminates in a district-wide learning fair to exchange ideas, acknowledge best practice, and celebrate success.

Passion and commitment, comprehensive resources, and an unwavering focus enable this learning community to meet its goals. The results are impressive. The district now sits among the top-achieving boards in the province—a win/win situation for students, their parents, and their community. (See the York Region District School Board Web site at www.yrdsb.edu.on.ca.)

Measuring the value realized from communities of practice (both qualitatively and quantitatively) is less debated than most knowledge management initiatives, where often the gain is in intangible knowledge assets that confound traditional dollars-out/dollars-in ROI calculations. Organizations such as Xerox have identified the cost savings generated by communities of practice. The company's Eureka community of service technicians has realized both a savings in cost of service (quantitative) and customer and employee satisfaction (qualitative). Lelic's (2004) collection of case studies highlights specific gains:

- Eli Lilly's InnoCentive community offers rewards up to $100,000 for ideas that the company believes would cost them more to develop.
- Halliburton's problem-solving community provides 350 percent return on investment.
- Caterpillar posted an estimated 700-percent gain in productivity and quality.

While we may never know the total value a community of practice yields, there is empirical evidence that the benefits are both real and significant for using knowledge to enhance practice.

The Dark Side of Communities

Just as we looked at the dark side of collaboration, in terms of *collaborating with the enemy,* communities themselves can pose a threat to an organization, especially when the notion that "membership has its privileges" becomes the operative. Wenger et al. address this issue beautifully in their chapter on "The Downside of Communities of Practice":

> *Communities of practice are not havens of peace or unbounded goodwill. They reflect all the strengths, weaknesses, and complex interrelationships of their human members. They have their share of conflicts, jealousies, and intrigues. But even when there are tight bonds between members, the result is not always positive. Tight bonds can become exclusive and present an insurmountable barrier to entry. They can even embolden members to act in ways that would shock outsiders. This downside of community is what gives rise to the mobs that would burn a witch, lynch*

> *an African-American, or guillotine an aristocrat. Without vigilance, having a community may create a toxic coziness that closes people to exploration and external input. In other words, too much community can become counterproductive.* (p. 144)

We saw this at Clarica Life Insurance Co. with The Agent Network—an exclusive group of independent agents (e.g., no managers had access). Members with an axe to grind on a particular agent-organization management issue hijacked the conversation, using the community platform to rally the troops in an e-mail campaign that flooded senior executives' inboxes, actually crippling the e-mail system. Needless to say, this action did not endear the community to senior management and caused further questions about the value of the community. The action was a great learning experience for all stakeholders, but the consequences later contributed to the withdrawal of organizational support to the community (Saint-Onge and Wallace).

Communities Fast Forward

For the foreseeable future, organizations are going to focus on how technology can be better leveraged in the workplace. Over the last decade, organizations have made a massive investment in technology—both in implementing it and subsequently upgrading it. New modes of communicating at even lower costs and developments in collaborative workspace tools, including focused suites or the integration of existing components, will continue to expand the possibilities to collaborate effectively within this global economy.

A structure as old as prehistoric hunting parties or medieval guilds, communities of practice are unlikely to go out of style any time soon. They are based on the fundamental social nature of human beings and enable the time-honored quest for new knowledge in pursuit of a better way of life. As an organizational structure, they will become further embedded in work routines, becoming part of the cultural fabric of "how we do our work around here." The conversation about communities may wane, just as sound business/organizational practice that reaches "fad or fashion" status due to hype in the management literature often does. However, communities will remain an integral element of our work life, just as other forms of community are central to our social life.

Learning from Experience

Simon Lelic, managing editor at Ark Group—a leading provider of information about knowledge management strategies and resources—gathered opinions from thought leaders and expert practitioners in a comprehensive report on the state of communities of practice as the

Communispace—Taking Communities to the Customer

Trimming research dollars, shortening time to market, and tapping into the unmet needs and new product opportunities that fuel innovation are three key reasons for creating customer communities. When online communities began to take off in 2000, start-up application developer Communispace Corp. entered the market with a product and service to support internal corporate communities. However, when market-driven companies like Hallmark, General Motors, and McDonald's suggested a change in focus for online communities, Communispace proved to be a willing partner to explore the possibilities. Based on the premise that trust, accountability, and empowerment are keys to authentic customer connections, and coupled with an expertise in customer-centered growth, Communispace worked with its clients to reposition the application to support ongoing, 24/7 customer conversations with a unique third dimension. Not only could a company or its customer initiate a conversation with one another, now customers could talk directly with other customers in a convenient and secure online environment.

Customer communities are leapfrogging more traditional ways of gathering marketing intelligence while strengthening a company's customer relationships and brand. Gaining customer insights through conversations has led to developing products that "hit the mark" rather than fail to meet customer expectations—increasing customer loyalty and market share in a time when obtaining the market's attention tips the balance.

For further information, see www.communispace.com.

"bedrock of the knowledge-enabled enterprise" (2004, p. 9). With 16 case studies from a wide range of organizations, the report delivers insights on the successes and failures of developing communities of practice.

The following list is a distillation and synthesis of the lessons learned. These lessons have been grouped by community components based on Chun Wei Choo's *The Knowing Organization*:

- *Vision and strategy*. The purpose and direction that keep the community focused on creating value for its members, itself, the knowledge domain or practice, and the organization(s).
- *Roles and responsibilities*. The people involved with the community either as members or enablers.
- *Policy, process, and procedures*. The formal and informal ways the community guides its actions and the activities that take place to create and share knowledge.
- *Content and capabilities*. The information and knowledge that inform the community process and provide the skills needed to develop community capabilities.
- *Enabling resources*. The tools and infrastructure (technical and nontechnical) that support the community's ability to achieve its vision and purpose.

Vision and strategy set the direction for the community, providing a rallying point and a way to create value for the various stakeholders involved in the community's life:

- Establish a clear purpose for the community to increase productivity. Long-term visions should not be ignored, but current needs should drive the central purpose.
- Provide resources strategically, encouraging communities that create business value to develop.
- Set reasonable expectations for what a community can achieve.
- Communities should generate valuable customer-centered insights and solutions based on knowledge shared and generated to address current problems and challenges.

- Communities of practice are not a panacea; they are a structure that can be effective but also has limitations. They are not solely knowledge or learning capabilities but an essential approach to creating tangible business results.

Roles and responsibilities outline expectations for how people within the community should function in order to realize the community's often multifaceted purpose:

- A catalyst that draws the community together plays a central role in getting the community off the ground.
- The community is responsible for selecting people to fulfill required roles.
- Recognize a core group of people who are essential for realizing the community's purpose, and outline the roles and responsibilities that they share in service of the community.
- Identify a facilitator who will help the community stay focused on its purpose and move the community ahead.
- Engage thought leaders to spark discussions and help develop the community's knowledgebase.
- Create a balance between the need for openness and confidentiality through a set of guidelines for community participation.
- Clearly defined membership criteria and a selection process help establish trust. Expanding beyond initial criteria may require legal agreements and/or disclaimers as a membership circle widens. But a diverse membership can increase the value created.

Policy, process, and procedures guide how the community functions with the primary purpose of creating a trusting environment where knowledge is created and shared:

- Starting with a pilot project in community development can lay the groundwork for success with a framework that provides legitimacy and encourages support.

- Develop a program schedule to facilitate relationship building and engage members in knowledge creation and sharing, remembering the value of face-to-face communication.
- Promote the community, creating awareness about the value that communities provide to their stakeholders.
- Interventions must be in line with community values and beliefs.
- Find ways to formally or informally identify community value and contribution to success as a way to sustain support and commitment from all stakeholders.

Content and capabilities represent the information and knowledge obtained, generated, and shared by the community in the course of fulfilling its purpose:

- Knowledge resides in the community—its members and its resource structures. Providing ways to access both tacit and explicit knowledge is critical for utilizing the community's knowledge.
- Anecdotes generate stories and act as a primary source of knowledge exchange.
- In addition to facilitation and problem solving, change management skills are key for keeping the community moving forward.
- Members' capability to utilize online options should be assessed and gaps addressed to encourage adoption.

Enabling resources provide the community with the capabilities it needs to function in the creation and sharing of knowledge:

- Identify a senior management champion who will validate the community's value and sustain middle management support for resources needed to support the community's efforts.
- Provide multiple channels to support communication, including an online option that makes the community available at the point of member need but that is familiar and integrated into work processes.

- Employ tools, such as social network analysis, to enable effective interaction.
- Create a resource team to provide expertise to the community's infrastructure support.

Conclusion

Collaboration is ubiquitous—not just a creation of the vagaries of management science. In art, Claude Monet is typically identified as the father of Impressionism, but it was actually his collaboration with Frederic Bazille that produced this famous artistic movement. Likewise in literature, T.S. Eliot's poetry and prose were developed based on his theory of collaboration—of jointly developing ideas and finding new ways to represent them. And more recently, mapping the human DNA sequence was accomplished by the Human Genome Project a year ahead of schedule, requiring revisions to the work plans because of its "accelerated progress." What we now know about human biology is attributed to the extensive collaboration of scientists from 18 countries—a feat that we cannot imagine being completed in our lifetime as an individual effort.

"Collaboration is cool" is not just the mantra of collaborative workspace software marketers. It is a fundamental tenet held by governments, educators, and business pundits. Visionaries are outlining new norms where collaboration is central to success, where organizations utilize their distinctive capabilities in partnerships and alliances with other organizations to meet the complex needs of their marketplace, and where there is a shift from competition to collaboration.

As a generative capability, collaboration has the unique quality of creating capabilities beyond the purpose of the collaborative effort itself. Problem solving, critical thinking, innovation, and knowledge creation are just a few of the "spin offs" possible from the interaction of varying perspectives, knowledgebases, and experience that come together in the dialogue of collaboration.

Within a community of practice, collaboration is responsible for leveraging the knowledge of the group, teasing tacit knowledge that may otherwise remain undiscovered. Through a dynamic problem-resolution process, community members unearth valuable experiences that help individuals and organizations avoid repeating past mistakes and reinventing the wheel, while innovating with the speed necessary to meet the increasingly fast pace of changing market demands.

Strategic partnerships, B2B alliances, supply chains, value networks, and joint ventures are a few of the types of inter-organizational collaborations that are gaining attention. However, in the rush to shape the organization of the future, one that can thrive—if not survive—in a networked economy, leaders are missing the need to develop the internal capabilities necessary to collaborate before they try to collaborate externally with key stakeholders.

Collaboration is a core capability that can distinguish any organization in its marketplace. People from around the globe come together as a community to address crisis—to aid victims of devastating clashes in nature and terrorism. The possibility of affecting change in the context of positive stimuli then has the potential for even greater contributions to the world in which we live and work.

Recommended Resources

When Kouzes and Posner were updating their book on leadership, their search of the Library of Congress catalog for works relating to collaboration identified more than 10,000 titles. A quick search of the Internet for this chapter yielded more than 33,500,000 entries. Obviously, people have a great deal to say about collaboration. The works listed here are meant as supplements to the works cited in the chapter (full citations can be found in the Bibliography at the end of this book), but even together, they do not approach a comprehensive literature review of the theory and practice of collaboration and communities.

Books and Articles

Drucker Foundation. *Meeting the Challenge Collaboration Workbook: Developing Strategic Alliances Between Nonprofit Organizations and Businesses*. San Francisco: Jossey-Bass 2002. See also the Leader to Leader Institute site at www.pfdf.org/collaboration/challenge/download.html.

Kim, A. J. *Community Building on the Web: Secret Strategies for Successful Online Communities*. Berkeley, CA: Peachpit Press, 2000.

Welborn, R. and V. Kasten. *The Jericho Principle: How Companies Use Strategic Collaboration to Find New Sources of Value*. Hoboken, NJ: John Wiley & Sons, 2003.

Web Sites

Human Genome Project Information, www.ornl.gov/sci/tech resources/Human_Genome/home.shtml
Oxford English Dictionary Online, www.askoxford.com/concise_oed/collaborate?view=uk
Webster's Online Dictionary, www.websters-online-dictionary.org/definition/collaboration
World Summit on the Information Society, www.itu.int/wsis

CHAPTER 6

Content Management for Intranets

Craig St. Clair
TKG Consulting LLC

In the 1957 movie *Desk Set*, Spencer Tracy and Katharine Hepburn engaged in one of their more famous onscreen battles, this time about how content and information are stored and accessed in the burgeoning Information Age. At different points in the movie, dialog from Tracy and Hepburn's characters goes something like this:

> *TRACY: You would be surprised how a little scientific application can improve the work/man-hour relationship ... the research worker types the question into the machine here, Emeric [the computer in this case] goes to work and the answer comes out here ...*
> *HEPBURN: I'd match my memory against any machine any day .... What's gonna happen when Emeric takes over?*
> *TRACY: Emeric is not gonna take over; it was never intended to take over. It's just here merely to free your time for research; it's just here to help you.*

Tracy and Hepburn hit on one of the central themes of modern knowledge management. What role should technology play in facilitating the capture and distribution of information for an organization? And, by extension, how can technology be adapted to help people store and manage information? Unfortunately for us, information retrieval was never as easy as the information-in/information-out scenario that Tracy described. Machines were simply not that smart in 1957, and while we have come a long way since then, they are not that smart today.

In this chapter, we will look at content and information management for intranets, specifically the following:

- How different types of content that have value across a larger organization can be efficiently stored, maintained, distributed, and accessed
- What online and offline tools and mechanisms need to be in place to make it all work

Before we begin our nuts-and-bolts discussion regarding content management, it is useful to look at why effective management of these assets is so necessary. We begin this chapter with some history about the development of intranets and a brief discussion of how and why content and information asset management has developed as a discipline.

Why Do We Need to Manage Intranet Content?

Historically, intranets have grown up organically within organizations. As soon as it was practical to put internal information on a Web site and distribute it securely via a browser, organizations seized the opportunity. The early promise of the intranet was clear: Because of the pervasiveness and flexibility of the Web browser, information and knowledge that was once hidden in file drawers or isolated in online file systems could be delivered to individual desktops throughout the organization, often for the first time.

The early stage of intranet development was characterized by ambitious in-house initiatives to digitize and distribute as much information as possible. The result was a veritable gold rush of intranet building. And like gold rush towns, departmental intranet sites sprung up overnight as departments hurried to tell their stories, prove their value, and increase everyone's productivity. Of course, just like a gold rush, there was no real coordination between departments, no centralized control over what was being built, and little consideration of how all this information was going to be maintained. And in the rush to build new sites, the actual needs of the end-user—the supposed consumer of all this information—was often the last to be considered (Figure 6.1).

It was not long before the sheer mass of information and mismatched and poorly designed intranet sites within organizations resulted in an information nightmare. Large companies typically

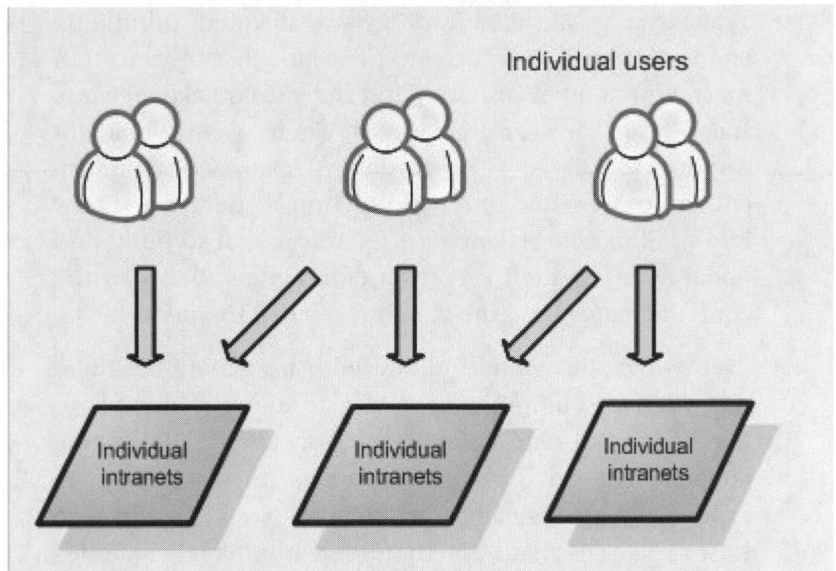

Figure 6.1 Beginning State: Multiple Disconnected Intranets

developed hundreds of unconnected intranet sites and hundreds of thousands of pages of content, each site with its own visual design and navigation scheme.

The sheer number of stand-alone intranets in organizations presented a confusing array to increasingly confounded users. What was worse, users often blamed themselves for not being able to find the information they were seeking. "I know it's there somewhere," said one user in a focus group about intranets, "I've just never had the time to figure out how to find it. ... Typically, I'll search for five minutes, then give up and pick up the phone and ask someone to send it to me."

In a very short time, the problems with this build-and-build approach to intranet construction became readily apparent:

- The separate nature of intranet sites within the same company meant that there was no common design, branding, or navigation schemes. The lack of common design elements and predictable navigation led to a jarring experience for users. Users had to re-learn navigation and content presentation schemes each time they visited a new site.

- Typically, a great deal of energy was devoted to building and launching a new site. After the launch, however, staff moved on to other projects, and the sites quickly became stale, out-of-date, and irrelevant. There was no efficient way to keep the sites up-to-date, because nontechnical content owners had to rely on technical staff to post new information. The reliance on technical staff to build and update sites created a constant bottleneck between the content creators and the site they needed to update.

- Even when sites were updated with new material, there was often no comprehensive way to identify, archive, or remove out-of-date information, so sites kept getting larger and larger. Because there was no mechanism to expand the site logically, new material would be added to existing sites in an ad-hoc manner, with no real regard for logical navigation. In very short order, existing information became harder to find.

- As the number of intranets increased, maintenance became a major problem. Because each site existed in isolation, there was no way to manage their maintenance effectively. Increases in the number of sites and pages meant corresponding increases in staff time devoted to site maintenance.

- Users had no way to search across multiple information repositories or multiple file types simultaneously. Users had to somehow know which intranet site, shared file system, or database was likely to have the information for which they were searching.

- Files stored on local drives in their native formats had to be converted to a browser-friendly format and be physically migrated to the intranet site. This resulted in massive migration efforts that often failed because they were too ambitious or poorly planned.

- In the push to make information widely available, the needs of end-users were often left out of the equation entirely. Content choices were based on what management thought users wanted and needed, and there was no facility for true information exchange and no ability for end-users to contribute to the knowledgebase.

- There was a one-size-fits-all approach to information distribution. Content owners and authors had no way of targeting specific content for specific groups of users.

Enter Content and Information Asset Management

If the unrestrained, and unplanned, energy of the early intranet boom often created more problems than it solved, how can we then bring sanity to the process and channel our energy to more productive ends? In other words, how can we ensure a more systematic and structured delivery of knowledge and information that is truly sustainable over time? If we extend the gold rush analogy mentioned earlier, the unplanned and unregulated exploitation and extraction that is typical of a gold rush is inevitably followed by a period of infrastructure building and innovation. While the discovery of gold leads to a chaotic and unrestrained atmosphere, the chaos and critical mass that are produced during the gold rush also jumpstarts the development of new processes and organizational structures. Ultimately, these new processes and innovative methods lead to more "civilized" practices and sustainable operations.

The same is true for content and information asset management for intranets. In the past several years, a good number of practices have been developed that help organizations manage assets more effectively. Software innovation has also kept pace with the development of tools for more systematic management of intranet content. When the software is at its best, it mirrors and helps to enable the innovative management practices that are being developed offline.

Gaining Intellectual Control Over Existing Content

Before we can ever hope to manage intranet content effectively, we need to have some grasp of what we are trying to manage. There are some basic parameters that can help us get our arms around the content. If we know these, we will be closer to gaining intellectual control over content and managing it more effectively:

- Where is the information stored and in what format?

- How is the information described in terms of subject, format, and specific business terms?
- How is the information maintained and what is its life cycle?
- And, most importantly, why does the information exist? How is the information used now and who are the current and potentially future audiences?

Translated into methodological terms, there are several mechanisms we can employ to help us answer the following questions and manage content:

- User interviews and surveys
- Content inventories and audits
- Content classification systems and taxonomies
- Content maps
- Content maintenance workflows
- Content life cycles

Taking the Lay of the Land: User Interviews and Surveys

Figuring out where content is produced, how it is maintained, and what content people need in their work, and then making the connections among content producer, repository, and consumer is one of the most basic and revealing ways to begin to look at managing content and knowledge assets for intranets. The best way to find out how individuals use content and what content they produce is to ask them. However, how we ask them and how we construct a valid and manageable mechanism for gathering this information is the central question. In terms of content and knowledge asset management, we need detailed, comprehensive information regarding what content exists and how it is used. It is not enough to get vague, impressionistic, or even great brainstorm ideas about how to manage and distribute content. We ultimately need to construct a model of content production and consumption within the context of a specific organization; to do that we need detailed and comprehensive data.

If we look at content producers and consumers as different sides of the same equation, we can begin to construct a mechanism to assess user needs and goals for both groups.

In constructing an interview plan for content consumers, consider the following guidelines:

- Identify a sample of the organization that is representative in terms of roles, businesses, product lines, geographies, or any other measures that are important to your organization.
- Map the demographics of interview subjects to ensure equal representation across the organization.
- Recognize that one individual can represent various parameters in the sample; for instance, an administrative assistant in the marketing organization in Germany can represent information needs on the basis of his role (administrative assistant), his organization (marketing), and his locale (Germany).
- Keep the sample small; recognize that as you move from interview to interview, common themes will surface very quickly.
- Devise questions for the interview that do not lead respondents or influence their responses.
- Use narrative techniques rather than direct questioning; for instance, asking "Tell me how and where you go about looking for this information" is much better than asking "How well do you think this source of information answers your question or solves your problem?"
- Extract various attributes from the narrative answers by focusing on the types of content that are useful, where consumers typically look for content, how they access it, and how often they need it.
- Produce a synthesized user profile from the data, capturing the patterns you see across the various interviews.

Content producer interviews use all of the guidelines just outlined, plus the following:

- Use the information gathered from content consumers to identify potential interview subjects among content producers. In other words, the rich sources of information mentioned by content consumers are excellent places to start looking for content producers.
- Ask the content producers to use narratives and a "talking protocol" to verbalize the process of content creation and maintenance. The narrative should result in a step-by-step process.
- Document why the content was created in the first place, how it was created, who approved it, and how often it is accessed.

Case Study: User Assessments

A recent intranet implementation project for a call center operation began with the admittedly broad question: "What intranet tools (including both content and functionality) do call center agents need to do their jobs?" After some initial project scoping meetings, we began to develop a user-needs assessment. We identified a cross-organizational sample of users, constructed an interview script, and defined a process for extracting and synthesizing the data. We developed an assessment process for both content consumers (in this case the call center agents and call center managers) and content producers. Specifically, this included the product managers who develop and disseminate information about the services the company provides and the client managers who contribute information about the company's customers/clients.

For the call center agent interviews, a sample was selected that included agents who serve various types of clients, specialize in major service areas, and sit in either of two call center locations. The interviewer asked the call center agent to lead her through several types of service requests. The interviewer took notes, focusing particularly on the following three aspects of the narrative:

- The *process* the agent used to find the information
- The *resources* that were used in performing the task
- The *barriers and challenges* that were encountered in the process

For the content producer interviews, we identified an interview sample from within the product development and client development departments. The interviewer asked the product and client managers to describe the content they produce and then describe the production process, from identifying the need or opportunity for content to authoring and posting the content on the intranet. Here the interviewer focused on the step-by-step process, the individuals and hand-offs involved, the sources of information, and any obstacles or barriers they typically encountered.

For about 400 employees, we conducted 20 interviews as follows: 10 call center agents from across the organization, three members of call center management, four product managers, and three client managers.

The interview data was distilled into a series of user profiles, one for each of the major employee groups: call center agents, call center managers, and product and client managers. Each profile included the following:

- An overview of the duties and concerns of the particular employee role and how that employee uses content or develops content
- A listing of the major content types used or developed
- A listing of functionality typically used (e.g., Internet searches, searches of internal databases, Internet authoring tools)
- A listing of barriers or concerns among both content producers and consumers
- The step-by-step process for content creation

The result was a manageable set of user requirements from both content producers and consumers with a consistent structure. The structured component of the user profiles is extremely important. Because we focused on extracting consistent data from the interviews, it was easier to see trends and patterns in the responses and to ensure that those patterns were captured in the profiles.

The user profiles can in turn be used to inform a more granular list of descriptions of how content is both consumed and managed, identifying the following:

- Where specific types of content are produced within the organization

- Step-by-step workflows that detail the process of producing content
- Gaps in the content production process
- The major types of content typically produced or repurposed from other sources
- How different groups in the organization use content differently
- Gaps between where content is being created and where content is required
- Gaps in needed online functionality in addition to more static content

While this information helps us understand how information can be managed from an organizational and process perspective, it is still not enough. We need more information about the nature and structure of the content itself, particularly if we want to use machines to help us manage our information and knowledge assets.

Taking the Lay of the Land: Content Inventories and Audits

Although this may be a rather basic point, it is worth stating: Consistent and reliable descriptions of content and information can lead to more intelligent decisions on how to manage that information. We already discussed the folly of individual content owners rushing to put any and all materials on separate, isolated intranets. What if we had a clear idea about what content and information was being stored and maintained by an organization before trying to make it more accessible?

While this may make sense in theory, it is not that easy. Even for small- to medium-sized organizations, completing a detailed content inventory, even in just one part of the organization, can be a daunting or even impossible task. Many organizations have begun trying to inventory their content and have become hopelessly mired in too much detail. Even the most industrious and steadfast content managers who actually complete a full content inventory are often left with spreadsheets of information that are too voluminous to digest and are therefore meaningless.

Instead, what if we described larger groups of content in terms of their source, owner, purpose, format, and audience? Broader descriptions of entire series or types of content can give a better idea of an organization's holdings at a more manageable level of detail. Instead of listing each page or item of content in an intranet, it really is more useful to list types of content produced by a particular department or organization. For instance, the fact that an IT department produces a series of FAQs (Frequently Asked Questions) that are designed to help employees diagnose and fix computer problems is of more value than an exhaustive list of each individual FAQ.

There are more dividends that result from describing content at this level of detail. First, it is easier. It is much more manageable if we hand content owners an audit framework based on types of content and ask them to write a brief description of their content corresponding to various content types. Second, if we concentrate our efforts on describing types of content from areas of the organization that we know from experience are holders of large amounts of useful information, we can more easily prioritize where we begin and what we capture. Finally, if we describe content in terms of set parameters, we begin to develop a classification scheme for the content that will become extremely useful as we move forward. In other words, describing content on the series level by a variety of attributes (e.g., content type, departmental owner, format, and audience) creates a series of classification terms that is the first draft of a useful taxonomy.

Case Study: Content Inventories, Audits, and Taxonomy

At a large company that I recently worked with, we were immersed in rebuilding the company's intranet within a corporate portal. In addition to anticipated benefits of better presentation, functionality, and usability, one of the major goals for the project was cleaning up the existing intranet content and smoothing and rationalizing an antiquated publishing process. The new intranet portal was regarded as a blank slate, an opportunity for a new beginning in terms of the content that was presented and the mechanisms used to publish it.

The first attempts at intellectual control over content came in the form of a highly detailed content inventory. Every content author in the organization was required to do a full inventory of the content they had created over the last several years. The result was long and detailed lists of discrete pieces of content. Since the content was housed in a static HTML intranet, the inventories described content page by page. At its conclusion, the aggregated inventories numbered nearly 20,000 lines representing the same number of intranet pages. The inventory entries included a page name, a badly written description that made sense only to the individual conducting the inventory, and the name and department of the content author. Since each inventory was conducted by the individual content owner, there was little consistency from inventory to inventory in terms of the way that content items were described.

Looking down the pages and pages of the inventories, one was at a loss for where to begin. The inventory project failed in at least two ways: There was no real consistency in how the content was described, and each inventory was a "laundry list" that lacked any prioritization or overall categorization. It was not just that the inventories were too detailed; it was also that there were no hooks to allow you to understand and prioritize the content at an organizational level.

A better attempt (and one that was ultimately successful) was to be more strategic than tactical about gaining intellectual control.

First, we established an overall goal of the first phase of the intranet project that would drive content selection and development. In this case, the stated goal was designed to provide employees with the tools and information necessary to be an "employee citizen." In other words, what content was necessary for employees to function as an effective member of the organization? Later project phases might include content and information that would allow employees to do their specific jobs, but this type of content was to be addressed after the intranet was up and running.

Next, we identified the major department areas that were likely to produce content that would fall into the first phase of intranet development. This was a relatively simple and intuitive process that was based on user interviews conducted across the organization. Several of the following content areas stood out:

- News and information about the company's businesses that would be of interest to a general employee population (news about company acquisitions, financial results, new product areas, major successes, etc.).
- Employee benefits and human relations information. This could include basic procedural information, frequently asked questions, as well as news about changes in benefits plans.

- Information technology information that keeps employees operational from an IT perspective. This included frequently asked questions, troubleshooting information, contact lists, and news of scheduled maintenance and systems outages.
- News and information related to a specific locale or geography. This included upcoming events related to specific offices, new location-specific programs and procedures, notices of scheduled building maintenance, etc.
- Departmental information. This included department descriptions designed to give employees a general overview of what various departments did and who key personnel were.

At this point, several important things began to happen, including the following:

- We had a clearer idea of what content matters to the larger organization and what should be developed or repurposed.
- We had the beginnings of a prioritized and phased approach to developing, migrating, or repurposing content.
- We had the beginnings of a categorization scheme that would help us describe and manage the content.

The categorization scheme included both consistent categories that described the content and controlled vocabulary for populating the categories. For this company and this particular project, the categorization schemes that emerged were the following:

- Department of origin (the department or group that authors and owns the content)
- Type of content (e.g., FAQs, business overviews, departmental overviews, news and announcements, contact lists, procedural information, etc.)
- Geographic location content
- Business unit content
- Product content

The categorization scheme (or taxonomy) can be extended and added to as we move into describing content in other areas of the company. One of the most important benefits of an organization-wide or corporate-wide taxonomy is that it allows us to describe content across the entire enterprise using the same terminology. This consistency and structure gives both humans and machines considerable leverage in managing content more effectively.

Putting It Together: Enterprise-Wide Views and Content Life Cycles

What happens when we combine what we learn from more process-oriented and qualitative user assessments and more structured content audits? We get quite a complete picture of how content is created, stored, and accessed within the organization, and we can begin to build tools that will allow us to capture and manage this information successfully.

From content consumer interviews, we gathered the following:

- We know what kind of content and knowledge users need to do their jobs.
- We know the process that employees go through to access information and where they go to get it.
- We have an idea of what information is most important and which information needs are most pervasive.
- We have an idea of what content is most valuable to a larger number of groups in the organization.

From content producer interviews, we learned the following:

- We know what type of content is being created by various organizations and departments.
- We know the steps that go into the creation and maintenance of the content.
- We know where the content is stored, in what formats, and how it is currently accessed.

From content audits, we gathered the following information:

- We know the type of content that is being produced in various departments.

- We have just started to describe the content in a uniform manner and in terms of set characteristics.
- We are now developing a classification nomenclature or taxonomy that describes content across the organization.

From these elements, we have the ability to map the content assets in two important ways: in terms of where it is created, stored, and consumed in the organization (often called content mapping), and in terms of its life cycle, detailing the steps that the content follows from creation, licensing, and repurposing, to deployment and use, and to archiving and destruction. Content mapping defines where the content originates and how it is distributed. Content life cycles define how the content is stored, how long it is stored, and who maintains it. Together, these mechanisms inform the configuration of enterprise content management systems in terms of security groups and rights, browse schemes, metatagging schemes, search terms, automated workflows, and automated archiving.

Three Models of Intranet Asset Management

Three models of intranet asset management are discussed in this section: the centralized repository model, the decentralized repository model, and a hybrid approach. Each model is discussed in terms of requirements, benefits, challenges, and when it works best.

The Centralized Repository Model: A Top-Down Approach

Thinking back now to the gold rush intranet scenario described earlier, a logical progression from separate, uncoordinated intranets in a large organization to a more rational model is to centralize the storage and maintenance of content in a common repository. In this case, content is combined in a single-file system or database, which users can access via a common interface. The repository is often combined with a publishing mechanism to push the content to various users via a variety of delivery mechanisms (intranets, extranets, Internet, mobile devices, etc.). Administration of the publishing process, categorization schemes for the content, and rights and permissions to access to the content are all highly centralized (Figure 6.2).

Requirements: Implementation of this model requires a strong centralized organization and infrastructure that sets policy and grants access rights regarding how content is stored and accessed.

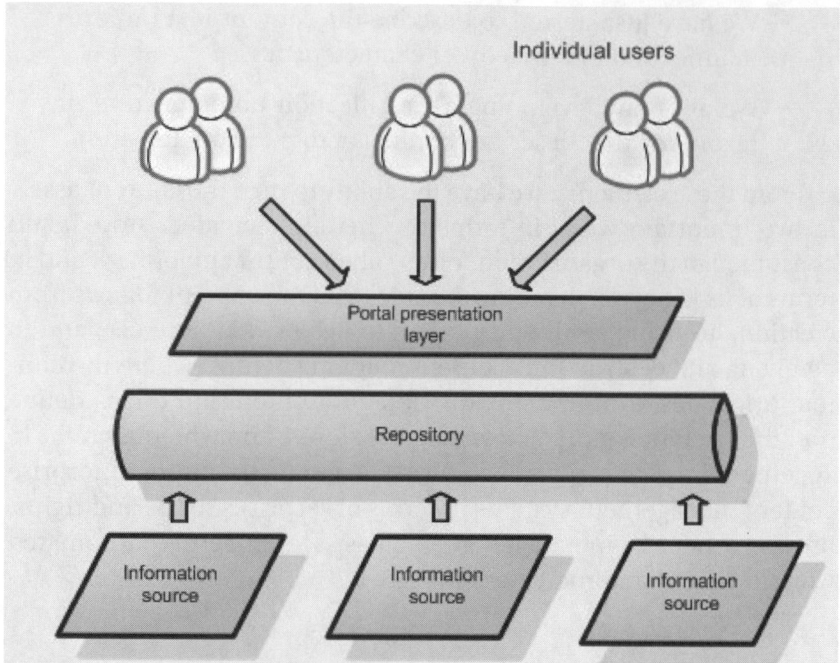

Figure 6.2 Centralized Repository

Likewise, individual departments are required to give up a good deal of control over how and where content is stored and the processes involved in categorization and publishing. This approach requires the implementation of a centralized document or content management system with large amounts of IT involvement.

Benefits: One of the results of a centralized repository and a standardized categorization and description scheme is increased document sharing, more reliable search results, and powerful publishing capabilities. When combined with an enterprise content management system, a single content item can be published to a variety of Web and wireless platforms. The organization's ability to publish and distribute content increases dramatically. Likewise, the ability to audit content on an enterprise-wide basis that satisfies legal and regulatory requirements becomes much more efficient. Ultimately, these efficiencies lead to corresponding decreases in cost and staff time.

Establishing a centralized repository also means that content will have to be moved or migrated in some fashion from its original location to its new home. While no one will argue that planning and executing a content migration initiative is any fun, it does allow organizations to look critically at the content they are storing and determine which content to move and which to leave behind. Content migrations also often translate into content standardization exercises. As content is migrated, categorization, metatagging schemes, and even the format of the content itself can be standardized, resulting in content that is easier to find, digest, and use for and within a variety of purposes and user interfaces.

Challenges: A more centralized management model is often a dramatic shift for organizational units that have historically been more autonomous. Complex publishing conventions have to be designed and put into practice, and users need to adjust to their new roles.

Manually migrating content to a centralized repository is slow and arduous. If the scope of the migration project is too ambitious, the project can run out of steam, or the organization can change its priorities before the project reaches completion.

Automated migration can help speed the migration process by migrating entire groups of content with a minimal level of human mediation. However, these methods require a broad-brush approach that invariably captures and migrates content that should have been left behind or discarded. Migrating out-of-date content negates one of the drivers behind setting up a centralized repository: Providing a "clean slate" that ensures that content in the new system is relevant and up-to-date.

When this works best: Centralized intranet models have been known to work well, particularly when the current system for content maintenance is in disarray and when the local publishing operation is not well-maintained or supported. In one organization where we were charged with implementing a centralized intranet, the team was concerned that the ambitious content migration plan we were proposing would run into resistance from local intranet "site masters." We soon learned, however, that these individuals were given intranet content maintenance duties in addition to their "real" jobs. They were quite receptive to having more centralized control with alternative processes available, particularly if it resulted in procedures that were more well-defined and offered better results overall.

The Decentralized Repository Model: A Bottom-Up Approach

As we have seen in the previous example, centralized content repositories have several distinct problems: They require a large, centralized infrastructure and centralized teams, and they typically involve major content migrations.

What if we could leave content where it naturally lives, in its original format, and provide access to that content via a single interface that reaches across various repositories? That would alleviate the need for massive realignment of roles in the organization and the need for massive content migration efforts. In this scenario, a powerful and intuitive search engine crawls and indexes content and assets in various parts of the organization and then categorizes and presents it in a consistent and useful way.

Requirements: This approach relies on (1) a powerful search and categorization engine that can selectively crawl, index, and surface content in a variety of formats; (2) a sophisticated categorization scheme and browse hierarchy that are meaningful to the entire organization; and (3) fine-tuned search results that deliver an accurate array of content.

Benefits: Because content is aggregated virtually rather than physically, there is no need for a laborious and somewhat risky migration plan. Moreover, since content is not moved from its original location, the traditionally decentralized content producers and maintainers have less impact, allowing them to go about their business with minimal procedural changes. In this regard, original workflows for maintaining the content are preserved. End-users access content and information via a single interface and can typically choose from multiple information search options, looking at natural language search, scripted searches that use set search criteria, or even more structured and hierarchical browse structures.

Challenges: It is important to remember that, ultimately, end-users are presented with a set of sophisticated, and hopefully, user friendly search results. Since the system relies on indexing engines, the results will only be as good as the search engine, the system design, and the original content. Since the underlying content is not being reviewed and filtered by a knowledgeable human, searches will invariably result in some out-of-date and irrelevant content. Content will always be mismatched in terms of format and structure and will therefore be more difficult to comprehend and use. Because content is stored in its original format, there is no real opportunity to publish it in a variety of ways in multiple-user interfaces such as Web sites, intranets, extranets, or handheld devices.

When this works best: For organizations with strong localized publishing procedures and a local autonomy that is working well from a cultural and practical perspective, a decentralized model for content management can be a real benefit. It provides enterprise-wide access with minimal impact on both the existing local organizations and the form and format of the original content. If local content maintenance procedures are delivering fresh and reliable content, we should not try to fix what is not broken. Decentralized models also work best for document-sharing scenarios where the original format of the content needs to be preserved and where content does not need to be repurposed or republished in a variety of forms and interfaces.

The Best of Both Worlds: A Hybrid Approach

The structure of content and the requirements of users are complicated, particularly in the context of large organizations. Forcing complicated content requirements to conform to simple content management models can be difficult and risky. We need to ensure that the content management model we implement is designed to fit the needs of the organization. What if we used end-user requirements to determine the structure of the content model? What if we pursued a more organic model for content management?

In this scenario, some content would be stored centrally (in a centralized file system or a centralized database), while other content would be stored locally and aggregated virtually via a common interface (Figure 6.3). Determining how and where the content is stored would depend on a variety of factors including whether the content needs to be preserved in its native format, how the content is typically used, who needs access, and whether a single content item needs to be repurposed in several forms and distributed to a variety of user interfaces.

A case-in-point illustrates this scenario: A company recently redesigned its intranet and recognized that the new site needed to serve multiple goals and various audiences. Once the company realized that "one-size-fits-all" information delivery did not work very well, it began looking at how different types of content were used by the organization. This helped inform not only the design of the intranet, but also how the backend content management processes were constructed.

The project team looked at the following content types:

- Business announcements from individual business units and corporate communications

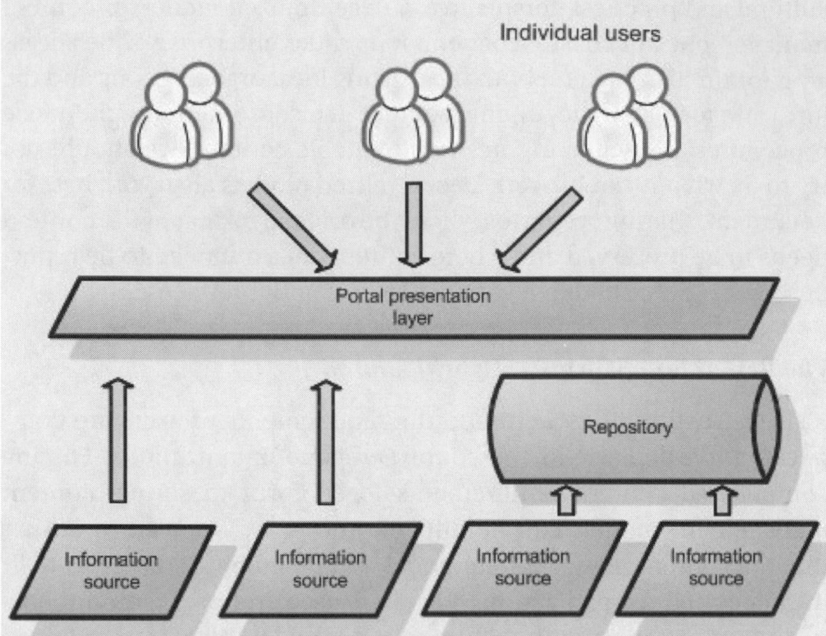

Figure 6.3 Hybrid Version

- Location-specific announcements about events at various company offices
- Press releases from business unit marketers and corporate communications
- Benefits plan information for U.S. employees
- FAQs and systems diagnostic procedures from IT
- Marketing collateral from marketing departments across business units in various countries
- Graphical digital assets from marketing collateral and corporate brochures
- Content in the corporate Web site and business unit marketing Web sites

For each type of content, the location, method of storage, and access requirements were considered. The intranet team created a construct that corresponded to different types of content and helped them determine how to treat the following content types:

- "Resource style" content had traditionally been isolated in local file systems but had a potentially large and distributed audience. The content needed to remain in its original format but needed to be actively shared among users around the world. Marketing collateral pieces and graphical digital assets were examples of resource style content.
- "Announcement style" content had a relatively short shelf life, a broad potential audience, followed a set structure or format, and had the potential of being used on a combination of internal and external sites. Examples of announcement style content were company-wide business announcements, local announcements, and press releases.
- "Library style" content was stored in local file systems but differed from resource content because it was actively and meticulously maintained and could not be easily moved. Examples of this type of content were IT diagnostic procedures, benefits plan information, and Web site files.

The resource content was migrated to a central file system so users could check documents in and out and share information seamlessly. Announcement content was authored directly into a centralized database via form-based content authoring tools. Library style content was left where it was and was crawled and indexed by the system and made available to users via a centralized search interface.

Requirements: This solution requires a combination of tools, including the following:

- A sophisticated search and categorization engine that can crawl and index file systems and databases across and even outside the organization
- An integrated database that stores structured content
- Authoring tools that allow nontechnical users to contribute specific types of structured content
- A central file system that stores both content and digital asset formats

Benefits: The system gives access to buried information and yields greater control over centralized information. It allows for a combination of centralized access, standards, and control, and decentralized content maintenance where it makes sense. In a very real sense, the form of the system follows the function of the content and the needs of the user.

Challenges: Solutions of this type require a dedicated centralized team with representatives from across the organization, a complicated and time-consuming design and implementation cycle, and a substantial financial investment. The key here is a sufficient upfront design that moves through user testing and content assessments to functional requirements and systems design.

When this works best: Solutions of this type work best in larger, more mature organizations that recognize the need for content and information systems that are flexible enough to scale and change with company growth. Typically, organizations that employ this model have tried more basic content management models and see the need for change. The good news is that integrated models of this type can be seen as part of a content management evolution. There is nothing wrong with moving toward this model after putting in place a more centralized or decentralized model; in fact, a staged progression is recommended.

Conclusion

In this chapter on content management practices for intranets, we have noted what happens to unmanaged intranets, taken stock of user-focused content requirements, looked at ways to assess and describe content, and put forth three structures for managing intranet content. Returning to the movie *Desk Set,* it is interesting to ask why the information automation project ultimately failed. Several points should now sound familiar:

- Spencer Tracy's character never asked users how they normally search for and find information.
- He tried to replace offline processes that were working well with online processes that did not consider established workflows and procedures.
- All content was entered in the system without regard to source, function, or format.
- Content stored in the system lost all its original categorization schemes and structure, resulting in mountains of data without context.

Fortunately, for Tracy's character, his failure in business did not also mean failure in matters of the heart. In the end, he got Hepburn's character to love him, and he learned something about the practice of content and information management along the way.

Some key takeaways from this chapter include:

1. Ensure that organizational change regarding content publishing goes hand-in-hand with technical infrastructure; you need to build content management duties into people's jobs.

2. Use online workflows for simple content contribution, editing, and approval, but don't use them to mirror complex offline processes; likewise, don't try to change offline processes so that they fit in linear online workflows.

3. Ensure that your organization can maintain whatever content management and portal infrastructure you put in place; there may be lots of energy around building a new system, but ongoing maintenance is the key to success.

4. The ultimate consumers of content are paramount; all decisions about what to publish should consider their needs first rather than a managerial notion of what is important.

5. Presentation of content and functionality at the users' desktop should be contextual, based on roles, lines of business, geographic locations, etc.

6. Developing a content technical infrastructure is important but not at the expense of the quality and freshness of content; in other words, content maintenance is king.

7. Build ways to access your employees' collective experience and promote a multidirectional flow of information as well as the more traditional top-down distribution of content; connect employees via expert directories and virtual groups.

8. Make sure that functional specifications directly correlate to business solutions; ensure that proposed functionality actually provides a business solution by rechecking original business requirements as the functional design is developed.

Recommended Web Sites

CMPros—The Content Management Community of Practice, www.cmprofessionals.org
CMS Watch, www.cmswatch.com
The Enterprise Content Management Association, www.aiim.org
Gilbane Group, gilbane.com

CHAPTER 7

Writing for Intranets

Cynthia Ross Pedersen
Adeo Communications Corp.

Simple Communication

With adult literacy at low levels, studies showing that reading online is more difficult than reading offline, and an increasingly global audience on the Web, never before has there been a greater need for a simple writing style.

Findings from the International Adult Literacy Survey (IALS) assessment indicate that only half of the U.S. adult population (16–65 years of age) reached Level 3, the level of literacy proficiency identified as a minimum standard for success in today's labor market (National Institute for Literacy). Canada shares a similar issue, according to the ABC Canada Literacy Foundation: "Twenty-two percent of adult Canadians have serious problems dealing with any printed materials. An additional 24 percent of Canadians can deal only with simple reading tasks" (ABC Canada Literacy Foundation; highlights from the original IALS report can be found at www.statcan.ca/english/freepub/89F0093XIE/highle.pdf). These North American issues are reflected in today's organizations and compounded by the speed that business demands.

When calling for a simple writing style, I do not mean a writing style that is somehow "dumbed down," but rather, a style that is aligned with the goals of the plain language movement. This writing is simple, uncluttered, and easily understood by a wide range of people.

Examples from the investment industry illustrate how plain language is applied. The following are headlines from analyst comments on tax legislation. I have presented the original and simplified versions. Try this exercise on sample content from your intranet and see the difference that simplicity can make:

> **Original:** Eliminating dividend taxation could prove a major lift for equity markets.
> **Better**: Equity markets would benefit from elimination of dividend taxation.
> **Better yet**: Removing dividend tax could lift equity markets.
>
> **Original**: Unintended consequences of U.S. dividend taxation have been negative.
> **Better**: U.S. dividend taxation has negative effects.

Plain language, sometimes called clear language, is both a concept and a movement that has quietly gained ground in the last 10 years. Organizations such as the Plain Language Action and Information Network (PLAIN) have been working to change the way government communicates with the American public. The organization states: "No one technique defines plain language. Rather, plain language is defined by results—it is easy to read, understand, and use." PLAIN's Web site (www.plainlanguage.gov) is a great resource on this topic.

Another strong reference is the Web site for the Plain Language Association International (plainlanguagenetwork.org). This site contains definitions, examples, contacts, and a listing of relevant initiatives and conferences across a variety of industries. Its definition of plain language uses the ROI equation: "Clear writing in plain language saves time, money, and lives."

Longer words don't make you sound smarter. Longer words simply put up barriers. Complex writing is understood by fewer people and, in these days of short attention spans, often dismissed. Rather than face the difficult task of reading complicated text, people opt out. Writing to explore the joy of words is a personal journey, but when it comes to your intranet, the goal of writing is to communicate a message. To ease this communication, I support and teach a simple style of writing.

Throughout this chapter, I will introduce some concepts from our Web Writers' Workshop. This writing workshop has been in operation since 1997 and prepares Web and intranet teams with the mind and skill sets to write online content. Over the years, we have worked with all kinds of organizations and all types of content—rethinking, restructuring, and rewriting corporate and government content. We have challenged conventions and presented a new way to write that is not only easy for writers but renders online content that is easily digestible to readers. I start my workshops with a self-introduction that states: "I've given up eloquence in favor of being understood by more people." This is a fundamental principle behind our methodology.

Top Lessons Learned

1. Content written just for the Web is always better than repurposed material.
2. Traditional writing styles are great for documents but not good for online content.
3. Getting rid of a document mindset is challenging.
4. Writing less is a win-win proposition—it's easier to read and easier to maintain.
5. Intranets tend to look like document repositories, but they should look more like Web sites.
6. Content cleanups are good preparation for content management system rollouts.

User-Centric Writing

One of the key differentiators of successful Web writing is that it is user-centric. It is aware of its audience and their needs. It is less about the writer or author and more about conveying the message. As Web writing is a subset of business writing, its purpose is to communicate an organizational message. User-centric writing proposes that:

> *I write this for you and with you in mind. I don't write it for me or the powers that be, except that it is my job to communicate messages related to my organization.*

So your first step is to identify who the audience is. There may be one or more—and likely several. Examine what content the audience needs and how they use it, finding commonalities to help you meet the needs of many without having to create a version for everyone.

Understand the situations in which they will be using your material. Is it used everyday or infrequently? Do users scan the content online, or do they need detailed material that they can take with them? Are they brokers for information, like an information center that may want to e-mail documents or hyperlinks to documents to people who have questions? Are they experts who need in-depth technical coverage of the topic or nonexperts who only need a high-level overview?

To understand the audience, you must also determine their technology and the circumstances in which this intranet content is being accessed. Are they in the head office, at a satellite office, or at home? What kind of computer are they using, and how are they connected to the intranet? This may limit the speed at which they can access information and the screen size that displays the information. A good test is to ask: How far can users navigate through your intranet in two minutes? How many layers or pages can they read and navigate through to get to the content they need? The answer to that test may influence how you structure and present the information. Something that works for head office staff may not work for a remote field office where the computer or connectivity is slower.

Then ask about their familiarity with the Internet, the intranet, and the content. This too will provide guidance on how to structure information. An expert can dive in and access lots of information all at once. Experts have the ability to sift through the information and will be comfortable with the interface. Users new to the Web may require less information at once and need a more explicit presentation of content and how to explore it online. For this audience, Web page content becomes more of an explicit guide and does not assume that the user knows all Web conventions. An expert user understands that a hyperlinked report name is clickable and will lead directly to the report. A novice may need a bit of copy to introduce a report and a specific call to action to present the available navigation.

Intranets Differ from Public Web Sites

Intranets are generally more complex than public Web sites. There are exceptions dictated by the nature of the organization, but in general, I would expect that for any organization, its intranet will have more content and serve more identifiable audiences than its public Web site. Intranets are created by larger and more diverse teams than public Web sites, and they are not generally funded or run by the communications or marketing groups that stand behind most public sites.

Intranets and the teams that support them need to work with few resources, and often with little focused attention, as the intranet is yet another demand on an already overworked staff. Beyond the resource situation, at the core, the nature of an intranet is different than a public Web site. It is an operational channel and support for communications and a self-service environment for employees. Intranets are sometimes viewed as the corporate library, other times as a portal to organizational applications, and yet for others as a collaborative environment. Regardless of the flavor of your intranet, it is a collection of a wide variety of material, each with a distinct purpose and use.

Online Content

Online content is a new category of written content that came with the introduction of Web sites. It is the content that many people forget about when they assemble material for intranets or Web sites of any kind. As intranets are not purely document repositories and portals need some glue to bind their applications together, this is the role of online or Web page content. Web pages provide context to the reader, and they provide related content that might not otherwise be found. They also encourage correlations and discovery that may lead to innovation.

The most common Web pages are the navigational pages that present menus of choices and lead users to content. However, Web pages can also be broker pages that introduce a topic or provide a central gathering spot for content geared toward a specific audience. Introduction pages for new employees are good examples of broker pages.

Web pages can be the end content as well. Online news pages or newsletters where the content only exists on the page are examples. Remember that Web visitors read as they navigate through a site—reading and clicking, scanning and clicking—they are accumulating information as they navigate through the site and validating that they are on the right path to what they are looking for. Depending on the depth of their information requirements, they may only need to follow a portion of the path to collect sufficient information.

Online content, especially home pages, section pages, and broker pages, are where the writer, Web designer, and usability specialist need to collaborate to provide the healthy balance of top line information and in-depth coverage to present choices and get users where they need to go quickly.

Most people write intranets top-down. They design a home page and then each successive layer of content almost predictably. You often see the hints of this approach with phrases like, "in this section, you will find," as if they needed to go through the process of writing the Web pages to determine what content they needed for the site. I recommend the opposite approach. Collect your content, and let *it* tell you its structure. Collect like-kinds of content by task or topic. Then tailor or add topic or contextual content with the end-user and their uses in mind.

The most distinctive characteristics of online content are its architecture and flexibility of formats. These characteristics empower users to make choices, allowing them to explore a topic to the level of understanding they need, investigate related content if they wish, and use a piece of content in a variety of ways. I would like to introduce the concept of scalable content, where you produce various sizes and versions of content to be used in succession or have it spread throughout a site to provide context and awareness. Follow my guidance on preparing scalable intranet content with the sizes and tone recommended for intranets, and you will have the makings of valuable intranet content—you just need to assemble it. This will provide your audience with just the right amount of information at the right time—providing enough content to satisfy situations where they need a little and where they need a lot.

Understanding Scalable Content Through Chocolate Cake

Since the concept of scalable content presented in connected layers is such a new idea for writing, I created the following story to help convey the concept:

> *I enjoy eating out with friends, and there are lots of restaurants for us to try in my town. Although I try my best to scout*

what people are eating when we enter a restaurant, I won't truly know what's good or bad until I try it.

It would be interesting if a restaurant would allow you to see and sample each of their main dishes in order to determine what you'd like to order; but that's not the case. Instead, they give you a menu with a brief title describing each dish and an additional line attempting to lure you to that choice with a further description of ingredients and preparations. On that little bit of text, you make your investment decision. Not unlike a home page that presents the options, and from there, it is up to you to make choices.

So here comes the chocolate cake part. When we're ready for dessert, out comes a small menu, again with choices ever-so-briefly described. Somehow, the chocolate desserts always sound marvelous; however, experienced eaters know that chocolate dessert can be greatly disappointing in spite of the description. So I propose that it would be interesting if you could order a taste of a dessert—a spoonful. As a non-dessert eater, I could use the spoonful to understand the dessert and fulfill my needs at that point. I have friends that enjoy chocolate and could use the spoonful to validate that it is worth ordering a full serving and then enjoy every last bite of it. And my other friends that want to explore further on consuming a full portion of the dessert might enquire as to the recipe. They may want to try making this same dessert at home.

Thus, I have described scalable content: from a line on a home page to a taste of chocolate cake to satisfy the light appetite or validate a heavier one; a full serving for those who want it, and the specifications, details, or recipe for the experts. Each audience gets what they want and learns more and more along the way.

Generally, we think in headlines for the home page with full servings of content. What Web writing wants you to think about is the taste of chocolate cake or snippets of content to give readers just enough of an introduction. Use snippets on broker pages to inform before linking to the main content, or use snippets at the sides of pages to present related content. Tastes of chocolate cake have many uses online, and do not forget to link to more detail or offer the full actionable path for users who want to go that far. Along with a full description of a program or product profile, present the links that will let the user complete an order form or explore technical specifications. This layering of content allows you to provide the level of detail that everyone wants. Users will explore to their own level of satisfaction.

Size and Tone

Remembering that the goal of Web writing is to communicate, we need to make sure that content is not only accessible but also absorbable. In addressing the size of content (Figure 7.1), I have found through study and practice that the following guidelines produce easier-to-understand content than with traditional writing:

- Words – Individual words should average between 10 and 12 characters in length
- Sentences – Full sentences should be about 20 to 25 words in length
- A bulleted point – Bulleted points should be shorter than sentences and amount to about 10 to 12 words
- Paragraphs – Paragraphs are one to two sentences in length and contain a maximum of 50 words

When it comes to style, the recommendation is a conversational tone. This is not the way traditional content is written, but it is the easiest to write and the easiest to understand. Plain language advocates and user-centric thinkers put the reader first. The conversational tone talks directly to the reader with an active voice. By its nature, conversational writing uses simpler words and shorter sentences. The active voice engages the reader and encourages them to read on. This is a standard approach for marketing and communications professionals—one that needs to be adopted by the general business community.

Words: 10–12 characters

Sentence: 20–25 words

Paragraph: 50 words maximum

Figure 7.1 Sizing It Right

Choosing Content Formats

Here is where I ask you to think wide and consider your users. Writers tend to think in documents. That is the way it has been for centuries. However, when it comes to putting content online, there are many format choices. While it is perfectly valid to use an intranet as a filing mechanism, a filing cabinet from which we retrieve documents, not all content is appropriate for this treatment. Fundamentally, you need to determine what content is meant for online consumption and what content is made for downloading (and most probably printing, with its consumption offline). You may choose to have multiple formats for a given topic or piece of content with the understanding that for different users or in different situations, a certain format may be needed. So let me take you through your choices.

A *native file* is a downloadable file in its original format. This may be a Microsoft Word document, a tool created in Microsoft Excel, or a brochure in Quark format. Generally, this is content that is meant to be used as a tool or template, and it expects that the user has the software to work with it.

An *Adobe Acrobat PDF file* is a downloadable file where the content is locked. This is common for documents where the integrity of the content is key, and this format makes it unchangeable. This format is also used when the software used to create the document is not generally available, but you want to distribute the content in a usable way. Contracts, policies, sample forms, brochures, drawings, and artwork are commonly posted in PDF format. Some organizations are using this format, and its ability to interface with data sources, to handle forms.

There is what I call *Webby material*—content written for online consumption. With the flexibility and reach of your intranet, there are a variety of Webby formats to suit the situation:

- *Snippets* are bits of content. These are quick summaries that can satisfy on their own or lead the reader knowledgably to a longer version.
- A *summary* or *topic-at-a-glance* is usually an introductory paragraph followed by bulleted content that provides a quick-to-consume overview of the topic.
- A full version is a deep exploration of a topic, but given that it is made for online consumption, it is optimally a mix of headings, bullets, paragraphs, and links to related

topics. It does its best to provide the kind of eye candy that makes a lot of content easy to consume online.

While you are considering formats, you should also address the need for multiple versions of the full content. You may need a version for experts and a version for people who are new to the topic. You may need versions according to job role, expertise, or language. Then, while you are trying your best to be user-centric, consider whether the audience needs a printable version and a version optimized for distribution via e-mail. Content management tools can help manage these multiple versions.

Tools for Intranet Content

Because an intranet is contributed to by many, but should be presented to the user as a cohesive collection of information, it is useful to have tools for contributors that encourage consistency. These tools can also help ensure that content is compliant with brand, legal, or communications guidelines. Tools are helpful to intranet contributors because many of them are not trained writers or experienced Web writers, so guidance on how to produce content is usually well received.

The starting tool is a style guide. These are common in communications departments, where they provide standards for terminology, branding, tone, and language references (dictionaries, stylebooks, etc.). For intranets, you should include these references, but also address the following unique facets of the Web:

- How to refer to specific Web features
- Conventions for presenting PDFs or other downloadable documents
- Size and overall style
- Tone guidelines for online content

Put this style guide content online and augment it with FAQs or a forum to engage your writing community.

Templates and examples are also tools. Templates are a basic of intranets and Web projects, but contributors need a more refined set of templates to support a variety of textual layouts. The conventional top-left navigation and footer, with remaining area for text, does not support best practices for content presentation. If your templates are few, perhaps examples are the best way of illustrating techniques for textual content. Again, add these links into an intranet contributor section of your intranet, and you will create a useful, centralized resource for this group.

To help set standards and identify good examples of online content, use your word processor. Although there are many sophisticated tools, Microsoft Word has a built-in tool for generating readability statistics. Once you turn the feature on, it will provide a quantitative and qualitative measure of your content. At a quantitative level, it will give you a structural analysis of the words, sentences, and paragraphs, so you can judge the size of your content. At a qualitative level, the readability statistics give you a grade level and readability index that will let you evaluate the complexity of the writing. Evaluate content and set standards using these measures, but use caution with the automated tools, as nothing compares to a human review of content.

The last recommendation is not a tool but a team. An editor or editorial team can provide support for your intranet contributors by coaching, ensuring compliance to standards, and cultivating best practices within your organization. These resources need to be positioned carefully so they do not become everyone's writing team, nor do they become an approval bottleneck for content posting. This person or team can consult with new contributors or with those dealing with difficult content. They can provide writing clinics and manage the contributors' section of the intranet. It is a great job for new grads with communications, journalism, or information sciences training.

Solving Common Content Issues

Now that I have presented a basic approach, discussed some of the tools that you might use, and the skill set to acquire, let's take a look at some of the more difficult content found in intranets, and the solutions that make this content more usable.

Policy and Procedure

Although people usually talk about this type of material as if policy and procedure were a single concept, they are related concepts but very different in use. Typically, I find that both types of content suffer from their history, generally having been written by the same people and rendered in a traditional if not formal approach. It is posted online in a similar format with a similar fate: It is unapproachable.

Skills and Competencies for Web Writers

Strong Web writers or content contributors are good writers who have a tailored set of skills made for the online medium. Look for the following skills in a Web writer:

- A simple writing approach that eases comprehension
- A journalistic style that puts the most important points up top
- A focus on always keeping the user or reader at the top of the agenda
- Knowledge of the technical and graphical elements of the Web medium
- Structural thinking with an understanding of information architecture
- An ability to help others understand how writing for the Web is different from traditional writing

Good Web writers can reduce existing documents or content to just the essential messages, eliminating redundancies and reducing content size by half or more.

Policy tends to be a reference or guideline organized by topic with content that explains an organization's position. Being able to find relevant policies, understand its background, author, applicable dates and scope, and even related policies make this content ideally suited to the scalable content concept.

Procedures outline the agreed-upon steps to do work that is inline with the policy. By its nature, this is best presented in a way that people can follow. In addition to a full version, a printable or e-mail version may be useful as you try to provide as much operational assistance to users as possible.

The biggest issue for this type of content is age. We call this legacy content, because it usually predates the current owner but its aura of importance means it is seldom challenged. The size and complexity of these documents make them forbidding to revise, and no one has the time or the inclination to change them. So up they go, posted as large PDF documents that are "available" online but seldom referred to.

Solving Policy Content Online

First, let's treat policy and procedure as two different but related concepts. For policy content, commit to a plain language approach. Sell this to senior management with the ROI that, if people can read and understand it, it is halfway to adoption. After all, isn't that what policy is all about—consistent practice? Another way to say this is that people cannot follow what they do not understand.

Next, pick a sample policy to rewrite using the following eight-step approach:

1. Clarify the content with a subject matter expert to ensure that the policy is current and correct. Since legacy content is usually 80 percent outdated or obsolete, do not fund this rewrite as an intranet project but as a compliance or governance project. In practice, most of the effort is not in rewriting but in confirming and updating the actual content.

2. With clarity over the policy, break the content into topics and prioritize the material. Identify the unique policy components and discard general material that is common and should already be on your intranet. To help with navigation, search engine tagging and titling ensure that topics follow the company taxonomy and identify synonyms that help employees locate this policy using their own words.

3. Decide where in your site structure this policy would be relevant and should be linked. This will help you decide on the various versions you need to write.

4. Now you need formats. Decide how this content will be presented online. You can use online content in the form of summaries, snippets, or full content pages. You can offer downloadable versions for printing. You may need a combination of formats.

5. And now you can start writing. At this point, engage the general rules of Web writing: simplicity, short sentences, and conversational tone. Ask yourself, "What's the minimum you need to write to communicate this policy?" For

longer online versions, use headings, groupings, and bullets to segment and present the content. Create eye candy to maximize content consumption and provide readers with instant hits. Read it to yourself aloud to hear how it sounds. While you are in the mindset of this policy, write a simpler version, a snippet, and alternate titles to be used as links, and perhaps a more targeted version for a specific audience. Now you have a selection of Webby content for this policy.

6. Time for testing. First you need to do your own testing. Run the material through the spelling and grammar checker in your word processor for structure and readability analysis. Highlight any section that you suspect needs further work, and see if the structure and readability scores indicate any problems. If you have a benchmark or guideline to follow for size and readability, ensure that your work conforms.

7. Take it back to the subject matter experts to check that you have preserved the policy and not simplified the content out of it.

8. Last but not least is user testing. You can perform usability testing on your content within the intranet site to check taxonomy and flow. You can perform comprehension testing to determine how digestible your content is to your target users.

Solving Procedure Content Online

The nature of procedure calls for a specific approach. It is a step-by-step approach and should provide all the information you need to produce a piece of work. This could include instructions on how to operate a physical tool or a software application, or it could be more of a guideline on how to create documents or documentation that complies with a specified policy.

Procedures need to be written with the user in mind. Ask yourself, "What is the readers' environment and requirement as they follow this procedure?" Are they in a call center, stepping a client through a process, or perhaps they are field workers who need to print the procedure and take it with them for easy reference? Maybe your content supports a manager who needs to use this content as a checklist or online form to support a human resources task. You might expect from these examples that the nature of the writing will be different. I would say that the format may change. Understanding the users' environment and requirement is key to producing online procedure that will be referenced frequently.

Tailoring Procedures for Call Center Use Online

The original procedures were converted to HTML pages, complete with navigation, but the content itself needed to be cleaned up and simplified in order to give call center staff the "at a glance" answers they needed.

Original Content
Eligibility Requirements for Clients and Mortgages
Eligibility requirements for clients are:

A maximum of two people can be insured on a mortgage.

To qualify for Property Life, and Disability Insurance, the borrower of an eligible mortgage, and one co-borrower or guarantor, must be:

- At least 18 years old and less than 65 years old on the insurance application date
- A U.S. resident (living in the U.S. at least eight months of the year)

To apply for Disability Insurance, they must also:

- Have Property Life insurance coverage
- Be actively working, on the date of application, in full-time employment, self-employment, or seasonal employment

Full-time and self-employment means actively working in the U.S. at least 20 hours a week for wages or expectation of profit in the regular duties of their employment or occupation.

Note: Actively at work does not include leaves of absence, including maternity, paternity, or sick leaves.

If seasonally employed and not working, they must be capable of performing their regular job.

To qualify as a seasonal employee, the work season must have a beginning and end, and they must have a proven work history as a seasonal employee with expectation of returning to the same occupation the next season.

TIP: It is necessary for an applicant to be working 20 hours or more per week to qualify to apply for disability insurance. There is no requirement, however, for them to remain employed in order to maintain the disability coverage.

Eligible mortgages are:

A mortgage that is secured by a residential property that is either your own home, a rental, or vacation property and that is not more than a multiple four-family-type dwelling.

Note: All mortgages must be denominated in U.S. dollars.

Webby Version

Eligibility requirements for Clients and Mortgages

<table>
<tr><th>Life Insurance</th><th>Disability Insurance</th></tr>
<tr><td>Qualifications
• Maximum of 2 insured persons per mortgage
• Borrower of eligible mortgage and co-borrower or guarantor, must be:
o Between 18 and 65 years old on the date of application
o A U.S. resident (living in the U.S. at least eight months of the year)</td><td>Qualifications
• Must have life insurance coverage
• Be actively working [link to definition], on the date of application, in full-time employment, self-employment, or seasonal employment
o There is no employment duration requirement to maintain disability coverage</td></tr>
<tr><td colspan="2">Eligible mortgages
• A mortgage that is secured by residential property, that is:
o The mortgagor's own home, rental, or vacation property
o A one- to four-family dwelling
• All mortgages must be in U.S. dollars</td></tr>
</table>

It is not uncommon to find that different formats or forms of the same procedure are needed for different audiences or at different times during a process. You might also post different versions of a procedure and evaluate them to see which ones are used more frequently. Analysis of Web usage followed by interviews or online polling will uncover the reasons behind the usage patterns, so start by identifying the target audience for the procedure. Try to determine its environment and how this impacts the form of the procedure for optimal use.

Next, you need your subject matter experts along with sample users to proof the procedure and ensure that it is both technically correct and applicable to the audience. This is not Web writing but more like procedure validation. Unfortunately, a well written but incorrect procedure is not helpful, although it may point out only too clearly how outdated the procedures are.

With content confirmed and each version targeted with an understanding of the related environment, you can begin the formats. Online forms, printable formats, downloadable templates, and online references each have their own layouts and information requirements. What procedural content has in common is a structured presentation of steps, probably with some branching for decision points.

Applying the Web writing guidelines, talk to the reader and provide instructions in a simple straightforward way. The focus is instructional content, so background material and policy can be linked from the sidelines as contextually relevant material, but try to stick to the mainstream, providing at-a-glance procedures.

Printed procedures can present more points on a page than the online version. However, since printable versions stand alone once printed, they need to have relevant material and references on the page. Onscreen versions need less information on the page as they can include links that will take the user quickly to related information. As with all intranet content, author, date updated, applicable scope, and perhaps who to call about this procedure should be provided to give context.

Now is also the time to think differently if your users are online when applying this procedure. Can an online form, decision tree, or online application aid the reader in applying the procedure? Just because the procedure was on paper does not mean it still needs to be available only in that format on the intranet.

At this point, snippets and alternative titles for linking should be created. Placement within the intranet should be determined based on the relevancy of this procedural content. Run the content through your spelling and grammar checker for structure and readability analysis, and adjust as necessary. Document your approach as a standard for all procedures. Then apply usability testing to ensure that it works for the most important people: your audience.

Legal and Compliance Content

Legal or compliance content presents the greatest challenges for the Web writer. Not only is it traditionalist writing, it is a type of content that has greater inherent risks than typical intranet content. It is written by and for specialists, and although these specialists are beginning to open up to a clearer style, it is not mainstream practice. That said, I have several approaches that seem to meet all needs when working with this kind of material.

Often, a simpler version can be provided and positioned as supplementary material, as long as the full, untouched legal version is available. These simpler versions can be presented as checklists or bulleted lists of key points, as long as reference is made to the full version. The full version is generally a PDF document that is ready to download and print or distribute.

With enough respect for the material and authority in the room, you can question which documents or collections of material really need the legal or compliance approach and which are really meant to be in plain language. Perhaps a collection of material was written at the same time, by the same people, and all given the same approach, when, in fact, some of the material was not intended to be formal. I have found this most often in the area of human resources, where schedules or sample letters were not intended to be legal documents. It takes a fresh eye and some common sense to gently question the nature of the documents.

Recommended Web Sites

ABC Canada Literacy Foundation, www.abc-canada.org

Adeo's Web Writers' Workshop, www.adeo.com/services/web_writers.html

Jakob Nielsen's Web Site (various studies, articles, and references), useit.com

National Institute for Literacy, www.nifl.gov

The Plain Language Action and Information Network (PLAIN), www.plainlanguage.gov

The Plain Language Association International, www.plainlanguage network.org

CHAPTER 8

Corporate Portals and Intranets

Craig St. Clair
TKG Consulting LLC

Jose Claudio Terra
TerraForum Consulting

No book on intranets would be complete without a chapter on corporate portals. In this chapter, we explain what corporate portals are, what they can do for your organization, and how they should be built and maintained.

Corporate portals directly address some of the most obvious needs of intranets:

- They promise the delivery of personalized internal and external content.
- They serve up content in a flexible, distributed way.
- They incorporate applications and collaboration tools via a single sign-on process and multiple-access devices.

The prospect of providing distributed and personalized content, and incorporating various online applications in one interface is indeed nirvana to many IT and business managers. It is, in many respects, the promise that everyone expects IT to fulfill and the goal that many software companies are relentlessly pursuing.

In a way, corporate portals are all about offering a user-centric solution with the perfect integration and total flexibility required to deal with fast-evolving business and IT landscapes. Are there any software solutions that offer a complete solution? Not yet, but it is good to know that software vendors and companies are heading in this direction. As we will see in this chapter, the "all encompassing solution" is a (moving) target worth pursuing.

The Concept of a Portal and a Corporate Portal

The first portals grew out of Web-based search engines in the B2C (business to consumer) environment. Since search engines had the capability of aggregating content from a variety of Web sites, it made perfect sense to direct this search and retrieval functionality to addressing the specific needs of organizations. Allowing search engines to crawl and index an array of Internet sites was a step in the right direction because it began to virtually aggregate distributed content in a single interface. Eventually, companies such as Excite, Yahoo!, Go, Lycos, MSN, and, most recently, Google started to offer exclusive content and a variety of online services. Currently, consumer portals have an ever-growing presence with hundreds of millions of people around the world. Corporate portals have a somewhat shorter lifespan, inheriting the metaphor and a number of the technologies and applications developed by consumer portals.

Corporate portals, as the name implies, were conceived as a gateway into a disparate array of functionality and content that was located both inside and outside an organization. In a sense, they were created in response to the confusion and disconnects that resulted from the ever-increasing numbers of mismatched online functional applications and content repositories. With the proliferation of Web-based, browser-enabled applications for everything from accounting processes to customer tracking to benefits forms, and the exponential increase in content and data repositories in a variety of forms and formats, some way of bringing order out of chaos was desperately needed. "Wouldn't it be great," said intranet managers and software developers at the time, "if there was a way to present all this information and functionality in a single interface?" This was precisely the need that portals were designed to fill.

Corporate portals in large corporations are still a rather messy subject. Historically, intranets and applications were not developed as part of a coordinated effort by a centralized organization. Yet, portals promise to offer a simplified and organized view of complex content scenarios, heterogeneous systems, and mission-critical applications. They also promise to deliver a user-centric experience and flexible architectures, as well as navigation and integration solutions that will keep the portal evolving seamlessly with the ever-changing business environment. But as we will discuss in this chapter, the promise of a single unified corporate portal is a goal that organizations have yet to realize. There is always more content to integrate and another application that is running outside the portal framework.

Despite their current limitations, corporate portals are undoubtedly here to stay. They offer great solutions for intranet managers. Intranet hot buttons such as modular page construction, personalization and customization, and intuitive search and collaboration tools have all been built into portal software in recent years. Since the late 1990s, corporate and enterprise portals have indeed become a mainstay of intranet design and construction. In fact, a list of what intranet managers regard as the most important intranet functionality is pretty much synonymous with the features offered by major portal software packages.

Assessing Corporate Portals: Four Perspectives

Because so many corporate portal solutions share so little in terms of technology, deployment, and use, we realize that a corporate portal cannot be easily described (although the idea of a central point of personalized access is often cited as the main characteristic that sets corporate portals apart from other IT applications). Instead, we like to talk about the attributes of corporate portals in terms of four perspectives:

1. Technology origin
2. Technical functionality
3. Focus
4. Scope

These four perspectives are presented in Figure 8.1 and can be used to assess individual portal offerings and to help find the proper solution for your organization.

Technology—Origin

Many portal solutions have evolved from other types of software. Although all major corporate portal solutions claim to integrate all sorts of functionality, it is very clear that the strengths and weaknesses of individual portal software packages are directly linked to the origins of the individual software solution. Often, portal software vendors have started with a specific type of software and then purchased and

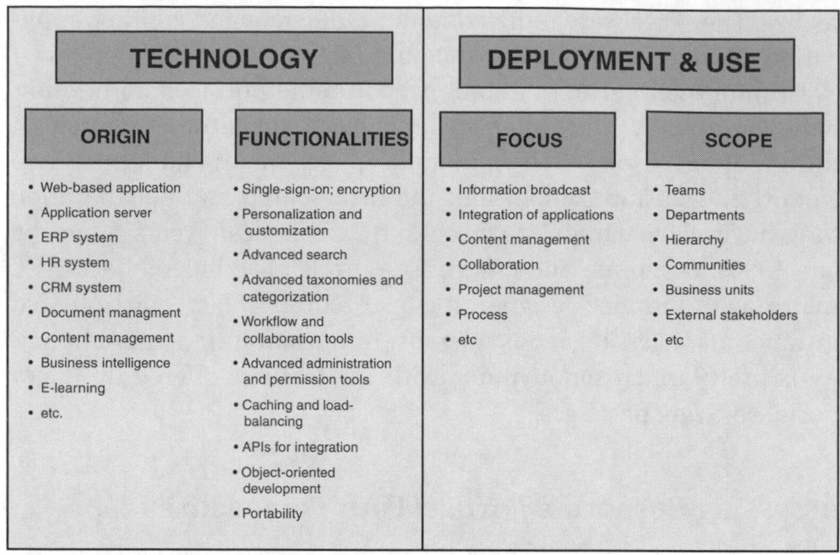

Figure 8.1 Four Perspectives on Corporate Portals

"bolted on" other software solutions in order to offer an end-to-end portal solution.

This often means that individual portal solutions are uneven in their offerings. Some portal solutions provide great out-of-the-box collaboration tools, some are great at integrating with front-end applications, others are much better at managing large amounts of decentralized content, and some may have strengths in true data integration. Anyone choosing a corporate portal solution needs to pay attention to the details of customization, integration, and the amount of work that is really necessary to achieve the functionality promised by the software.

Technology—Functionality

After understanding the core of a corporate portal framework, the next step in technology assessment is to undertake a detailed analysis of the functionality included in a specific software solution. Our advice is to ask vendors to create a quick prototype; that is when many differences tend to emerge. It is also particularly important to think about the portal from the point-of-view of end-users and non-IT professionals. Some corporate portal solutions deliver types of functionality in friendlier ways than others. Finally, one of the toughest things to evaluate is performance. Although reading technical specifications may help, it is important to look at actual deployments of a similar size, the distributed nature of the user base, and the complexity of required integration.

Explaining Personalization and Customization

While portals enable access to content and functionality across and even outside the enterprise, intranet managers and portal developers also recognize that full access to every online resource for every user has not always been advisable or preferable. User requirements (the notion that user interfaces, content, and functionality should fit how people naturally work and complete tasks) have informed not only *how* content and functionality is presented in the portal, but also *what* content and functionality should be available to different users within an organization.

The technical response to different user requirements has come in the form of personalization and customization. While the terms "personalization" and "customization" are often used interchangeably, we will make an important distinction here. Personalization refers to system-driven presentation of content and functionality; content and functional applications can be pushed to specific groups of users, while not appearing for other users at all. Customization, on the other hand, is user-modified presentation. Users themselves can select and arrange content and functionality according to their own preferences. So while the aggregation capabilities of portal architecture can make for a dizzying amount of content and functionality in a single interface, the personalization and customization aspects of the architecture ensure that the user only receives relevant content and functionality.

In the case of personalization, content and functional applications can be pushed to specific groups of users by matching descriptive attributes of content or functional elements (metadata) with descriptive attributes in a user profile that is accessed by the portal. The relationship between the attributes attached to content and functionality and the attributes of the user profile are defined by a set of business rules. This can be illustrated in a simplified model. A content subject attribute of Buffalo, NY, (content about Buffalo) could be associated with a user whose office location is Buffalo, NY, via a business rule that basically says: When user location attribute equals Buffalo, serve content with attribute tag Buffalo.

For customization, users themselves select and arrange content and functionality according to their own preferences. In a portal, user customization is typically associated with a "my pages" concept, that is, a page or series of pages designed and constructed by individual users. Typically, users can select and arrange on a single page favorite tools, such as stock quotes or industry news; they can construct a list of favorite links, or they can save a list of Internet searches. The actual construction of the pages is enabled by the portal interface and a series of very user-friendly construction screens.

Customization and the "my pages" concept works on an individual, user-by-user basis, and personalization and business rules are generally defined for groups and subgroups of users. Users can of course belong to multiple groups, each with access to a specific set of content and functionality. User groups are often built along the natural divisions of company organizations, such as roles, lines of business, products, and office locations. Combining various types of user groups allow organizations to serve a targeted array of content and functionality to groups with specific demographics.

Deployment and Use: Focus

Although related to the choice in terms of technology, it is also clear that the design and deployment of corporate portals has evolved substantially from mere broadcast tools to a highly complex solution that allows knowledge workers to use the portal as *the* tool to do work. When designing the portal, it's important to have a clear idea of what users need from the system and what user requirements the portal is required to solve. Sophisticated corporate portals will not force users to choose one specific focus (for instance, broadcast, data integration, content management, collaboration, and project management or process); rather, it will allow the user to configure the portal through many facets simultaneously. In fact, the main challenges are often related to how users decide to solve the user requirements in terms of information architecture, navigation, taxonomy, customization, and personalization strategies. While users of sophisticated portals may have substantial choices in customizing different views of content, applications, and tools, the portal design team will play a significant role in prioritizing different focuses for the evolution of the corporate portal.

Explaining Different Focus Areas for Portals

Although there is a certain evolutionary pattern in the various portal focuses presented later in this section, more advanced portals will include all of these perspectives simultaneously.

Information Broadcast

The earliest (and yet highly relevant) portals were concerned with providing access and organizing vast amounts of information. The earliest portals were search engines directed toward specific sets of content. When considering the growing array of content repositories, however, simply listing search results was not enough. The single interface view needed more structure so that users could make sense out of large amounts of data. Soon portals also allowed organizations to categorize search results in ways that were relevant to them. Companies or organizations could create a specific categorization scheme and taxonomy that was relevant to the entire enterprise and subsequently build that structure into the portal. Users could browse through a hierarchy of terms and search results that would be returned in the context of the aforementioned categories and subcategories, allowing users to see content in terms of subjects, sources of information, and document formats.

Integration of Applications

Managing content repositories and Web sites are just part of the challenge in large organizations. The other challenge includes integrating applications. Before portals were as important as they are today, companies were developing separate online functional applications that were browser-enabled as well. During the Internet revolution, there was a veritable avalanche of traditional client-server applications that were translated into browser interfaces. While browser-based applications eliminated the need to load individual clients on every desktop, the separateness of each application created its own set of problems, not the least of which was multiple open browsers on everyone's desktop and separate logins for each application. Portals let browser-based applications be "ported in" via separate modules (sometimes called portlets or Webports) and to appear alongside one another in the same portal interface.

The functionality that emerged ranged from a variety of personal tools, such as newsfeeds, currency converters, and stock quotes, to enterprise-wide applications, such as customer relationship management (CRM) applications, Web content management systems (CMS), and human resource management tools. As the vendors of these more functionally dedicated applications saw the emerging power and potential of corporate portals, they also decided to enter the corporate portal arena. As a result, many Web-based applications evolved to be repackaged and offered complete portal suites. This was a clear "me too" move on the part of application vendors. However, since the focus was still heavily centered on their respective applications, the overall portal architecture suffered in most cases.

Regardless of the drawbacks of those Web-based applications that were converted to corporate portals, it was clear that for the first time, business managers and portal interface developers could imagine a scenario where content (knowledge repositories of various types) and functionality could be united in a common interface. This was a powerful concept. While content and applications were not integrated with each other in the strictest sense, they could be associated with each other in the context of the portal page and, more importantly, in the context of how the user executed job-related tasks.

Content Management

The deep integration with solid content management systems (CMS) provided corporate portals not only the ability to organize and distribute information but also to decentralize the administration of content in a controlled and granular way. The same issues of broadcast portals apply in this context, but there are also important issues in terms of governance and the ease with which the publication of material is decentralized to people other than IT or Web-design professionals.

Collaboration and Project Management

The aggregation and distribution model described for portals so far suggests a unilateral distribution of knowledge and information, from an organization to users. Recognizing that knowledge does not flow in only one direction in an organization, portals were used to facilitate other types of knowledge sharing as well.

To facilitate information and knowledge flow across groups within the organization, portals established secure "members only" areas that included a number of tools designed to connect groups often located in distant offices. These tools typically included or addressed project management, threaded discussions, document sharing, chat, or instant messaging (IM) functionality.

Using the personalization capabilities described earlier, portal designers began to provide secure members-only areas within portals and built a variety of collaboration tools to fill them. For some portal vendors, these community or group collaboration pages became the central organizing principle for the portal's architecture, resulting in a central navigation that consisted of access to group areas for which the user was a member. Users could either subscribe to the secure pages or automatically became a member based on their administrative rights. Once inside, they could use a variety of tools that were available only to the users who were members in that area of the portal.

Process

A powerful organizing principal in modern companies is to identify and address a collection of processes that need to be reinvented, discussed, and constantly optimized. Processes, however, need individuals to act upon them. In this context, portals can be a great help in streamlining core business processes. Processes cut across functional areas, applications, content, and even the organizational borders. Thus, the use of portals for enabling processes requires a deep understanding, reflection, and optimization of core processes. The risk, which already occurred during the business-process reengineering craze of the 1990s, is to simply automate the existing processes without rethinking them in light of the business challenges, the stakeholders involved, and the new collaboration possibilities that can be enabled by technology solutions.

Deployment and Use: Scope

What kind of scope defines the use of a corporate portal? Some large organizations have been paralyzed by the idea that a corporate portal should be the solution for all employees and, thus, implemented primarily from a top-down perspective (i.e., taking into consideration some key business goals and a broad IT perspective). One of the most important lessons from corporate portal projects is that corporate portals will serve different audiences in very different ways.

Some audiences may get very little benefit from the corporate portal, while other core audiences will have their work profoundly affected by it. Another consequence of this focused-audiences concept is that corporate portals can start small and evolve to encompass more and more internal employees and even external stakeholders. Generally speaking, though, there are high costs associated with a corporate portal solution. To avoid duplication of efforts and technology implementations, good portal deployments start with a set of applications, content, and tools that benefit a large number of employees. A second set of more focused applications, content, and tools may need to be made available, focusing on smaller groups such as teams, departments, hierarchy levels, communities (internal and external), and people involved with specific processes (internal and external).

Case Study: One Company's Move from Static Intranet to Corporate Portal

For three years, I was involved as both an interested spectator and ultimately a designer/manager in one company's journey from a static, "homegrown" intranet to a corporate portal. It is useful to look at this company's experience in terms of an evolutionary process and lessons learned.

In this case, the story started in the IT department and actually did not immediately involve the company's already well-established intranet. The immediate impetus and application for portal software came in the form of online document sharing between specific groups of users. IT viewed the portal as a platform that would make use of its online document management system (which suffered from low user acceptance and was the source of many complaints) easier, more targeted, and more secure. In this initial implementation, the portal allowed a minimum amount of collaboration in the form of document sharing and centralized announcements for project teams with members scattered in different geographic locations. The portal also enabled crawls and indexing of the company's public-facing Web sites and intranet, links out to popular search engines, and listings of purchased newsfeeds.

While this was a step in the right direction, the limitations of the implementation were immediately apparent: Online collaboration beyond secure document sharing was not part of the mix, and the information imported into the portal was narrow and of inconsistent value. Because the implementation was installed project group by project group and because the ability to adopt and maintain the portal differed from group to group, adoption was slow and time consuming. As soon as one group was up and running, an earlier group would drop off or stop active use of the portal.

The next portal project on IT's list was one designed to extend the same limited portal functionality to partner organizations outside the company. This allowed secure sharing of documents with various marketing and research and development partners. While there was a distinct value in sharing workspaces with outside partners, the necessary provisions for maintaining mutually secure environments meant that use of the system (involving secure ID tokens and much paperwork) was difficult and cumbersome.

After two years of slow and inconsistent adoption, the corporate communications department stepped into the project with an agenda of its own. A portal, with its ability to aggregate both content and applications and present a specific mix of information and functionality to users across the enterprise, was viewed as a logical replacement for the company's aging static intranet. The company's intranet was typical of most intranets of a certain size and age: It was plagued with huge amounts of out-of-date and irrelevant information, illogical and inconsistent navigation, and nonexistent design standards.

Rebuilding the intranet in the portal involved several major steps:

- To create content directly in the portal, content management functionality needed to be added to the portal's native content aggregation and search capabilities.
- The portal's navigation system needed to be customized to behave as a more standard intranet style navigation system.
- A new information architecture system needed to be created that provided an intuitive, hierarchical arrangement of content.
- A new governance system and publishing procedures needed to be designed and implemented.

It was initially believed that the largest hurdle to providing a new home for the intranet was the portal's lack of content management functionality. While this was a basic functional requirement, it paled in comparison to other requirements, namely the systematic transfer of huge amounts of content and the building of new (and largely offline) publishing and governance procedures. The intranet phase of the portal program was plagued with technical delays in the form of system and software upgrades, expensive customization, and prolonged and difficult content migration.

In the end, however, the company migrated to the new portal platform and was better for it, particularly in the areas of publishing processes, rationalized navigation, more targeted, personalized content, and a more scalable technical architecture. Painful as it was, it was widely recognized that the company's static, patched together intranet no longer matched the size and complexity of the company, and that portal building and migration was a necessary byproduct of organizational maturity.

Standardization and Enterprise Suites

Corporate portals have not evolved to the point where companies can scrap other important software solutions such as CMS, DMS, CRM, collaboration tools, or Microsoft Office applications. Their interfaces are also not as friendly and flexible as a typical intranet, and integration into legacy applications is still quite difficult (no matter what the vendors say). Having said that, it is important to highlight that corporate portal technologies have improved a great deal in the past five years.

As we have seen, early portals basically consisted of user interfaces that collected and provided access to different types of content and functionality from a variety of sources and locations. This worthy goal was developed in direct response to the proliferation of applications and content repositories throughout organizations. It soon developed, however, that mere aggregation of content and functionality was not enough. The trouble was that porting all the content and applications into the portal took a long time and required lots of hard work.

Content and applications from a variety of sources could indeed be brought into the portal, but they retained their separateness in terms of sources, repositories, and formatting. Content was aggregated or, more accurately, associated, but it was not integrated. Likewise, applications could be surfaced in the portal by building "mini" interfaces. However, each interface had to be built separately, and they remained that way. Again, there was association but not really integration. Applications could also be developed specifically for the portal, but these too had to be built individually.

As a result, early portal implementations were often dismissed as empty frameworks without much content and functionality, with long and painful implementation cycles. In one portal implementation example, the company's legacy intranet was crawled and brought into the portal. This resulted in a thin portal layer that quickly brought the user back to the familiar (and much maligned) intranet. "Why," one user asked, "should I use the portal if it puts me immediately back to the old intranet? What is the value in that?" The user had a point.

Almost as soon as portals were implemented, users asked for more native functionality that would help them develop content directly for the portal and to use out-of-the-box functionality that would help them access a basic set of tools. The enterprise suites, or corporate portals, from major vendors now offer many of these possibilities. Through the use of single sign-on, out-of-the-box functionality and applications, deeper and easier integration and configuration, and the introduction of more effective development environments, corporate portals are finally making life much easier both for IT and business users. The real issue remains in the alignment of portal implementations with concrete business goals and the organizational dynamics that will support the portal over the long run.

Looking into the Future

As the concept of portals and extended collaboration evolve, it is possible to view corporate portals not only as a substitute for current intranets but also as a *de facto* platform for how work is done across organizations. People are increasingly wearing many hats both within a single organization and across many organizations. Corporate portals have the potential for mirroring how people work based on self-described identities, corporate-assigned identities, and personal digital patterns. The concept of individual portals that recognize the many relationships, roles, and interests of its users is not a far-fetched concept. Ultimately, portals will be accessible through any digital device that the individual prefers. Embedded geo-referencing tools will also make portals location-sensitive and more intelligent about what kind of content or applications to present to the user.

Corporate portals will have delivered their promise when users say "I cannot live without my portal," and when the software can integrate seamlessly with existing IT platforms with manageable effort. While this is a formidable task, it is the direction in which leading vendors and organizations alike are currently heading.

Conclusion

Portals have a primary role on the intranet today, with many changes foreseen for the near future. In considering a portal implementation, consider the following elements:

1. Limit technical customization of the portal to items planned for by the software supplier or easily accommodated in the software.
2. Fully understand the logic of how the individual portal software approaches content publishing, information architecture, and collaboration spaces before designing the portal—in other words, do not try to radically adapt the portal to your preconceived notion of how it all should work; use the software's design to achieve your goals.
3. Do not underestimate the time and effort of content migration (in a recent project, migration of 20,000 pages of static intranet content took one year to complete).
4. Avoid duplicating the problems of the old intranet in the new portal by working with content owners to migrate content item-by-item rather than page-by-page (try to break content into distinct individual content items rather than relying on the old page structure).
5. Map the individual content items to individual portlets or content modules (use a content inventory listed on a spread sheet), and then assign content modules to pages—fully understand and take advantage of the distributed nature of portal content publishing.
6. Be sure content owners and their organizations are prepared to take on content maintenance before beginning the migration process. Emphasize that starting with a simple set of content is a good thing—complexity will come soon enough.
7. Recognize that content migration is a golden opportunity rather than a necessary chore; you will never have a better chance to clean up out-of-date content and navigation again.

Recommended Web Sites

BRINT, www.brint.com/intranets.htm
CMS Watch Enterprise Portal Reports, www.cmswatch.com/Portal/Report
Destination KM, elibrary.destinationkm.com/rlist/term/Corporate-Portals.html
Gilbane Group, www.gilbane.com
Portals Magazine, www.portalsmag.com

CHAPTER 9

Information Architecture

Mike Crandall
University of Washington

The most visible organization in the information architecture (IA) arena today is the Information Architecture Institute (IAI). Its definition of IA seems a good place to start when exploring the boundaries of this discipline. According to the IAI, there are three parts to IA:

1. The structural design of shared information environments
2. The art and science of organizing and labeling Web sites, intranets, online communities, and software to support usability and findability
3. An emerging community of practice focused on bringing principles of design and architecture to the digital landscape

These three components reflect the interdisciplinary nature of IA and hint at a few of the threads that have coalesced into what has become one of the most important fields in the all-pervasive digital environment we live in today. Practitioners in the field come from backgrounds as diverse as computer science, library science, design, MIS, psychology, and anthropology. Each contributes a particular perspective to the challenges and problems of the design and delivery of information to meet user needs and business objectives.

Although it is clear from the definition that IA can be applied to many different environments, one of the most challenging areas of practice today is in the design and management of intranet portals and search engines. The scale of these enterprise information networks requires nearly every skill and technique available to the IA practitioner, and it provides fertile ground for those who are helping to shape this growing field.

It is also interesting to note the third part of the definition, because as an emerging discipline, this community of practice helps define the direction and refine the definition on an ongoing basis. Part of the nature of the discipline is the moving target of its coverage, which provides ample material for ongoing discussion and debate in conferences and online discussions.

History

Recent debates on the origins of the term "information architecture" have placed it in various disciplines at different times. Richard Saul Wurman, coming from an information design perspective, is often credited with coining the term in 1976 with his use of the phrase "Architecture of Information" for the 100th anniversary conference of the American Institute of Architects. He subsequently published a book with the phrase in the title—*Information Architects*—in 1996. In the 1980s, the term was used in enterprise information systems contexts as it became clear that system integration was only part of what was needed to make enterprise technology work; the information also needed to be integrated along with the technology (e.g., see Brancheau, Schuster, and March, 1998).

However, it was in early 1998 that the term really began to be used in the modern sense with the publication of the first edition of Rosenfeld and Morville's defining work, *Information Architecture for the World Wide Web*. Drawing from their background in library and information science and several years of consulting work through Argus Associates, they provided the world with a summary of their lessons learned and insights into the practice and theory of IA. It is still considered a classic reference for those wishing to get started in IA and is a handy guide for those who need to educate others about some basics of the discipline. A second, revised edition was published in late 2002, followed by a third in 2006, each including several case studies of organizations that provide good examples of IA in action.

In 2000, a collection of leaders in the field organized the first Information Architecture Summit in conjunction with the American Society for Information Science and Technology (ASIST). An Information Architecture Summit has been held every year since then and provides a gathering place for people around the world to share their latest practices and research with the community. It also offers an opportunity for ongoing discussions on the nature of the field and where it is headed (the Summit Web sites are all available through the ASIST Conference Web site: www.asis.org/past conferences.html).

The Asilomar Institute for Information Architecture (AIfIA) was established in 2002 and became a center point for growth of the field. It now provides a long list of resources to help both novice and experienced professionals orient themselves in the discipline and is an important starting point for those wishing to delve further into the field. In 2005, the institute changed its name to the Information Architecture Institute (iainstitute.org). The IAI continues to influence the development of IA through research grants, education, sponsorship of local workshops across the world, and the active promotion of discussion into the nature and direction of IA as a discipline.

How Does Information Architecture Fit into an Intranet?

Returning to the definition proposed by the IAI in the first paragraph of this chapter, it should be clear that IA is an essential underpinning of the infrastructure used to deliver information through an intranet. This information structure should be distinguished from the technology used as the basis of an organizational network, but the two are closely intertwined and require close cooperation and understanding of distinct yet linked objectives.

Relation to IS Infrastructure

When authors in the information systems field began speaking of IA back in the 1980s, their focus was on integrating data contained in existing legacy systems that support an organization's finance, human resources, and production data. The IAI vision of IA focuses instead on delivery of content available throughout the organization, usually (although not always) through a Web browser at the end-user's desktop. It sits on top of the enterprise information systems layer, and in many cases, it takes advantage of these resources to help enrich and augment the services and applications delivered to the user.

A recent article in the information systems field by Roger and Elaine Evernden (2003) provides a useful way of thinking about this evolutionary change in the information systems version of IA, and it helps to

Generation	Focus	Driven By	Content
1st Generation 1970s and 1980s	Systems as standalone applications within individual organizations.	Increasing functionality and sophistication of standalone applications.	Explanation of the need for an architectural approach; Analogies with building architecture; Simple 2D diagrams or frameworks providing overviews of the architecture.
2nd Generation 1990s	Systems as integrated sets of components within individual organizations.	Growth in system complexity and interdependence; Demand for software reuse.	Extension and adaptation of diagrams from 1st generation architectures; Population of frameworks with industry reference models.
3rd Generation late 1990s and 2000s	Information as corporate resource with supporting IT tools and techniques.	Emergence of the Internet, e-commerce, and an increase in business-to-business applications; Growing interdependence among organizations; Adoption of knowledge management, systems thinking, and a more holistic view of information as a resource.	Explicit definition of principles and background theory; Development of multi-dimensional architectures; Customization of information frameworks to the needs of individual organizations; Generic information patterns and maps.

Figure 9.1 Features of the Three Generations of Information Architecture (Source: Evernden, Roger and Elaine Evernden. "Third-Generation Information Architecture." ***Communications of the ACM*** **46.3 [March 2003]: 95–98)**

put the current approach in the context of other enterprise activities that either complement or support it. Figure 9.1 outlines the features of the three generations of information architecture.

It is obvious that third-generation IA (from the information systems perspective) is concerned with much more than dealing with data living in legacy systems; it is focused on the organization's use of knowledge rather than the underlying technology. This is convergent with the more recent activity in the content-based IA movement and points out the shared goals and focus on user needs that have come to dominate both approaches.

It should also be apparent that there is a close marriage between what an IA in the IAI sense and an IA in the information systems sense are trying to achieve and that both are important components needed to achieve success in an enterprise setting. An article by Maloney and Bracke (2004) examined this close linkage in a library setting, and it concluded that the information architecture must be closely linked to the system architecture for either to succeed. Figure 9.2 shows their conceptualization of this relationship.

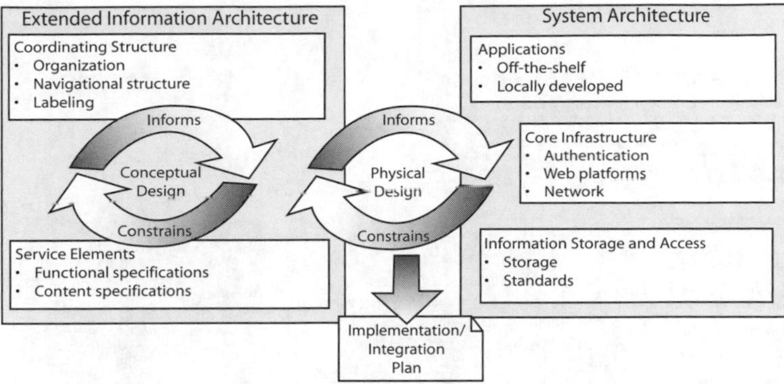

Figure 9.2 The Interrelationship Between the Conceptual and Physical Design of the Library Web Site (Source: Maloney, Krisellen and Paul J. Bracke. "Beyond Information Architecture: A Systems Integration Approach to Web-Site Design." ***Information Technology and Libraries*** **23.4 [December 2004]: 145–152)**

For the purposes of this chapter, we will be focusing primarily on the Extended Information Architecture side of this diagram, but it is important to remember that this activity is closely linked with, and dependent upon, the systems architecture and with the direction being highlighted in Everndens' third-generation information systems IA.

Relation to Other Disciplines

Having placed ourselves in the larger context, let us return to the IAI sense of IA, and examine how the components and elements of this definition might fit with other disciplines that work toward the same objectives stated in our working definition. As always, there are many ways of looking at this environment, but one of the most widely known is that proposed by Jesse James Garrett in 2000 and is shown in the Figure 9.3.

This diagram places IA under the broader umbrella of User Experience, as a means of enabling the structural design of information in order to provide easy access to content (part one of the IAI definition). The activities contained in the second part of the IAI definition clearly extend above and below the IA plane shown in this diagram but are integral to providing the final deliverable: user-centered, information-driven interfaces that provide access to the information contained within the system.

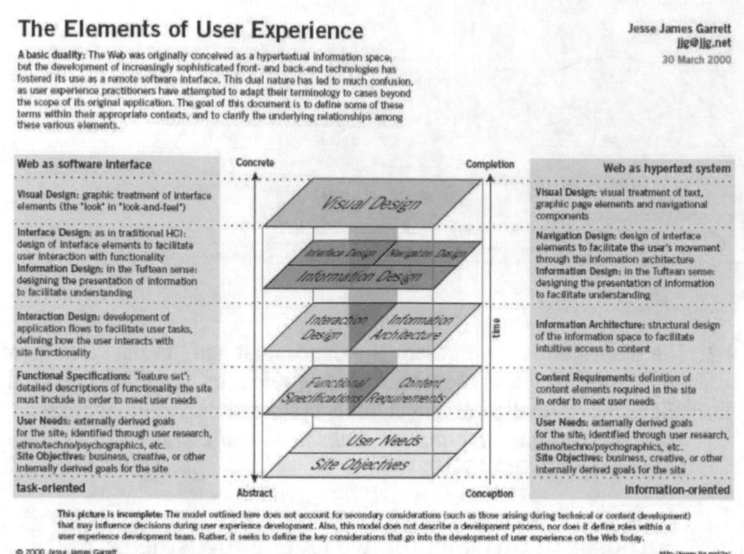

Figure 9.3 The Elements of User Experience (Source: Garrett, Jesse James. *The Elements of User Experience*. March 30, 2000. www.jjg.net/elements/pdf/elements.pdf [accessed April 24, 2005])

A continuing debate within the IA community is pertinent here: namely, the distinction between what is called "little IA" and "big IA." The distinction between the two has to do with the scope of activities associated with IA practice: The "little IA" focuses more narrowly on the skills and techniques associated only with structural design of content, and the "big IA" reaches even more broadly into business strategy, requirements gathering, and design than is shown in Garrett's diagram.

When focusing on intranets, it is most likely that IA roles will lean more toward the "big IA" side of the debate but through an organizational rather than individual lens. In other words, an IA role will be part of a larger team and may assume different roles at different times during the life of a project as the need arises. Some of these roles may in fact be "little IA," others may lean more toward the "big IA," but all of them can reasonably be included in the reach of activities that an IA should be able to understand and support, if not actually doing it themselves.

Martin White writes in a brief overview of IA in 2004:

> *I suspect, and indeed hope, that information architecture will be rather like information science, a set of tools and approaches that can be used by professionals from a wide range of backgrounds to solve an equally wide range of information management problems.* (pp. 218–219)

Key Components of IA

Chris Farnum, a former consultant with Argus Associates, identified the following six key components central to IA in a 2002 article in the *Information Management Journal*:

- Simultaneous architectural design from the top-down and bottom-up
- Information organization
- Navigation
- Search
- Labeling
- Taxonomies

These closely align with a similar division made by Rosenfeld and Morville in their 2002 book and provide a convenient way to think of the different components involved in IA.

Architectural Design

The overall goal of IA is to provide a logical, coherent design for the movement of information from sources to the user. To accomplish this, an architectural framework must be developed to guide subsequent steps in the design process. Most IAs work from both the bottom and top levels of the information within the scope of the project, whether it's a single Web site or a large intranet. From the top, an IA works down from the main information gateway and draws a picture of the complete organization from the information available within the site. From the bottom, chunks of content are analyzed and labeled based on common criteria, and over time, patterns of usage and description help to flesh out the details of the top-down view and may actually contribute to a redesign based on what is found. Both contribute to the overall architecture and inform the development of the framework that can be used to manage the information over time for the business and the users.

Information Organization

Organizing the information depends on the business drivers and audience needs that are defined for the site. It may well be that one set of information is organized in different ways at different times based on these requirements. The IA analyzes requirements and helps to frame an approach to organizing the information that is flexible enough to meet the varied needs but can be managed over time as changes occur or new information is added to the resource pool. This organization provides the working structure for the information and is independent from the user interface. Ideally, a change in look and feel should be possible without changing the underlying information organization, because it will be flexible enough to allow differing presentations based on changing user needs and business drivers.

Navigation

"Wayfinding" elements are an important part of user experience in moving through large sets of information. These clues help a user know where they are in the set of information and how to move from one area to another. Commonly seen on Web sites as page navigation elements across the top of the screen or on the left-hand side, they may also be displayed as tabs, breadcrumb trails showing the path the user has followed to get to the present location, or links to related material based on the content the user is currently seeing. Site maps, indexes, and tables of contents are also examples of navigational resources. Each of these examples is tied closely to the organization of the information, at a higher level than search, and is supported by the overall architecture defined at the outset.

Search

While it is unlikely these days that anyone will build a search engine from scratch, buying a product turns out to be the easiest part of enabling effective search in an intranet environment. In most cases, full-text search will not be adequate, even with the improvements Google has brought to our lives in finding critical information on a site or across the intranet. One of the key offerings an IA can provide in this area is integration of the various components of the information architecture with the search function, providing better results for users, and linking the search function to other similar offerings through navigation and labeling elements.

This is perhaps one of the most complex areas of an IA's job, and it often requires a specialized background in information science to understand whether the chosen search engine works well enough to integrate it with the overall IA of the site. In some cases, integrating a search engine with database queries may be required, and in other cases, an IA may need to fine tune the ranking algorithm of the search engine itself. In all cases, the search results will need to be displayed effectively for the user to take advantage of the results, and they must be segmented in ways that reflect the information organization.

Labeling

All of the elements on a site need names, and those names are often important as locators and identifiers for other systems and the users themselves. Integrating these labels into the IA provides coherence to the system and a better user experience throughout the information landscape. Page titles, link names, names applied to taxonomic elements, and names applied to drop-down list elements all need to be consistent throughout the site and must reflect the users' needs and the overall business objectives of the Web site or intranet. This requires someone skilled in analyzing user terminology and providing mechanisms for translating it into the language used in the content underlying the site. On large intranets or multilanguage sites, this can be a daunting task made even more difficult by multiple users' information sets and content chunks.

Taxonomies

Finally, underlying all the other components, and, in most cases, providing a kind of glue that binds them together, are the many vocabularies, thesauri, lists, and other collections of organized terms that are created to support the tagging, labeling, and other activities surrounding the organization of information being managed within the IA space. A background in library and information science can be invaluable for this part of the IA activity, since it is core to that discipline. However, an IA has to blend that skill set with a good sense of requirements and understand how best to use these taxonomies to drive the user experience and the overall purpose of the site. On an intranet, this can be a major task since preexisting taxonomies often need to be integrated to provide a common vocabulary set for users, and they may require full-time staff dedicated to just this portion of the work.

The IA Process

Rosenfeld and Morville call out three key aspects of the IA methodology that distinguish it from other approaches and drive the approach used to implement the components just described: content, users, and context. Analysis of the content provides the raw material that is used in combination with user behavior and needs analysis to develop the components, while the context determines how this data is used to design the Web site or intranet portal.

A variety of techniques are used to analyze content, ranging from crawls across existing Web sites to mining databases, gathering search logs, looking at existing taxonomies or organization schemes, analyzing content management systems, and much more. The user needs are collected through marketing materials, interviewing and surveying techniques derived from ethnography or market research, and prototyping or testing sessions throughout the design phase in order to validate and correct the information gathered. Context is gleaned from both the content and the users but also from the organizational environment through stakeholder interviews, organization charts, past history, historical evaluation results, and discussions with the team charged with managing and running the site.

Throughout the design and implementation process, IAs capture their results in many deliverables that communicate to designers, programmers, stakeholders, and users the information required to move the project to the next phase. Rosenfeld and Morville discuss many of these items in their book, such as wireframes, blueprints, content maps and inventories, design sketches and prototypes, and style guides. Each is used to capture and document specific information necessary to reach the next stage in development of the architecture and the resulting Web site or portal.

Once it is complete, the cycle often begins again, since no organization is static, and user and business needs change with time. The advantage of the artifacts produced during the IA process is that these documents can be used as baselines for subsequent redesigns, and they often provide benchmarks that can be used to measure the success of particular approaches or design choices.

Looking back at Garrett's diagram in Figure 9.3, it will be evident that parts of each of these activities fall outside the narrow plane of IA, so it is often necessary to work with others to gather the information and build the results necessary for successful completion of the job. An IA must be skilled in working as part of a team, knowing when to seek help and how to get it, and being a good communicator and strategist in many cases.

IA for Web Sites vs. Intranets

All of the concepts previously mentioned can be applied to either a departmental Web site or cross-enterprise, but the scale of effort is clearly different depending on the scope and reach of the effort. When moving beyond local control, the complexity multiplies tremendously in each area, and the organizational and political factors often outweigh the technical ones. It is in the intranet that IA can provide the most return, but it is also the hardest to do. As Tony Byrne (2004) notes in his article on IA for content management in enterprise scale implementations, "IA evaluation methods, designs, and (especially) governance models become much more complex."

The concepts and processes described here are still key in an enterprise information architecture (EIA) setting, but the number of organizations, stakeholders, and user populations involved make common agreement much harder to achieve, and the architecture becomes much more complex to design and manage as a result. Byrne calls out the following three central practices that must be considered when working in an enterprise setting:

- Balancing central versus local needs and authority
- Tactical versus strategic approaches
- Understanding (and acting on) the different (but related) EIA problem domains

The good news is that EIA can provide not only better results for users across the intranet through common access to information, but it can also result in cost savings and increased efficiencies in managing information on an enterprise level. Microsoft's intranet portal, MSWeb, followed the approach outlined by Byrne in its IA, and by careful design and strategic and tactical engagements with groups within the company, it was able to reuse its backend IA for search and taxonomy management across a number of other groups without additional investment. The resulting savings in development costs and rework were substantial, and both users and cost-center managers were extremely pleased with the results. Details on this case can be found in Rosenfeld and Morville's *Information Architecture for the World Wide Web.*

Current Developments in Information Architecture

Given the rapid emergence of IA as a discipline in the last decade, what can we extract from the work that has been done? As IA has moved from solving immediate problems to trying to understand what approaches work best in the long term and over increasingly broad enterprise spaces, some general models have emerged that attempt to provide a context for thinking about IA in the larger enterprise. These have direct application to the use of IA in intranet and portal design and support, since this is the primary delivery method most organizations are currently using for their information.

One of the most interesting visualizations of the complexity of IA in an enterprise setting is a diagram developed by Lou Rosenfeld as a roadmap for EIA (see www.louisrosenfeld.com/home/bloug_archive/images/EIAroadmap2.pdf). In this diagram, he attempts to show the multiple paths that IA takes within an organization, and the steps that are necessary to move from one stage of development to another. He recognizes several levels of activity, ranging from top-down navigation to bottom-up navigation to search "guerilla" information architecture, and he gives examples of where those might be applied in an enterprise IA strategy. This is all related to near-term, long-term, and long-range activities for each initiative.

It is evident from this diagram that IA is not a one-time event but a continuing and integral part of a well-planned organizational strategy. This is perhaps the most significant takeaway: Making IA a permanent part of the picture is the only way to be successful. Organizations need to commit resources and attention to the elements of IA to succeed in the enterprise and intranet portal space.

Future Developments

Rosenfeld points out that it may be a little strange to think about the future of a discipline that is scarcely a decade old. However, as our information environments become more complex and central to the operation of an organization, it is certainly not premature to try to understand how IA fits with other activities in the same area and what it can bring as a unique offering to the table.

The AIfIA (now IAI) conducted a survey of practitioners in several areas early in 2003 to get their take on what the future of the profession would look like. A few excerpts from that survey point out some major themes that will impact the future of the discipline, and they identify areas that will be important to pay attention to as IA evolves into its next stage.

Solidification of the Discipline

> *We're experiencing a transition from the pioneer period (where ideas about how to describe and do IA were important) to the performance period (where what's important is doing good IA within real world situations).*
>
> *The academic teaching of IA as well as the creation of standard work methods and tools.*

Given the short lifespan of IA as a discipline, it is not surprising that the need to solidify the underpinnings of the field was pointed out. A key element in defining a discipline is being able to show what impact it has in practice and in identifying and establishing a common set of tools and methods that can be taught and used in practical situations. A research agenda must also be created in order to move the discipline forward, and this requires the development of a strong academic discipline that can provide the critical mass necessary for this to happen. We will look later at a snapshot of the current state of education in IA, but it is clear that this is in its nascent stages and will take some time to build.

Broader Reach

> *Maturity of intranets will lead to enterprise information architectures in the majority of large companies. These projects will be immense, but the only way for companies to*

be able to cope with large amounts of information, reduce costs in a bear market, and improve employee satisfaction.

IAs hold the key to the future of everything from usable wireless devices to artificial intelligence. Not as interface designers or usability experts or strategists, but as professionals whose narrow focus is the organization, categorization, and labeling of information.

These comments point out two areas of growth for IA, one related to broader reach across enterprises, the other driven by the increasing diversity of delivery platforms. The second comment also emphasizes the core skills of IA as the critical elements enabling this reach. The underlying architecture is what allows information to flow across boundaries and through multiple interfaces, and it will take increasingly sophisticated practitioners to deal with the added social, organizational, technical, and political complexities that go along with that reach.

Measurement of Results

Developing tools to measure and qualify various implementations of IA will help us evolve current standards.

I see IA more and more interconnected with (some parts of) project management. Not the management of hours and money, but planning of process and tasks, and setting project scope.

Building in metrics and relating those metrics to project management and business drivers will be an area that draws increasing attention as IA becomes more commonly practiced. Development of measurement systems such as the Software Engineering Institute's Capability Maturity Model Integration suite for IA will be necessary to advance practice and justify expenditures for more and better work in this area. This goes hand-in-hand with the development of an academic base and the associated research agenda, but it also depends on standardization of tools and methods by practitioners and the development of commercial products to support those tools by industry.

Integration with Business Strategy

> *The most important development I've seen exemplified at the large financial institution where I currently work is the growing role of information architecture in business strategy. As human faces become computer interfaces, information architecture becomes the conduit for communication both within the organization and between the organization and the folks outside. If business folks aren't thinking about IA concepts and IA folks aren't thinking about business strategy, the consequences are real and quantifiable.*

The integration of IA with overall business objectives has yet to occur on a wide-scale basis. It is still too soon to tell how and where this will happen, but as more case studies and examples are made available to the community, showing how IA has in fact produced the business results that it promises, adoption by larger institutions will become more widespread. Of course, the early adopters will reap the competitive advantage of being first out of the block, so do not wait until everyone else has seen the light before trying IA yourself.

What Makes Sense for Your Organization?

Tony Byrne points out that starting small might be the way to put your toe in the IA waters. Working vertically to integrate a single unit's information resources, both legacy data and the more free-form content generated through the modern Web-based delivery platforms can provide a good example to show others what works. The MSWeb case study mentioned earlier is also an example of this in a slightly different manner: The Microsoft team took two components of IA, search and navigation, and provided a cross-silo service that managed to provide common structure with flexibility.

This flexible and tactical approach to IA is often the only way to begin in a large organization where organizational silos are deep and entrenched. Building bridges over time, showing small successes and best practices, while continuing to make strategic alliances with groups that have the ability to bring resources to bear when the timing is right to initiate a larger initiative, seems to be the way many successful IA campaigns have been waged.

On the other hand, you may be able to start an enterprise initiative from scratch if the conditions are right. Marc Solomon (2005) quotes

Christy Confetti Higgins from Sun Microsystems Sun Library about starting a fresh EIA project:

> *You can really structure the right type of team with the right skill sets that you need. The focus then needs executive formal level funding and support in order to really make an impact in the organization.*

She also points out that communications must be tailored to the workflows and details of each business unit to show that their needs are being considered and met by the project.

In some cases, it may be more useful to outsource parts or all of your IA to a vendor, but Solomon notes that this must be done carefully to avoid mismatch of service expectations and ensure that the vendor fits with IA components that are still kept inside the organization. In many cases, a vendor's tool will only replicate the problems you already have, because it is not the technology but the organization of the information itself that is lacking. This is the IA's job, and good vendors will work with you to structure your information in a way that will take full advantage of their technology's capability rather than leaving that for you to figure out after you have written the check.

Managing and Staffing for IA

Roles and Responsibilities

In a small organization, one person may perform the multitude of activities discussed earlier, jumping from content analysis to design to taxonomy development to prototyping to strategic engagement with stakeholders to every other component involved in successful IA. However, in larger organizations, this is often not possible (or desirable), and teams that are focused on IA for the enterprise may develop or be created from scratch for large projects. A good example is the team that assembled for the MSWeb intranet IA project described earlier (see Figure 9.4). Each individual on this team had specific roles to play in the development and management of the IA used to drive the intranet portal and the other customer portals serviced by the Information Services Group.

Note that many of the roles are focused internally and provide the details that are necessary to build, process, and maintain the components of the IA used in the offerings. However, others are

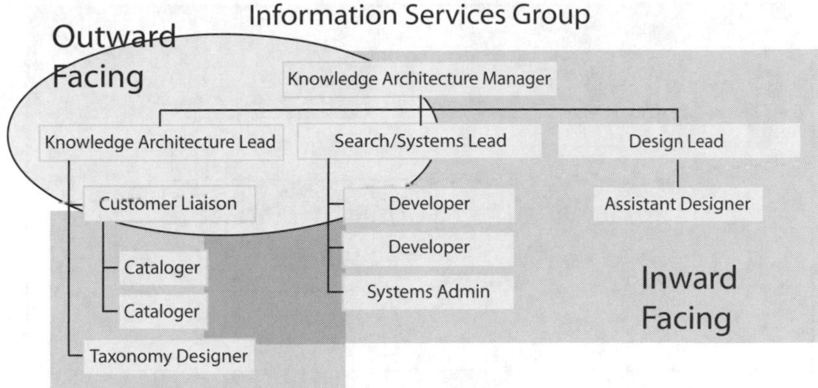

Figure 9.4 Example of Information Architecture Organization for Intranet Portal

external-facing and spend much of their time working with other organizations to gather requirements, understand user needs, and provide the strategic and tactical linkages that ensure continued support and success for the initiative.

Without this dual emphasis, it would be virtually impossible to succeed. Byrne also points out, however, that in many organizations, outside help may be critical for success in negotiating the politics and power struggles necessary to achieve success in the enterprise arena. The MSWeb team did this through careful alliance building and role definition in the larger enterprise, involving stakeholders and other key organizations in the decision-making process, while maintaining ownership of the core IA role (see Figure 9.5).

Skills and Competencies

A self-assessment of practicing IAs conducted by IAI in 2004 (see iainstitute.org/documents/research/results/IA.comptencies.graphs.pdf) provides an enlightening view into the difficulty of describing what exactly it is that IAs do. A list of more than 80 skill sets were identified as being within the scope of IA, clustered into larger blocks that map closely to the activities discussed earlier; focus areas were identified in Content, Business, Users, Technology, and Design. This diversity emphasizes the need for collaboration and teamwork to accomplish the desired objectives. No one individual is likely to have all these skills, but being able to draw them together is critical for IA success.

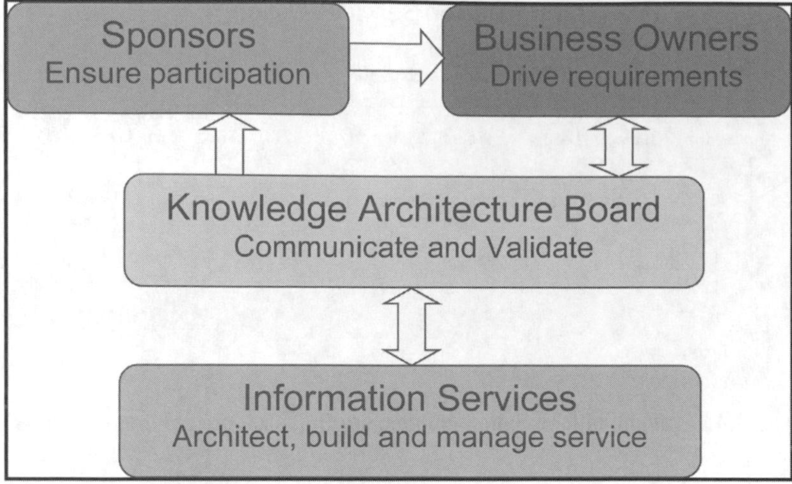

Figure 9.5 MSWeb External Relations

Job Descriptions

Over the past several years, job descriptions have varied tremendously for IA positions, as might be expected from our earlier discussion of the fuzzy and ever-changing boundaries of the discipline. Art Ignacio synthesized a survey of these postings for the Society for Technical Communications Information Design Special Interest Group, as shown in Figure 9.6. This provides yet another window into the variety of skills needed for success in IA.

Education

One of the best benchmarks for the maturity of a discipline is the depth and breadth of offerings related to it in institutions of higher learning. Since IA first became popular, courses have been offered in universities and colleges focusing on the concepts of IA at varying levels of detail and coverage. In recent years, some institutions have begun offering more substantial programs that allow for specialization in IA as part of a degree in Information Management, Communications, or Library/Information Science. The IAI conducted a survey in 2003 of institutions offering degrees that might lead to employment in this area (see iainstitute.org/edu/2003/AIfIA_List-of-IA-Programs.2003.pdf for the results).

At the present time, most practitioners in IA are self-taught or come from a background that lends itself to success in one of the key

Information Architect - Requirements
The following requirements were collected from job listings with the term "Information Architect" in the posting's title. An attempt has been made to categorize the requirements. Where meaningful, items within each category are listed in order of increasing level of requirement. Information Technology (IT) is the most technology-centric category, with requirements outside the norm, but representing some employers' views of the position. This list was originally developed for the STC Information Design SIG.

- User, usability
    - Conduct user surveys
    - Perform task analysis
    - Perform heuristic evaluations
    - Determine audience needs
    - Create task flows
    - Define user scenarios, persona development
- Business requirements
    - Manage stakeholder expectations
    - Deliver status to senior management
    - Perform comparative, competitive research
- User interface development
    - Produce mockups, wireframes, flowcharts, storyboards, content inventory, site maps
    - Develop working prototypes, perform rapid prototyping
    - Demonstrate UIs and test functional alternatives
    - Perform iterative UI design
    - Possess facilitation and interpersonal skills; able to work with cross-functional team
    - Translate user research to design decisions
    - Develop functional specifications, page specifications, visual specifications
- Implementation
    - Develop templates
    - Establish standards, guidelines
    - Manage 3rd party vendors, contract staff, work with remote teams
- Web technologies, experience with the following
    - Web site tracking and analytics
    - Data modeling, databases, XML, taxonomy, hierarchy, classification, categorization
    - Search, form filling
- Tools, experience with the following
    - MS Office, Acrobat Distiller
    - MS Project
    - Visio, Photoshop, Illustrator, FreeHand, Dreamweaver, HTML, CSS
    - JavaScript, Flash, Flash ActionScript
    - Adobe Premier, Windows Media, QuickTime
    - CMS, Documentum, TeamSite
- Information Technology (IT)
    - Develop workflow, logical processes, h/w, os, interfaces between systems
    - Experience with application, data, middleware
    - Create entity relationship diagrams
    - Create CRUD (create, retrieve, update, delete) matrices, data modeling
    - Experience with Web-based application frameworks (.NET, JSP, ASP, PHP, etc.)
    - Knowledge of Internet and email standards and UNIX system administration
    - Evaluate tools, technologies
    - Work with application vendors to understand direction, roadmap
    - Experience with WebLogic, WebSphere
- Education
    - Art, Graphic Design, Fine Arts, Industrial Design, Interface Design, Technical Communications
    - Cognitive Psychology, Human Computer Interaction, Human Factors
    - Instructional Design, Library Science, Information Science
    - Information Systems, Computer Science
    - Business Administration

Figure 9.6 Information Architect Requirements (Source: Ignacio, Art. "Information Architect—Requirements." Developed for the STC Information Design SIG. April 15, 2005. www.info-design.com/ID/InformationArchitect.htm [accessed April 24, 2005])

concept areas that are the core of IA. As time goes on, it is likely that these practices will be more firmly entrenched in the academic world, and a new generation of IA will be born with a body of research and history to pass on to subsequent practitioners.

Checklist for Success

The Australian Government Information Management Office has developed a series of excellent checklists with detailed explanations for each item that provides a handy way to calibrate your efforts against best practices in the area of intranet and Web site management and design. Its checklist (shown in Figure 9.7) for Web site information architecture provides a good starting point for anyone beginning work in this area. There is clearly much more to each of these steps, but as a practical guideline, a beginning IA may find these helpful in laying out a strategy for a smaller project before diving into an enterprise-level effort.

For those ready to move further and tackle the major challenges posed by working across an organization's many vertical silos of information, Solomon (February 2005) provides a series of checkpoints mingled with case studies in his look at best deployment practices for EIA (Figure 9.8). A quick study of this article will flesh out these checkpoints in more detail and offer a look at how others have managed to move through large-scale IA deployments with more or less success.

Conclusion

Whether starting small or attacking the entire enterprise, IA is becoming a key component of an intranet strategy. With a clear understanding of the relationship of IA to other enterprise information strategies, a grasp of the key concepts of IA and the processes behind the methodologies used, a sense of organizational readiness for implementation, and the right people on the team, IA can have a major impact on business processes and the bottom line. As the discipline matures and a deeper core of practice and knowledge becomes available, this impact will become more visible, and organizations that have not already adopted IA as part of their ongoing practice will find themselves left behind. They will be far behind in the use of their own and others' information to further their business

SUMMARY OF CHECKPOINTS

EARLY PLANNING

- ☐ Identify the business goals of the website
- ☐ Identify the target audience and their needs
- ☐ Determine what services, functionality or information will be provided via the website
- ☐ Describe how users will interact with the website to meet their needs
- ☐ Consider what type of website structure will be appropriate

DEFINING THE CONTENT

- ☐ Identify the content required to support the services that will be provided on the website

GROUPING AND LABELLING THE CONTENT

- ☐ Determine how content will be grouped on the website
- ☐ Determine a logical content hierarchy
- ☐ Identify other grouping methods
- ☐ Identify related information
- ☐ Create labels to represent information on the website
- ☐ Map content to the IA

DOCUMENTING THE IA

- ☐ Document the IA

REVIEWING AND IMPLEMENTING THE IA

- ☐ Review the initial structure
- ☐ Test the proposed structure with users
- ☐ Design navigation elements
- ☐ Monitor and evaluate use of the website

Figure 9.7 Information Architecture for Web Sites Checklist (Source: Australian Government Information Management Office. *Better Practice Checklist 15: Information Architecture for Websites*. Version 1 2004. April 24, 2005. www.agimo.gov.au/__data/assets/file/33933/ BPC15.pdf)

objectives. IA may only be 10 years old, but it is growing fast, and those who have had an opportunity to use it will not turn back.

Examples and Lessons Learned

- *Findability.* Peter Morville discusses the concept of findability (www.infotoday.com/online/nov05/morville.shtml)

- Reach across disciplines
- Lay the foundation for the project team
- Provide direct engagement between system designers and users
- Build vocabularies through working relationships
- Conduct needs assessments in practical terms
- Evaluate query logs
- Conduct a detailed use case analysis
- Develop a detailed system architecture
- Recruit allies
- Create roles, responsibilities and take ownership
- Isolate the essentials
- Manage your outsourcers
- Keep your improvements continuous
- Identify unifying concepts
- Map workflow to regulatory sensitivities

Figure 9.8 Checkpoints for Enterprise IA Projects (Source: Solomon, Marc. "Under Budget, on Time, and in Sync: How to Stage Successful Rollouts." *Searcher* 13.2 [February 2005]: 28–39)

and how IA (information architecture) helped win the 2005 Webby Award for Government sites for the National Cancer Institute (www.cancer.gov). While not an intranet, this is a good example of the use of IA in the design of a complex, content-rich site. More than 550,000 pages are now accessible for the general public and health professionals through well-labeled, tightly organized pages, taking advantage of rich metadata defined by user surveys. The site was developed through a collaborative effort among external consultants and an internal information architecture team.

- *Navigation and faceted classification.* Case study showing steps and methodologies used in the development of a faceted classification scheme for a global chemical company (www.iasummit.org/2005/finalpapers/50_Presentation.ppt) to be used in browse navigation and search for a large Web site. Audience and content analysis techniques are discussed, as well as methods for extracting and organizing terms for the classification.

- *Controlled vocabularies and schemas.* The IBM Intranet team offers a good case study (www.iasummit.org/2005/finalpapers/106_Presentation.ppt) of top-down, bottom-up architecture, using a large internal team with skills focused on various aspects of IA and associated disciplines.

Development of controlled vocabularies, schema integration across multiple business units, and the use of labeling and interface design to provide easy access to information brings out many best practices and lessons learned in these areas.

- *Navigation and labeling.* Vanguard offers a great example (www.iasummit.org/2005/finalpapers/101_Presentation.ppt) of development of navigation structures and labeling for a heavily used Web site. Methodologies are explored for gathering and organizing navigation labels and relationships and integration with the overall site architecture. The importance of clear, audience-focused navigation labels is emphasized and demonstrated through examples.
- *Top-down/bottom-up architecture.* A case study from PeopleSoft (www.asis.org/Conferences/Summit2002/peoplesoft_case_study_FINAL.ppt) is a great example of top-down and bottom-up architecture in a large enterprise setting. Details of taxonomy construction, navigation design, and cross-platform integration are discussed, with screen shots and samples of the actual artifacts used in the process. It provides a good overview of a very large, complex IA project.
- *Taxonomy integration and faceted labeling.* This case study is the integration of multiple taxonomies within an organization to meet user needs (colab.cim3.net/file/work/Expedition_Workshop/2004-04-28_Multiple_Taxonomies/Dutra_20040428.ppt). It addresses the relationship of the IA team to the enterprise architecture team (be sure to examine the appendix for slides relating to the Zachmann Framework). It provides good examples of complex faceted taxonomies, with a live demo showing use in a search engine.

Recommended Resources

People

Andrew Dillon, www.ischool.utexas.edu/~adillon
Lou Rosenfeld, louisrosenfeld.com

Peter Morville, semanticstudios.com
Christina Wodtke, www.eleganthack.com/blog/index.html
James Robertson, www.steptwo.com.au/columntwo

Lists/Blogs

Boxes and Arrows, www.boxesandarrows.com
CHI Web, sigchi.org/web
IASlash, www.iaslash.org
Infodesign, www.informationdesign.org
SIGIA, mail.asis.org/mailman/listinfo/sigia-l

Web Sites/Organizations

ACM Special Information Group on Computer-Human Interaction, www.acm.org/sigchi
AIGIA, journal.aiga.org
American Society for Information Science and Technology, www.asis.org
Center for Human Information Interaction, www.ischool.washington.edu/chii
IA Summits, www.asis.org/Conferences/index.html
Information Architecture Institute (formerly Asilomar Institute for Information Architecture), iainstitute.org
Interaction Design Group, www.ixdg.org
Step Two Designs, www.steptwo.com.au/papers/index.php
Usability Professionals Association, www.upassoc.org
UXNet, uxnet.org

CHAPTER 10

Intranet Search

Avi Rappoport
Search Tools Consulting

Why Bother with Intranet Search?

Search is one of the "killer apps" of the World Wide Web: Imagine if there were no Google/Ask.com/Yahoo!. We would never find anything at all; we would be trapped in our little comfort zones, unable to take advantage of the great information out there. Similarly, intranets need a search engine to let people find information in corporate networks flexibly, without having to wait for someone to catalog or organize that information. For example, an oil company once called because it discovered that its Jakarta office was bidding against its Dakar office for contracts. With an automated search engine that indexed all the corporate intranet servers, it could check before starting the bid process. Obviously, a better solution would be to automate its workflow, but sometimes you cannot wait for the best and get a good deal of value out of a "good enough" solution. Likewise, after a sudden event, such as a newly designated product name, corporate merger, or a hurricane, it may take some time to update a portal or adjust the navigation. A search engine can index and make searchable information in near-real time, providing ad-hoc access when it is most needed. Search is a part of Information Architecture (IA): It can take advantage of the organization and consistency that IA brings, while supplementing it by allowing new vocabulary and unexpected connections.

The ROI of Search

Intranet search engines are infrastructure, like e-mail servers: They do not have an obvious dollar value, but without them, people would waste time trying to do their work. Intranets generally see a reduction of average per-employee calls and e-mails to the HR department, internal ordering, and internal support departments after installing and configuring a search engine. As employees become accustomed to self-service, they will ask fewer repetitive and low-level questions. However, this is not the main value. Analysts such as Susan Feldman at IDC have estimated the time knowledge workers spend not only looking for information but also re-creating documents that already exist. If intranet search can reduce this waste by 1 percent, it can certainly pay for itself.

Defining the Requirements for Intranet Search

While it is easy enough to install a search engine, start it up, and advertise it as a service to find documents on an intranet, that is the least valuable approach. It will tend to frustrate people because the default installations cannot solve the specific information needs of any specific organization. As part of the intranet implementation, you need to do an information needs analysis. This removes the guesswork and helps you focus where the current systems are weak. By concentrating on these areas, you can truly help people do their jobs. In my experiences, I have found the following kinds of information needs:

- Everyone needs basic information, such as the holiday schedule, how to get business cards, file an expense report, find a report template, and deal with heating problems. Up to 80 percent of intranet traffic can include these topics, especially if the portal interface has weak navigation.
- Sales and marketing people need information about products and services.
- Researchers need scientific and technical information from both inside and outside the company.
- New employees always need more information, because they do not have existing networks and systems. They tend to use whatever tools are available, including search. If you do a good job, they will be the best advocates for your systems, because they will always use them.

Once you have done some interviews and have some ideas about areas where a search engine could provide significant help, recruit a small panel of advisors. This should be drawn from various parts of the institution and include influential stakeholders who can help champion your project. Present them with your preliminary plans, but be prepared for brainstorming and sudden changes of direction.

It is also useful to set up personas to provide context for your decisions. Personas are not real people, they are representatives of a few classes of people. "Lee, the VP of finance," "Dave in tech support," and "Juanita starting a new research group" provide diverse examples with both similar and very different information needs. Making explicit and strategic decisions about how to serve these constituencies is far better than proceeding in one direction and finding that it only addresses one kind of information need.

Technical and Organizational Aspects of Search Implementation

There are several parts to running a search engine: finding content, indexing, responding to queries, displaying results, analyzing search activity, and maintaining the system. Figure 10.1 presents the main parts of the search process. Consider the process in the work of running a search engine.

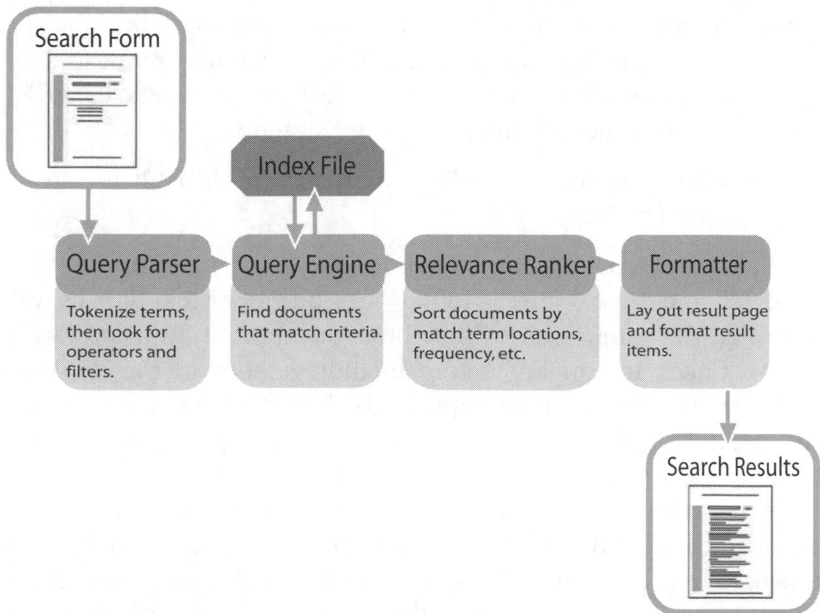

Figure 10.1 Parts of the Search Process

Finding Content

The easiest way to start is to install a test search engine with a robot crawler, set it to go slow for any one server, and give it a list of all the known servers in the intranet, allowing the crawler to find other servers by following links. Note that even with this setting, your search engine crawler will be putting some pressure on some internal servers that have not had any traffic for a while and may crash them. If you notice that, try to contact the server administrator and work with him or her to improve the robustness of the server. If it is terribly fragile, you may have to remove it from your allowed list of servers.

Common issues when crawling intranets include the following:

- Servers that have "robots.txt" files rejecting robot indexing.
- Pages with problem links, including JavaScript indexing, incorrect relative links, capitalization, frames, redirects, and refreshes (see searchtools.com/robots/robot-checklist.html for additional information).
- Infinite links and loops are links that either go into the future (such as automated calendars) or call themselves with a slightly different URL, forever.
- The robot crawler will follow all the links, even the mistakes—and bring up pages that have never been requested before. This has been known to crash some servers, especially very old or database-backed systems.
- Obscure or very new file formats can be difficult for an indexer to read.

Most search engines can also index server file systems, so if you have a shared drive or public folder, you can gather that data as well. Note that these repositories may have private and duplicate documents: Check for quality before including them in the deployed index. There were some attempts in the late 1990s to index employees' desktops, but privacy issues caused a huge uproar, and I do not recommend trying that. In addition, intranets tend to have one or more "data silos"—an application with valuable data that can only be accessed through its special interface. One common example is the e-mail server: There are often valuable public discussions that can address employee questions. Rather than forcing people to search inside the e-mail system, you can incorporate that data in the general intranet search. There are a number of ways to handle this: The most frequent solution is to write an HTML form front-end to the silo. Then you can create a form that asks for every record, as an HTML link, and follow those links to index the data. Other solutions are to write a connector using the search engine's API (application programmer interface, "hooks" to access data) and the data silo's API, or to use the more modern Web Services approach. In all of these cases, when a user does a search and clicks on a link on the result page, it is as though they filled in a query form.

Content Quality

There are always amazing amounts of ROT—a term coined by Peter Morville and Lou Rosenfeld to describe Redundant, Outmoded, and Trivial information. In one installation, we found a server with thousands of tiny Web pages, each containing a tech support call report on a product that was no longer available—completely trivial. You can work with the intranet server maintainers to identify the definitive version of redundant information, label the outmoded stuff, and get rid of the trivial content. It is better to do it as part of the intranet information architecture than to just leave them out of the search engine—they are time bombs if left accessible in any way.

For companies with a long and valuable history, such as pharmaceuticals, manufacturing, and consumer products, defining certain servers or directories as archival and indexing them in a separate collection is a good way to provide access without cluttering the standard search results. This is the time to check for sensitive documents accidentally left on servers. The search indexing process exposes problems with access control, so take some time to look for sensitive words, such as product code names, salary and payroll terms, and legal terms.

Security and Access Control

The search engine should never show results to employees who are not authorized to see them—it should not be the weak point in your data security. You need to work with the security team in the organization.

The first solution is to exclude sensitive data from general search entirely. This is the cheapest and safest way to go. To provide search access, implement a special limited-access search engine, for example, searching patient records or salary information. If you do this, be sure to secure the physical server, as well as encrypting transmissions from the search server to the end-user browser.

For relatively low-level control, you can connect your search engine to your security system and require users to log in before they can search a collection. One step beyond that is "hit-level authentication," where the search engine queries the access control system to see if this user is permitted to see a document before even displaying the results page. They will only see results they have access to, avoiding any reverse-engineering or clever ways to peek at documents.

About Indexes

The index is the file or set of files storing the words for searching and document information. Generally, these are inverted indexes, storing the words in alphabetical order (the inverse of sentences). This is extremely efficient for searching since it only takes a few steps to match any word. Research-oriented search engines may have more complex index structures.

Each entry for a search word must also include the ID of the document from which it came. Other information may include the position of the word in the document (useful for finding proximity); whether the word is within any tags, such as H1 or "meta keywords" tags; if it is in the URL; and other in-document context information. Note that intranets can trust metadata because it is within the enterprise, where public Web search engines have been abused by spam in metadata.

Stop Words

Older search engines were extremely concerned with index file size, and they often excluded articles (a, an, the) and other very frequent words, such as "copyright." This causes significant problems for search retrieval, because it means that these words simply cannot be found. Modern search engines generally index everything.

Stemming

Similarly, older search engines would stem words: Reduce them to their root, so "run," "runs," "running," and "ran" would all be treated as the same word. This was done to match more documents, because in this paradigm, there were not that many documents, users would enter complex queries, and wanted complete answers. In the current era of millions of documents, short queries, and "good enough" answers, this is entirely inappropriate. The example I always use is that a person searching for the Japanese film *Ran* would not be happy to see a match on the German film *Run, Lola, Run.*

Search Usability

Keep the system simple! If it is harder than Google or Yahoo! Search, your users will grumble, and reasonably so.

Search Interface

Put a search field on every page of the intranet that you control. Make sure the search field is long enough for at least 20 characters—the longer the field, the more likely users will type longer and clearer queries.

Query Languages

Despite the wishes of librarians and information retrieval specialists, search users generally want to type in one or two words and get useful results. So you should not require Boolean operators or long well-phrased questions—accept simple search terms and do the best you can. Despite this, having an additional advanced interface and query operators will help power users and allows you to set up complex queries for other people.

Handling Queries

Search engines generally run a small HTTP sever on port 80 or work with an existing server as a CGI or servlet. They accept an HTTP URL query, which can be created interactively with an HTML form, just like a guest book or e-mail form. Once the search engine receives the query, it tokenizes it, separating multiple words. In Roman script, this usually just handles punctuation, but in Asian scripts, the words may not have any space between them, and it is up to the search engine to recognize the words. In most cases, converting queries to lowercase expresses user desires properly. People search for "ssl" far more often than for "SSL," and they do not expect to find anything different. You can allow users to type quote marks to indicate an exact match in case, as well as phrase matching.

If there are any operators (plus, minus, quotes, Boolean AND, etc.), any field definitions, or other control parameters, the search engine has to extract them and store them in a useful format.

Query Stemming

Many search engines do a lightweight stemming at this point, mainly handling plurals so that people searching for invoice also find documents with invoices. In most cases, this is entirely the right thing to do—users will not even notice, except that the result is better.

Synonym Expansion

Another possible function at this point is searching for synonyms. For example, a transit company may use the word "coach" at all times, but many users type in "bus" (the search engine could search for both and find the desired result). Similarly, if a healthcare company writes out the full text of "Preferred Provider Organization," but everyone says "PPO," automatically expanding the query can improve results.

Spell Checking

Queries can be misspelled or mistyped (including missing spaces between words), leading users to believe there is no content relating to their topic. Search engines can use the searchable index as a spelling dictionary, suggesting spellings that relate to the specific vocabulary. This solves the problems of using generic dictionaries, which may recommend words not in the content on the intranet, and cannot recognize specialized technical terms, internal jargon, code names, abbreviations, and personal names.

Some search engines have used fuzzy matching to handle the problems with typing, but that turns out to retrieve far too many inappropriate results. By using that fuzzy matching, among other algorithms, specifically on the search terms, and suggesting alternatives (especially when there are no matches) rather than automatically retrieving all possibilities, the spellchecker narrows its focus to the most important situation. If your intranet has a great deal of e-mail and other unedited content, the spelling may be erratic at best. In that case, some search engines can provide a threshold before suggesting, requiring multiple instances of the same spelling, to avoid suggesting misspelled words.

Retrieval

Retrieval is the term for finding the documents that match the search terms. This is relatively easy for single-term searches, but once there are two words in the query, it gets harder.

Matching Any vs. Matching All

Search engines may default to finding only those documents that match every term (Boolean AND) or any term (Boolean OR). There are advantages and disadvantages to both approaches:

- Very large intranets (and the Web-wide search engines) generally default to matching all terms, because the results set is more manageable that way.
- Smaller intranets may find that users are upset at getting no results. If a user types "HP laser printer," you may want to retrieve documents that mention HP printers, even if not laser printers.

Older search engines often only matched documents with the exact phrase in them. This turns out to be a mistake, because the document may cover the topic in slightly different wording, and it is very frustrating for users. Recognizing quote marks in the search field as a command to search for phrases solves that problem while still providing better results in general. In addition to finding all documents matching the query, the search engine must check for matches in any fields and areas, or search zones, that the user has specified.

Why There May Be No Matches

- The search may be for a topic not in the intranet, such as a commercial product or a Web site.
- The spelling, typing, or spacing may be wrong.
- The vocabulary may not match the words used in the enterprise.
- If the default is to match all words, some may not be found.
- The user may have typed in an unsupported complex query.

There are a number of things the search engine can do to avoid this problem or address it when it happens, including spellchecking, automatic synonym expansion, and options to search for any word instead of every word.

Relevance Ranking

Relevance ranking means showing the matched documents in order by their relevance to the search. However, most queries are very short and therefore it is not clear what the user is really asking for. "Relevance" as a concept is situational—even longish queries can be referring to multiple aspects of the same topic. So search engines do the best they can with algorithms, heuristics, and human judgment.

Relevance Algorithms

These are the mathematical formulas for comparing documents and defining the more relevant one. The simplest system is TF-IDF (Term Frequency—Inverse Document Frequency), which involves counting the number of times the search words appear in each document and then giving extra weight for rare terms. In its purest form, it can cause odd results, with pages that have some rare terms but none of the common terms coming at the top of the results list. It works fairly well for short queries when adjusted to give more weight to documents containing more of the search terms.

Other relevance ranking algorithms use document vectors for comparison, statistical analysis, and other mathematical processes. None of these seem to perform much better than the others with the short and imprecise queries we see in intranets. They may be helpful in more complex research systems, such as scientific research and competitive intelligence. Unfortunately, the "PageRank" system used by Google and similar in-linking and authority algorithms used by other public Web-wide search engines to identify relevant pages do not perform well in intranet search settings. They rely on the value of Web pages creating meaningful links to other pages. Intranet links are generally navigational, pointing at home pages rather than richly informative pages deep within sites.

Relevance Heuristics

In this context, heuristics refers to commonsense rules that improve relevance ranking. Documents where an entire phrase matches the search terms are more likely to be relevant. Search terms in the title tag, the keywords tag, or an H1 tag are also good matches. As you can guess, phrase matches in the title tag are very likely to be relevant. If they are not relevant, at least the user will understand why they are in the results. In addition to these document-based rules, search administrators can specify certain hosts, directories, or document types as more likely to be relevant, giving them extra weight to improve their rankings in results. Public Web-wide search engines cannot know how important the main HR department is or how obscure certain content may currently be. But search administrators can make value judgments based on their knowledge of the enterprise.

Search Suggestions

No matter how good a relevance algorithm is, it cannot substitute for human judgment. And many pages make relevance impossible: Their text is within graphics, or they have confusing titles, or they use vocabulary (such as marketing jargon) that does not match the words that employees use. The best solution is to incorporate Search Suggestions (also called Best Bets or Recommendations) in results pages. These Search Suggestions are manually created by search administrators or librarians, based on search traffic, and are designed to send people to the best landing pages for specific topics. For example, if the old name for your bonus program was "BHA" and the new name is "LifeStar Plus," long-term employees are likely to miss all the new information. By creating a search suggestion for BHA that directs searchers to the appropriate landing page for the new program, you acknowledge human inertia and provide useful information. If there is an Information Architecture system and controlled vocabulary, you should integrate the suggestions and their synonyms, rather than recreating the process.

There is a danger with search suggestions of going overboard by trying to deal with all possible searches. This has a high cost, and it is better to be balanced and follow these procedures:

- Extract a list of the most frequent queries from the search logs.
- Starting at the top, perform the search and look at the results.
- If the results are good, go on.

- If the results are not so great, try to figure out why. A page may be missing or in a funny format, or a title may be missing. If you can, improve the page and get it indexed.
- If there is no way to make the standard results better, put in a search suggestion.
- Repeat for the top queries that get significant traffic.

Search Results Pages

The only visible aspect of the search engine is the results page. This is where the user interacts most with the search engine, and it is important to present the content as clearly as possible. The elements of this page include the general design and navigation, the search header and footer, the list of results, and each of the results items.

Page Design

The search results should clearly be situated within the intranet. This page should have the same standard look and feel as the intranet or portal: the same colors, graphics, page layout, and navigation elements. This reminds users that they are in the same context, and there are alternatives if the search results are not satisfying.

Search Header and Footer

Search header and footer refer to the sections providing information about the search as a whole: the query terms, the search form, the number of results, results navigation (next page), and special features. This requires some user interface testing for the wording and concepts. It should balance the values of exposing useful features while not overwhelming the user. For example, view the Stanford Search page in Figure 10.2.

In reviewing Stanford's Web site, note the following key takeaways:

- Always include a field to search again, fill it in with the existing search terms. Users can then instantly see what they searched for, but also change it with minimal fuss.
- Include a link to the Advanced Search interface for power users. While even experts start with simple search, they will appreciate the option.
- Provide transparency: Be clear how many results are on the page and how many were found. It is a quick way for

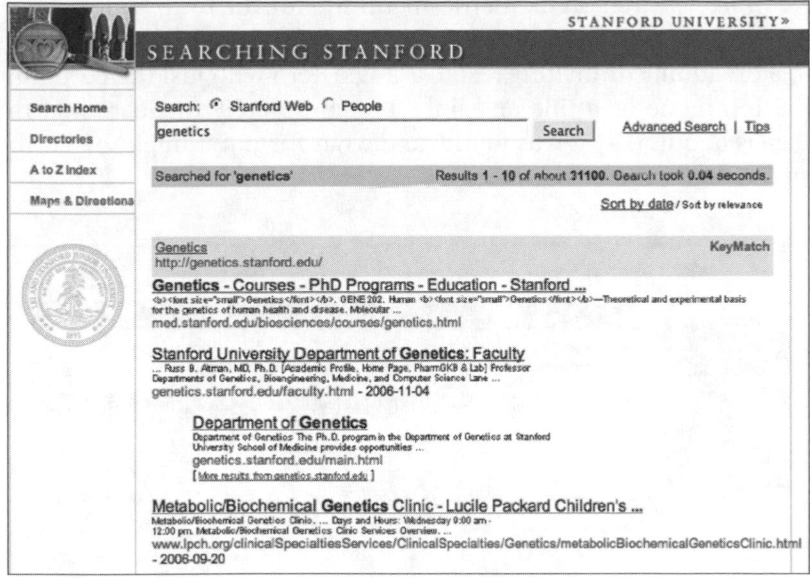

Figure 10.2 Stanford University's Search Page

users to calibrate popularity of their search terms on the intranet.

- Provide a simple page navigation interface.
- When appropriate, display a search suggestion (here called "KeyMatch") for the most common queries.

Why Result Lists Instead of Visualization?

There have been many attempts to create powerful interactive search results interfaces. None of them succeeded in the simple search space, because they require too much effort by users. When trying to find the FedEx instructions, the last thing an employee needs is a 3-D interactive flythrough of all related topics. Search administrators should save complex information mining tools for specific research areas and stick with the tried-and-true list of results for simple search.

Results Items

Each result item should express as much useful information as possible, without overwhelming the user. Figure 10.3 illustrates a bad example. A search on the Bertlesmann site for the term "sarah" (as in McLachlan, the singer highlighted in the lower right corner) brings up a dreadfully uninviting result, a single item with just the corporate division name as a title and link. It is completely unclear what the page is about, why it was found, and what format it might be in. You can do better than this!

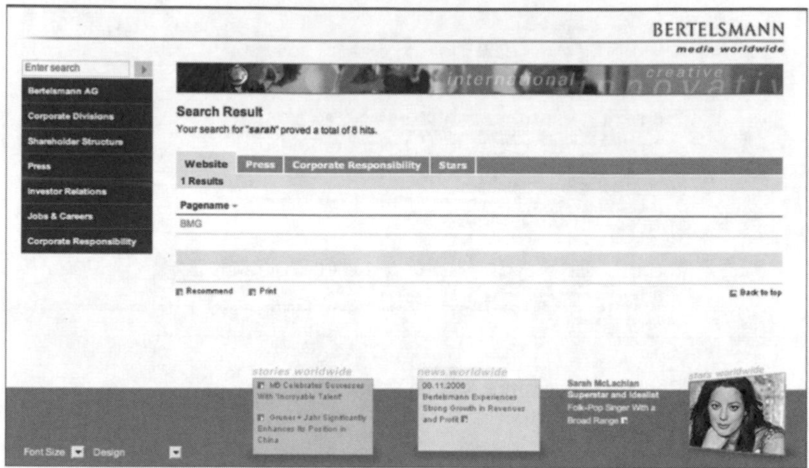

Figure 10.3 Bertelsmann's Search Page

Compare that with the Harvard University search shown in Figure 10.4. It provides significantly more (perhaps even too much) information about the results: not only the title, text snippet, URL, and size, but also a calculated relevance rank and graphic, and links to search for similar documents or to view the cached document as HTML.

Based on Figures 10.3 and 10.4, the following advice is given:

- Page title:
  - Show the Page Title, clearly marked as a clickable link.
  - If there is no <title> tag or Property, your indexer may be able to extract a useful title from the text.
  - Otherwise, use "untitled" or the name of the document.

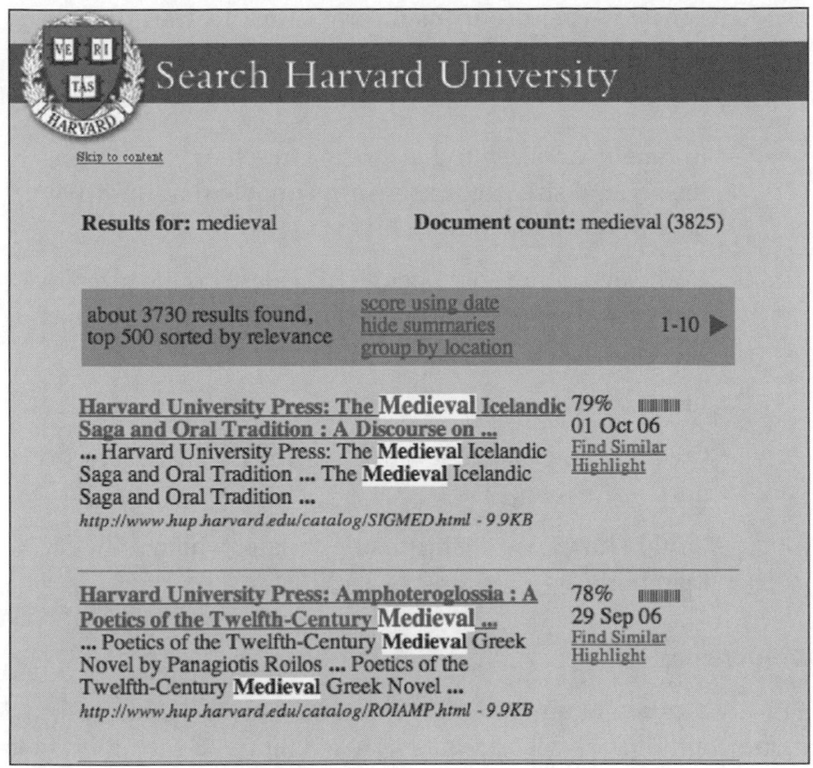

Figure 10.4 Harvard University's Search Page

- Extracted text from the page, showing the matched term in context:
  - Explains clearly why this document was matched.
  - May answer the question immediately.
  - Helps users decide which is the most fruitful page to click on.
- URLs:
  - If the URLs are meaningful, they provide another form of context.
  - If they are simply numeric, as in some CMSs, don't display them.

  - For File Type, use icons or bright text to warn people about non-HTML files.
- File size:
  - Intranets are likely to have very large files, so showing the general size is good. It warns people that they may have to download quite a bit.
  - However, do not force people to calculate file sizes in bytes. Give people a general sense of the size, such as 4K, 280K, 3.4 MB.
- Date:
  - Great to show date, if it is trustworthy (most servers are not).
  - Could show "not changed since" date, which is better than nothing.

Maintenance

Like all other enterprise software, starving or ignoring search engine maintenance will inevitably cause failure. In the other direction, it can soak up enormous amounts of resources. Here is some advice for charting a middle course.

Server and Software Updates

Eventually, the server hardware and OS will become obsolete, so be sure to include the search engine server in your upgrade plans. Monitor the disc and related hardware for errors, as the constant indexing and querying within the search engine puts a lot of strain on the system.

As your searchable intranet grows, the index file itself may become too large to fit on any old disks, or the software may not be able to scale properly. Start by purchasing a search engine that can handle significantly more data than you have, and upgrade disks and software as you reach their limits. You may need to partition the index or add a RAID for better response time—check with the vendor or user community to learn from others' experiences. You may need to add disc storage or upgrade to a faster chip if search response time starts slowing down due to increases in use. While search does not have to support many concurrent queries (people spend most of their time typing or looking at results), with intense use, the system will be unable to keep up and must be scaled up.

There are several reasons to update search engine software. One is simple file format compatibility: Old versions will not be able to read files created by new versions of Microsoft Word or Adobe Acrobat. They also are compatible with new standards, such as SOA/SOAP, providing better tools for indexing content. And finally, the newer versions of the software have new and valuable features, such as spellchecking and match terms in context.

Index Currency

Obsolete documents in the searchable index makes users (rightly) frustrated and angry. They do not trust the search engine if they look for something and it gives them old documents. The search engine should check the documents for changes very frequently and follow links to find new documents. When new servers and new content come online, it is a good idea to feed the indexer a new starting point, and let it go from there, rather than waiting for it to discover the new area by following links. The search engine should automatically remove pages that are inaccessible, so users do not click on a result and get a "Page not found" error.

Information Needs

In addition to the technical aspects of maintenance, the search administrator should consider the enterprise's information needs. Some of these are ongoing, involving improvements to the search engine as described here, while others involve new lines of business, mergers, and other significant changes to the institution.

Search Log Analysis

Search logs have many things in common with Web logs: They generally have large amounts of data such as the query terms, parameters, referring page, browser, user agent, IP address, and date stamp, and so on. However, Web traffic logs are mainly known data, whereas search engine logs contain search terms, which are somewhat less amenable to data mining. This can be done—it just takes different tools.

Traffic and Metrics

Certain types of metrics are useful and easy to compile:

- Number of searches per day, week, and month

- Number of searches with no matches
- Percentage of most frequent queries (tends to be very high)
- Number of queries with at least one click in the results list
- Average response time

Query Analysis

The idea is to find out what people are looking for and whether they are finding it. The reality is trickier. Counting the number of each query will find the most frequent ones, though if the search engine does pluralization or stemming, the log analysis should probably follow suit. In most cases, there will be a steep slope and a long tail, because there are generally a few frequent queries and a large number of unique ones. For instance, Figure 10.5 shows the "zipf" distribution of a log analysis of a public site. In this particular case, there were 2,398 instances of the most frequent query, and thousands of unique and almost-unique queries. The more queries fall into categories (such as part numbers or domain names), the easier it is to understand what people are looking for.

Click-Through Analysis

While a few searches can be satisfied by simply looking at the search results, such as the spelling of a name or the age of an item, most require the user to click on a results item and view a document. In the best case, they can tell which document is the best from the results and click on it, so each session has a 1:1 ratio of searches to clicks.

Putting together the total number of searches on a term and the number of clicks gives you an approximation of this ratio. The most interesting cases are below 1:0.05, in which case the search results are clearly inappropriate to most users, or above 1:2, in which case many users clicked on two or more results and were therefore unhappy with the first one found. Analyzing the most frequent problem click-throughs indicates areas where the content should be improved, the titles should be improved, or a Search Suggestion added to point users in a more fruitful direction.

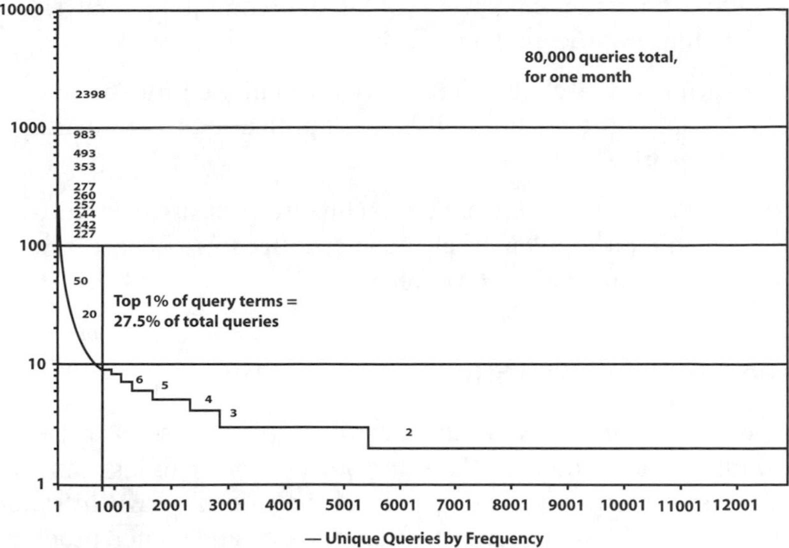

Figure 10.5 Query Frequency Distribution

Ad-Hoc Session Analysis

When there's a particularly confusing query—when you look at a common search term and ask "Why on earth would anyone look for that?"—you can try to track down their intent by looking at the query in context of a query session. A session can be as simple as the same IP address or ID, with search interactions (queries, clicks, next-page navigation) sorted by date and time. With a set of these, it is possible to get an idea of what the user thought they wanted and how they set about finding it.

Conclusion

In summary, the chapter seeks to aid information professionals in managing the search functionality of an intranet. Key takeaways include the following:

- Intranet search requires an investment in both configuration and maintenance, but it pays off in reduced repetitive support and expensive duplication of labor.

- Many Web-wide search standards can be applied to intranet search but not all. On the other hand, intranet search engines can leverage metadata and query analysis to improve the interaction.
- Intranet search is often navigational, helping people locate content and Web-based applications within the enterprise.
- Working with information architecture, search engines can offer a supplemental and alternative form of access to information within the enterprise.

Recommended Web Sites

Intranet Focus Ltd., www.intranetfocus.com – Offers useful articles on intranet search and related topics from a U.K. consulting company.

Intranets: Enterprise Strategies and Solutions, www.intranetstoday.com – Presents news of intranet search and related products.

Search Tools for Web Sites and Intranets, www.searchtools.com – Provides articles and lists of search engine features from Avi Rappoport.

CHAPTER 11

Designing the Ultimate End-User Experience: Separating Presentation and Content

Eric Hards
Lockheed Martin

Good intranet design starts with an understanding of several elements beyond the "look and feel" of the site. At the end of the day, this is the first impression a user or stakeholder will have of the work an information professional does. The design elements include the following:

- The requirements from the content providers
- What type of content will be made available
- How users are expected to use the content
- How users actually use the content
- Good understanding of basic design concepts

Most intranet professionals are faced with designing Web pages or Web sites without understanding what content will be used. Sure, it can be done, but the time it takes to create the finished product is excessive, and the site will not look or work as intended. Many intranet professionals make the mistake of starting with the "look and feel" of the intranet before they truly understand the requirements for the Web site. Moreover, without having the content for the intranet before the design begins, the design will eventually fail. The reason is that "mock-ups," prototypes, etc., are all based on a perfect design where everything fits, graphics are well designed, and navigation slots into the allotted space. Once the content has been developed, the prototype design will probably not be correct based on the needs of the users and the content provided.

The design of the intranet needs to start with a thorough understanding of the site requirements. This is usually accomplished much sooner in the development phase of the project, and it is essential for the designer to develop a usable Web site. Additionally, understanding what content is available and how the intranet manager would like users to access the content is also paramount to the Web designer. Overall, it is the designer's task to create a framework for the intranet that can expand as the intranet grows and that will allow users to easily understand new content and quickly find existing content. The design must not get in the way of the users' workflow. Users of intranets have specific tasks to accomplish. This could include things such as viewing their 401(k) balance, retrieving an approval form, or simply finding out when the parking lot will be paved. The designer must listen to management, program managers, developers, content providers, and, above all, users, taking into account all stakeholders' requirements before beginning to piece together any design.

Is Intranet Design Different from Internet Design?

Users have tasks to complete. Whether it is the purchase of a book or making updates to dependent information for tax deductions, users want to accomplish a specific task on the Internet and the intranet. However, many tasks completed by users on commercial Internet Web sites are conducted on company Web sites with the sole purpose of selling a product or service to the user. Even if the user is there simply to pay a bill, additional information has been designed into the Web page to advertise additional services, related products, and, in some cases, unrelated products. Even companies such as Amazon.com, which aim to make available the shortest path possible to purchase, continue to offer additional items throughout a user's shopping process. Imagine how annoying this would be for users who want to ship a package, find the correct forms to place an order for a computer, or fill out a time card. If the users of your intranet were bombarded with unrelated information while trying to accomplish their given tasks, not only would they become frustrated, but they may also become distracted and lose sight of their original goal. Consequently, companies will lose employee productivity during this "surfing" time. However, many companies still treat their intranets as simple Web sites with many separate and dramatically different sub-sites.

A 2002 study about how people are interfacing with the digital world shows that more people are going online, and the number of users who have never used the Internet has fallen. More importantly, users are expressing more satisfaction with online activities (NFO WorldGroup, 2002). What does this mean for your intranet? It means that your employees want the same experience on their intranet as they have with Amazon.com, Bestbuy.com, or any of the other numerous e-commerce Web sites that understand users' needs. Therefore, designing an intranet is not just creating a well-designed page. Instead, every aspect of the company intranet needs to be examined in order to provide a seamless user experience to your employees. The important theme here is that designing the pages (which we will cover later) is most likely going to be the easier part of creating your intranet. Making all the Web pages, sites, and applications work together so that users understand them and can use them quickly and efficiently is the more challenging goal.

> *Graphic design is essentially about visual relationships—providing meaning to a mass of unrelated needs, ideas, words, and pictures. It is the designer's job to select and fit this material together—and make it interesting.* (Rand, 1985, p. xiii)

Internet design has come a long way since Tim Berners-Lee created the first pages in August 1991. We have had 15 years of the Internet, thousands of studies, intranets, Web phones, e-mail, and handheld devices, and in general, we still are in our infancy of understanding how to consistently design good Web pages. We have had more than 450 years to understand how people use the printed language. We understand how to get users to read a particular part of an advertisement or to structure a piece of research so that information is easy to find; however, we still do not completely understand the best way to design information for electronic media. Nevertheless, we have learned a few things from some of the many user-studies conducted that ask the question: How are Web pages interpreted while looking for information or trying to solve a task?

Many studies have shown that users tend to expect certain things when using Web pages. Whether those pages are on the Internet or intranet, users have developed domain knowledge of how Web pages and sites function. However, many Internet sites still continue to do things differently, wanting to forge their own path and create their own unique look and feel, which has become confusing to our Internet users and consequently our intranet users.

Intranet users expect the intranet experience to be seamless. Navigation elements are always in the same place, and these elements all interact in the same manner. Multiple Web sites, navigation schemes, layout design, and construction are confusing to intranet users. Users expect instant feedback on choices that they make. Whether it is a click, a dialogue box, or a new page, they want things to happen quickly. If pages take too much time to load, users become uneasy, and they believe that there might be something wrong. If they are asked to make a decision regarding input without verification of what will be submitted, they begin to get worried and may need to ask for help. Users also expect interfaces to be easy to use, intuitive, and simple to understand. Not all users know how to use dropdown menus or collapsible navigation. Moreover, users expect good design. Pages that are well designed and function correctly instill trust in users. When employees are making changes to their benefits information, they want to trust that what they submit will be accepted and has been completed correctly. This is accomplished through good Web design and usability testing.

These items represent the primary factors for determining how well your intranet is accepted by your employees. Users want a friendly and easy-to-navigate site where they can easily find what they need and accomplish their task so they can move on to the next task. They expect fast response times, and feedback is required when activities take longer than expected. Finally, and most importantly, they want relevant, frequently updated content that they can trust and rely on for timely information about their job and company.

The Design

Now that we have determined what we need, the big question is how do we accomplish this in our intranet development or redesign project? First, we have to realize that we may not all be starting in the same place. You may be responsible for the first undertaking of an intranet for your corporation. You might be responsible for reworking and redesigning a disarray of multiple Web pages, Web sites, and Web applications, or you might have a well-functioning intranet but want to redesign the site to better deliver information to your users. Additionally, you may or may not have control over how the site is developed. Your IT department might be the developers for all Web sites and Web-based applications, each department within your company might create its own Web pages, or everything might be controlled by one department within the company, such as communications or HR.

While the starting point for the design of your intranet might be one of many stages, your first step is to fully understand the team that will be involved in the design process. Designing your intranet without understanding all "stakeholders" will ultimately lead to an intranet that does not work well for the parties involved. Key elements to designing an intranet are the following:

- Learn how to identify and manage the stakeholders
- Develop the command structure so decisions can be made
- Understand the information and applications that will need to be a part of our intranet
- Identify your users and their individual goals for using the intranet

All of these items are extremely important for the Web designer to understand before constructing the final design for the site. Do not attempt to design the site without first understanding this information.

Starting the Design

In addressing the information architecture (IA) of your intranet, information is organized and categorized in a logical manner. The Web designer will rely heavily on this information structure to develop the design of the intranet. It is the Web designer's responsibility to take the structure developed by the information architect and represent it visually in such a way that it is intuitive to the users in regards to where they will find the information they are seeking.

The Web Designer as Technologist

Web designers are more than artists. They are more technologists than designers. Web designers must have a core set of skills that allow them to produce designs that are visually pleasing, offer credibility to the site, and keep ease-of-use paramount. To create a quality experience for users on the intranet, Web designers need to understand many disciplines. Web designers should possess traditional design and art skills along with basic understanding of Web technologies, information architecture, usability testing, sociology, and psychology. When asked why this is the case, I always respond with the following: "Look at the complexity of the Web!" The Web is far more complex than any printed medium, video production, or multimedia CD. Therefore, it requires many more skills to master, and the designer will need these additional skills to be successful. The recipe for a good Web designer includes a foundation in traditional design, a good understanding of current Web technologies and, finally, an ongoing study of how users use the intranet.

Design the Framework

The designer will need to understand the IA of the intranet before he can begin. Additionally, he will need to understand if there are any existing Web pages, Web sites, and/or applications that will need to be included in the final design. These will also need to be examined for content that may need to be dissected and moved to more prominent areas of the intranet design.

In a given portal design (Figure 11.1), information about employees' vacation days, absent days, holiday information, and floating holidays have been moved to the home page. After talking with users, it was determined that a large amount of time was spent digging into the company's time and attendance system to find information about vacation time and absent time. By moving this information to the home page, users were able to find this information quickly and continue with other work tasks without losing productivity. Because the

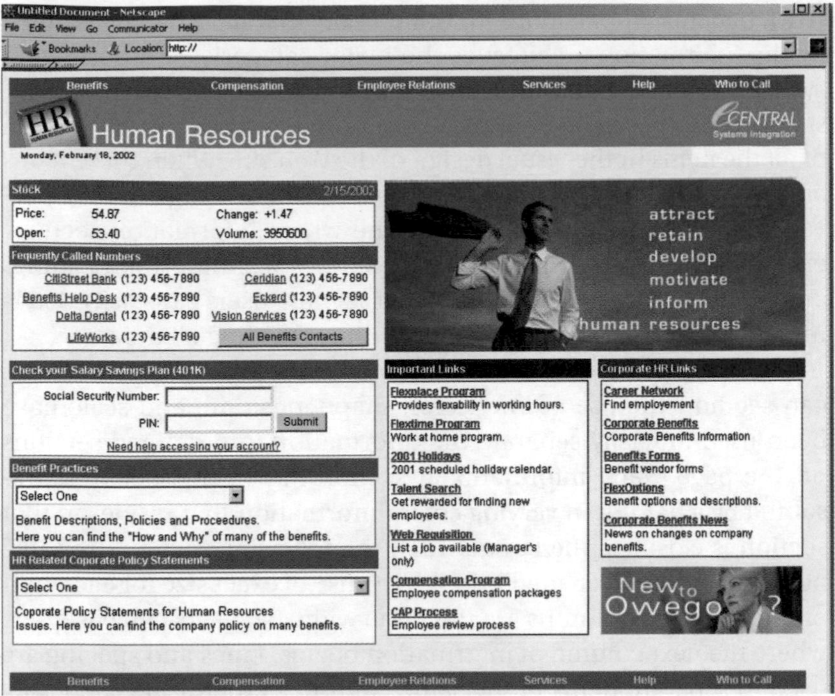

Figure 11.1 Moving Information to the Home Page

designer consulted with users, determined that moving this information to the front of the site would save employee time, and understood that this information could technically be extracted from the given application and placed on the home page, the design was very successful.

The designer will need to examine all the information available on the intranet and prioritize this information into the overall design. They will also take the information framework developed by the information architect and use this as the starting point for the navigation design of the site. The visual design will rely heavily on the information structure of the overall site.

While the information architect has developed levels of precedence and hierarchy for the information that will be displayed in the intranet, it is the designer that will apply visual design so that users can easily interpret the structure of the Web site. Major topic areas will become the main site navigation. These are usually generic titles that will hold more specific information, such as human resources

(HR), benefits, applications, or other items that have been identified by the information architect as the major categories of information for the intranet. Similar to an outline, the designer will use size, shape, color, position, and scale to denote importance and location of all the items in the visual design of the Web site. When these items are used correctly, users can more easily scan the page to find relevant information. They can determine where information sections end and when new ones begin. By simply scanning the headings and/or titles of information in a given section, users can easily determine the nature of the information without reading all the text.

In this simple rendition of an intranet home page (Figure 11.2), we can see how the use of line, color, shape, position, and scale have been used to easily separate the information into defined sections on the page. Each informational section has been visually represented by a banner in varying color. Information that resides in that section is closer to the banner than the following section. Invisible borders have been created through the use of exact size for each unit of information. Columns are the same width, so users can easily see where the next column of information begins. Lines and spacing are used to separate items in the same column so that users can easily read the section heading of each information area and determine if it is of interest without reading all the information in that section. This is extremely useful for areas that have hidden information, such as the dropdown menu navigation in this example. The titles of each dropdown menu help the user determine where to start looking for additional information.

Users do not need to be entertained by their intranet. They would prefer it to be simple, easily navigated, and easy-to-use. While Internet technologies can help in the process, adding graphics, animation, video, and/or audio for the sake of generating interest is a very common mistake that should be avoided by the intranet designer. Graphics can be used for visual interest, and they can be used to help separate sections of information. They are certainly welcome in areas where users need a visual representation to make informed decisions and to help clarify information. These can include pictures for news stories, graphs that represent complex numbers, icons that can be used in complex interfaces, or artwork used consistently to help separate information sections. Navigational elements can also be graphics, helping to generate interest in the intranet. Users still tend to expect buttons to look like buttons and links to look like links.

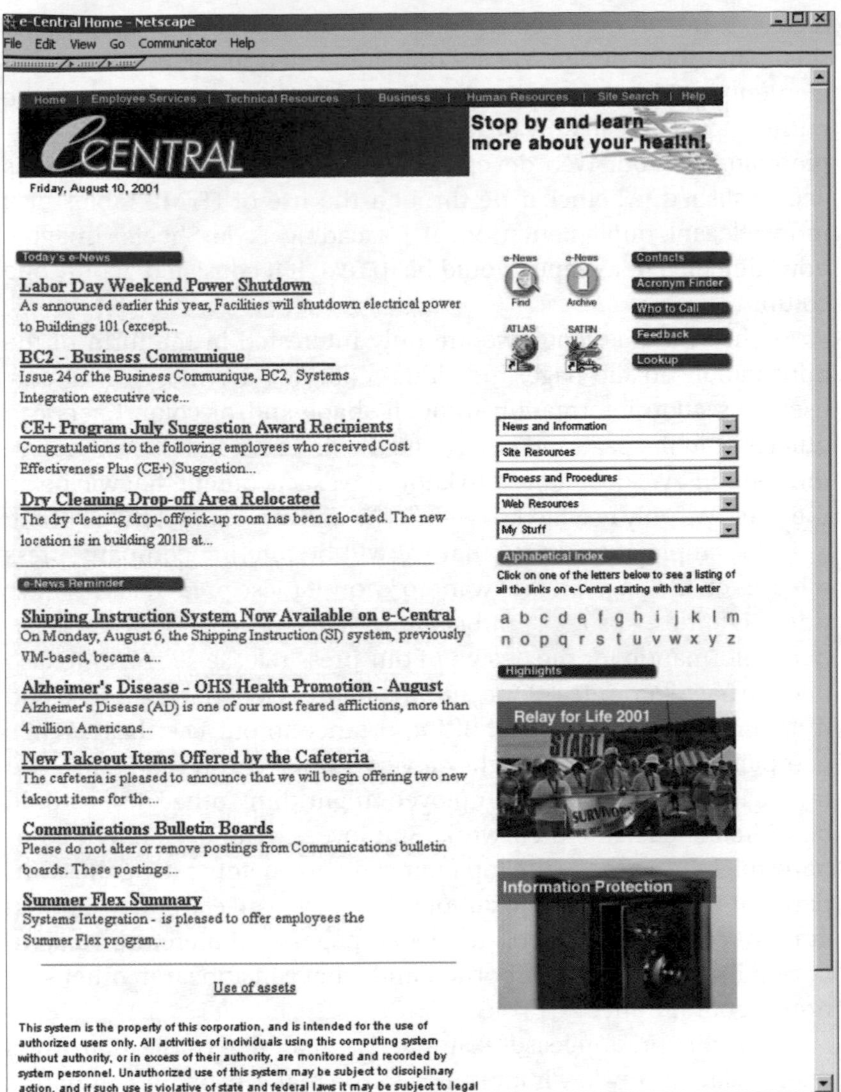

Figure 11.2 Using Visual Design to Facilitate Scanning

> *The real truth is that everybody is afraid of honest simplicity, because it hides nothing.* (Paul-Jacques Grillo)

Basic Page Design

When starting to design the visual structure for any intranet, it is important to realize that we do not begin by addressing "look and feel." We are not overly concerned with color choices or graphics at this point of the design. We are only interested in the positioning of elements within the overall page. First and foremost, we must use the entire page. This can only be accomplished through the use of multiple columns. Your Web developers will determine just how this is accomplished, whether it be through the use of HTML tables or a more elegant implementation of Cascading Style Sheets. Imagine how difficult a newspaper would be to read if it consisted of only one column.

As the visual designer, we are only interested in the form of the information on the page. Individual columns are most commonly used to section information through shape and/or color. Users can quickly scan the page and determine the nature of the information in the columns. We do not need to know the exact content that will be on the page: We only need to know the type and structure of the content.

For example, if we know that we will be offering company press releases on the page, we will want to know if these press releases have titles, subtitles, abstracts, publication dates, photos, or other pertinent information for the design of our press release section. We also need to have some idea of the number of press releases produced and most importantly their level of importance to our user base. While company press releases might be very important to marketing and management, the average employee might think other news would be more beneficial to their work. Employees of an investment company might want to see the top financial news before seeing the company press releases, for example. We have an extremely limited amount of space on the top-level Web pages, and therefore, need to determine what is truly important and what can appear in other sections of our intranet.

Given our press release example, we may determine that press releases are of very low importance to the majority of our company's employees, and we might just have a simple link that says "Press Releases" on the navigation area of the home page. This would then take our users to the press release section of the intranet where we can then design the space based on how press release information should be presented to our users. As the visual designer, we always have this option. We can take information that has been deemed "not important enough to appear on the home page" and move it to a second-level page or to its own section of the intranet. This is one of the most powerful tools visual designers have. Remember, not everything is of equal importance. Therefore, not everything will appear on the home page, a second-level page, or even its own page. The designer can determine the location of the information through relevance, precedence, and importance, instead of simply by how things look on the page. Key steps in visual design are:

- Determining what information is available
- Determining how much of this information is needed to make an informed decision by the user
- Determining which information is important enough to appear on the home page

This will require some research on the Web designer's part, talking with all the stakeholders to determine what information is needed to make decisions and get tasks accomplished.

This task can be accomplished through a simple outline as shown in Figure 11.3. Here we see the items that will be on the home page along with any additional information that will accompany those items. We see the company news section will have a title and a brief line from the first paragraph of the news article. For HR stories on

- **Home Page Outline**
  - Top Navigation (links)
    - Employee Services
    - Technical Resources
    - Human Resources
    - Business Tools
    - Site Search
    - Help
  - Identification Banner
    - Site Name, Logo
    - Informational Advertising Banner
    - Date, Time
    - Company Name and Logo
  - News Section
    - Story title
    - First sentence of story
  - Human Interest News Section
    - Photo
    - Story title
    - First two lines of story
  - Company feature story
    - Photo
    - Story title

Figure 11.3 Outlining the Home Page

employees, we will have a picture and a title. For financial news supplied by a third party, we will just post the headline as a link. The outline will help you determine what sections will be needed on the home page and also allows you to move sections to lower pages if there is too much information to display on the home page. It is also useful to show the outline to the stakeholders in the project. They can help determine if something might be taking too much space or if items are missing.

Sketching

Now that we know we will be using columns for the page design, and we have a good idea of the type of information that will be on the page, we need to determine how the page will be laid out. Before reaching for the computer, I would suggest using pencil and paper to help determine the design of each section of your intranet. There are several reasons for this. First, you will not limit yourself to the design tools you have on the computer. You might be an expert with HTML or you may have difficulty spelling HTML. Either way, we can all use pencil and paper. Secondly, drawing on paper allows us to explore different ideas. We can start with one design, grab another piece of paper, and change it slightly. Thirdly, pencil and paper allow us to "sketch" our ideas. We do not need to make things look finished; we only need to identify where things will be on the page, show how items will be separated and easily scanned by our users, and determine where common items will be located, such as navigation and the location of information. Finally, it allows us to take a "big picture" look at our developing structure. By spreading our pieces of paper on a table, we can see if information is consistently located on each page, if navigation items are always in the same location, if we are using the same header sizes for main and subhead information, and so on.

Sketching on paper is one of the best ways for the visual designer to work during these beginning phases of design. It also lets the designer easily ask users how they might use the page. Showing a sketch to someone is far less daunting than asking him or her to go to a URL and give feedback. Users tend to feel that designs are more difficult to change once they see things in finished form. They believe that a good deal of work has been undertaken to get to this stage, and they may be reluctant to comment on large-scale changes. Sketches are less foreboding, and users feel they can easily make comments without causing large amounts of additional work to occur. Also, the designer can easily receive feedback on changes by simply sketching over an existing drawing or beginning a new sketch with users present and giving feedback in real-time.

The sketch will need to show the location of all the items to be included on the page. While the page structure may be different for the home page as opposed to the second-level press release page, we will need to have some consistency between these pages for our users to understand how to navigate through the intranet. Therefore, we want to begin with the location of our navigation elements and our identification banners. For the majority of Web pages, the identification banner will be at the top of the page, and the navigation will run along the top or left side of the Web page. Our intranet can also use a combination of navigation locations.

In Figure 11.4, we see the use of global navigation for the intranet, including simple buttons such as Home, Search, Employee Directory, and the use of the company logo. We then have the identification banner, followed by the site's high-level navigation. Additionally, we have a secondary set of navigation on the left side of the page that is dedicated to this section of the intranet.

Obviously, there are many ways to use navigation elements on pages. Multiple tabs can be added or subtracted on the top of the page, depending on which section we are in, or secondary navigation can be included on the right-hand side. Dropdown or pop-up menus can also be used. However, it is important to maintain consistency within the pages of your intranet. Thus, we will want to determine where and how navigation will be used for all the sections we are designing.

Use of Lines, Size, and Shape

As we begin to sketch our intranet pages, we need to start separating information elements so they can easily be scanned, inspected, and digested by our users. In most cases, your intranet home page will be very similar to the contents pages found in magazines. Readers can easily scan the magazine's contents (once they actually find the contents page in the magazine), allowing them to determine the different departments or sections that are in the magazine, together with article titles (some of which have brief synopses). For those of us who spend a good deal of time wading through information, we know how helpful a quality magazine contents page can be. We can easily see if a title is intriguing. We might want to quickly see what products are being reviewed, and, further,

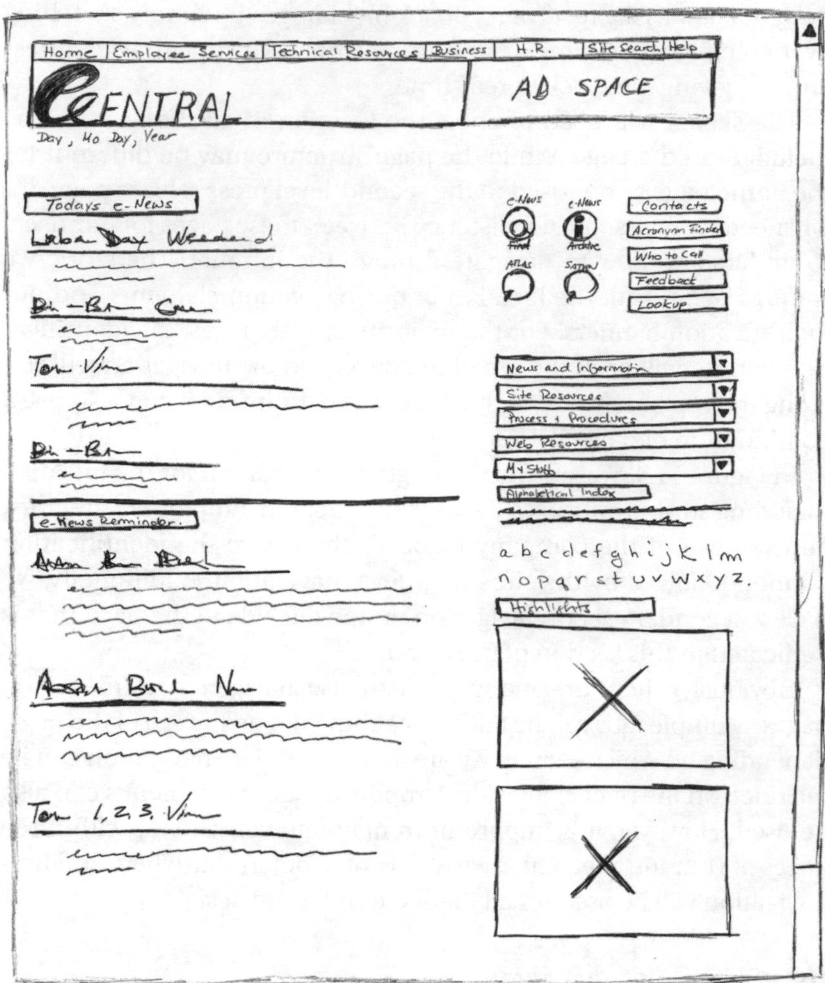

Figure 11.4 Initial Sketch

we can read the subtitle if the title is somewhat ambiguous. All of these things allow us to decide easily if we should go ahead and read the magazine. A common practice for Fortune 500 executives is to have secretaries rip out articles from a magazine on their behalf. That way, they do not have to waste time looking at the advertising, and they can focus their time reading the articles. This is why the contents page is so important. For our users to easily scan our contents page, we will want to incorporate many of the design techniques used in print.

Figures 11.5 and 11.6 are before-and-after design samples of the home page for MiamiDade.gov. Figure 11.5 consists of a simple home page, while Figure 11.6 is a redesign of the page in Figure 11.5. The information has stayed mostly the same; however, the information has been sectioned through the use of lines, size, and shape. While the example in Figure 11.5 does use columns and some size differentiations, they are not used effectively or consistently. This makes it very difficult for the user to understand (1) what defines a section of information, (2) where one section starts and the next section begins, and (3) what the different types of data are that are offered to the user. There is very little differentiation between global navigation and sub-level navigation. The user does not know if "bold" items refer to the beginning of a new section, or if they highlight the title of an article.

The redesigned page takes advantage of consistent use of lines, size, and shape. We can easily determine where the navigation for the different sections of the Web site is through the use of shape (note the buttons along the top) and lines (note the border around the navigation on the left). We have chosen not to use underlined hyperlinks for navigation elements so that users can identify with navigation as opposed to text links. We have used a slightly larger font, giving "bold treatment" (size) for section titles along with the use of borders (line), fills, and negative space (shape) to section the

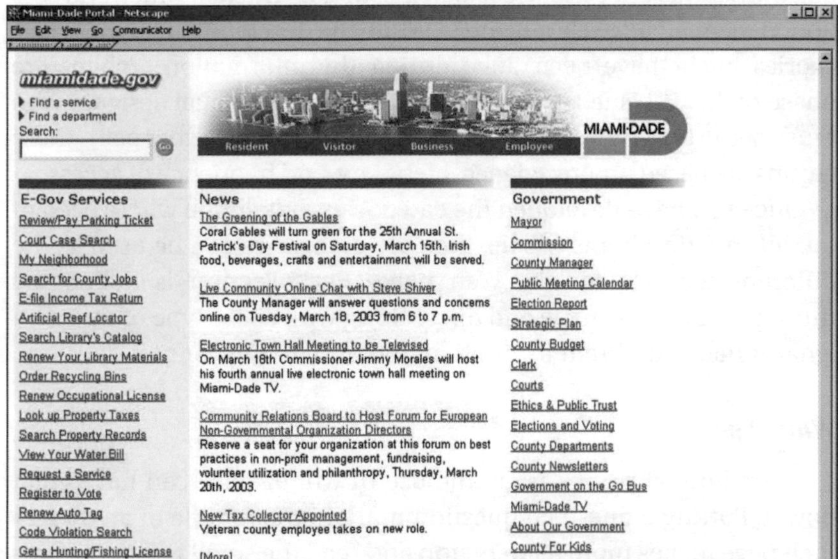

Figure 11.5 MiamiDade.gov Home Page Before

Figure 11.6 MiamiDade.gov Home Page After

information into compartments, thus allowing the user to easily scan the page and determine where information starts and ends for each section. Also, when comparing the two designs, you can see how we have taken what was once a long list of items, in no particular order, and sectioned them off into relevant areas. While the development of these categories might have been done during the information architecture phase of the Web site's development, it is often the visual designer who must decide how these should be grouped on the page. Again, these groups are based on precedence, hierarchy, and frequency of access.

Once you have developed the categories that define where each of the information items will lie, then the categories can be used as the different sections for the Web page. Each section is delineated through the use of shape and lines, along with some type of title designator that is different in size than the underlying content.

White Space

In traditional print design, the use of white space can have great power. Putting a one-inch question mark in the middle of an 8½ x 11 inch page makes more readers stop and read the small text at the bottom of the page, curious to find out what the connection is between the question mark and the text. This has always been the case for print media, where the cost of space is expensive. Make the page larger, and it costs more to print. With the Web, we do not have to worry about space. We can make pages longer, wider, and add as many pages as we want without any additional cost. Therefore, the impact of white space is not the same on the Web. Additionally, for the intranet, our users are looking for a small information item in a sea of information. Imagine if they needed to wade through several pages of white space with a single title on each page—not very efficient. As visual designers, we want to put information on every part of our page, and through the use of lines, shape, size, and color, we can allow the user to easily scan through the information and find what they want without wading through several intranet pages. Look at the *Wall Street Journal* for a good example of how well this works. The front page is packed with information that can easily be scanned by the reader and areas of interest are identified simply by understanding what a title is, where an article stops or starts, and where each section begins. This is all done through the use of size, shape, and lines without any white space involved.

Type

For any designer, type is one of the most powerful design tools. A designer can instill mood, attract attention, make things more readable, or make dull information interesting simply by choosing a different typeface, size, or style. However, while type choice, style, and size can be used in intranet design, it is no longer as important for the designer. The intranet is designed to convey information, and therefore, the designer will use the appropriate font, style, and size to make information readable and easy to find. Since much of the reading will be on a computer screen, it is important for the designer to choose fonts that are easy to read in this environment. Additionally, for the designer to be somewhat confident that what they have designed will look correct on other computers, it is important for them to take advantage of Cascading Style Sheets when choosing fonts, styles, and sizes.

Fonts should be chosen based on commonality for your users. This is usually easier for intranet designers than for Internet designers. Most companies have standardized their computer equipment to save on cost. This means that the designer can have a good idea of the type of fonts that are readily available on the users' equipment. In most cases, this will include simple fonts such as Arial, Times, or Courier. These will be the fonts that will become the staple for your design. Additionally, the size and style you choose will be based on the content displayed on the page. Due to the low resolution of computer displays (as compared to print), sans serif fonts, such as Arial, are easier to read on screen than serif fonts, such as Times or Courier. This would be the exact opposite for print. However, the computer display has difficulties displaying all the intricate designs found in serif fonts, and this causes problems for on-screen reading. Using sans-serif fonts for displaying long passages of text is usually the best choice for designers.

Controlling size is also very important for the designer and the reader. For areas such as navigation and section headings, the designer will want to "lock down" the size so that the overall design is not compromised due to the changing of font sizes by the user. This can easily be accomplished by using pixel sizes in the style sheet. However, designers will want to give their users the ability to enlarge text that must be read on-screen, such as company procedure and benefits information. This allows individuals who have problems reading on-screen to enlarge the text for an improved experience. This can be accomplished using the same style sheet with the use of percentages or point sizes for fonts. Additionally, by using style sheets for all text within the design, a designer can easily change the entire intranet design by making simple changes to font, size, style, and color within the style sheet. In most cases, you cannot go wrong using one or two fonts—usually a serif typeface such as Times and a sans-serif typeface such as Arial. Remember, as the designer for the intranet, it is your duty to get the information across to the users using the best method possible. The goal is not to make things look "pretty." Additional fonts are not needed for text information within the site. Keep in mind, however, that different fonts and styles can easily be incorporated into banners, section headers, and navigation through the use of graphics.

Figure 11.7 is an example of using a single font for an intranet page. Here we can see how the use of size and shade allows the font to easily separate the information on the page. Bold type is used to help designate different sections of the page, and size helps to denote areas of importance. Also notice the use of a different typeface in the banner at the top of the page. This page uses a single font; the readability is good and the design works well.

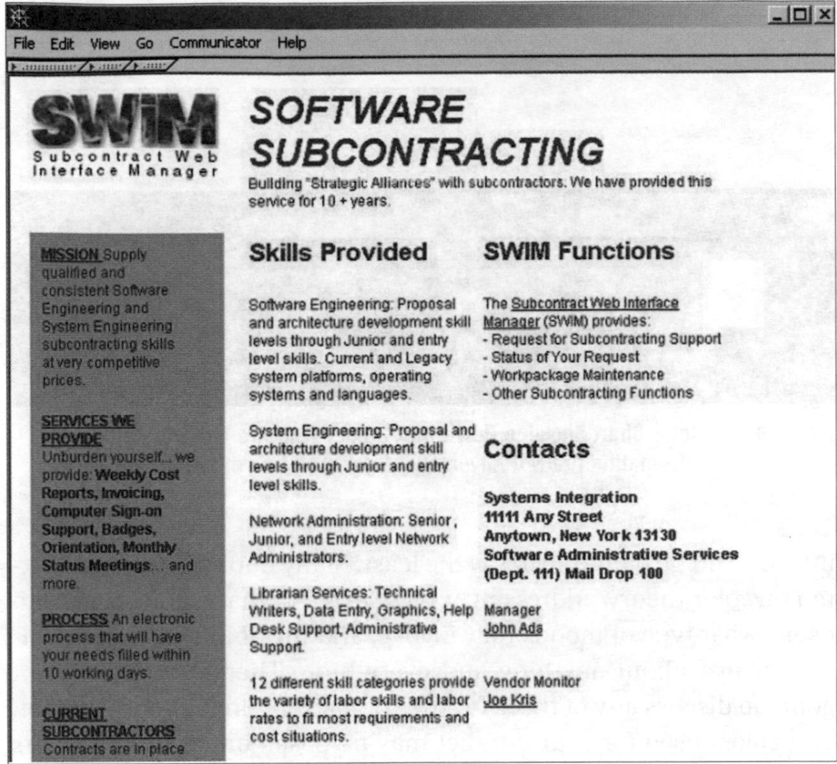

Figure 11.7 One Font Only

Color

In almost all cases, there is no better background for reading text than white. Why is this important to state now? Because almost every intranet team will have at least one stakeholder who will want to do something “different.” There is no reason to use something other than white as the background for your intranet pages. It offers the most contrast between the (black) text and the background color, and thus makes it easier for on-screen reading. Additionally, any other colors that are used on the page for separation of information are not adversely affected by the use of white (see Figure 11.8). Color for intranets should be used to separate information, graphics, and navigation—not as page backgrounds.

Choosing colors for your intranet can be both exciting and difficult. Computer screens are capable of displaying true color with more than 16 million possibilities. Choosing the right colors for your

Figure 11.8 Color Chart Showing How Other Colors That Are Used to Separate Information Are Not Adversely Affected by Use of White

intranet can be daunting to say the least. Many books have been written on color theory, addressing topics such as: what colors suggest to users, what type of moods they invoke, and the ability to choose colors for just about anything and everything. Therefore, we are not going to discuss any of these for the color selection for your intranet. The colors used for your intranet may be based on corporate colors or they may result from a selection by your stakeholders. However, there are some important things to remember about using color on your intranet.

While computer screens today are capable of displaying 16 million-plus colors, intranet designers only need a few of these to be effective. In fact, starting with the 216 Web-safe colors, you can stay within a manageable palette and not get too lost in a rainbow of color. Starting with a basic palette of colors for your intranet can be accomplished by choosing several colors for the use of separating information. For the simplest of palettes, only a single light color and a single dark color need to be chosen. Assuming we are using white for the background and black for displaying text, then we only need color to help separate areas of information. Light colors are used to help create areas of information, and dark colors can be used to help separate related information within a section. Figure 11.9 illustrates the use of just a few colors to help separate information. This page uses white for the background, black for the text, a light blue for sectioning information, and a dark blue to designate information breaks such as titles and subheads. Through the use of these colors, it is very easy for

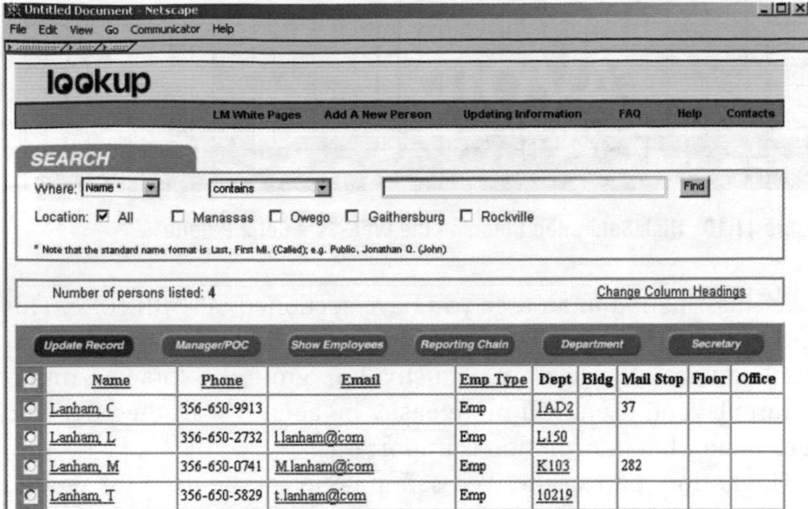

Figure 11.9 A Few Colors Are Sufficient to Separate Information

the user to process the different information sections on the page and quickly find the area or areas in which they are interested.

When choosing the color scheme for your intranet, it is important to incorporate both light colors and dark colors to allow for separation of information. However, when choosing these colors, there are some areas of the 216 Web-safe colors that should be avoided. The colors that have extremely high saturation, along with brilliant hues, are very difficult on the human eye. When these colors cover large areas (e.g., backgrounds or information sections), they become irritating to users.

Figure 11.10 exhibits how high saturation colors take up a large portion of the Web-safe color palette. These colors can still be used in small amounts throughout the intranet, but they should be used sparingly. In most cases, they might be used to call attention to a headline or a small graphic, but nothing more than that. As designers, we are most interested in the colors at the top and bottom of this palette.

The top part of this palette represents the colors we would use for sections of information. From the previous example, we saw the light blue bar long the left side of the page. This area is instantly recognized as being different from the area of white on the right. Users can quickly scan the section heads in the light blue area to determine if the information in that section is of interest. If not, they can skip the section altogether. Keep in mind that you will want to put

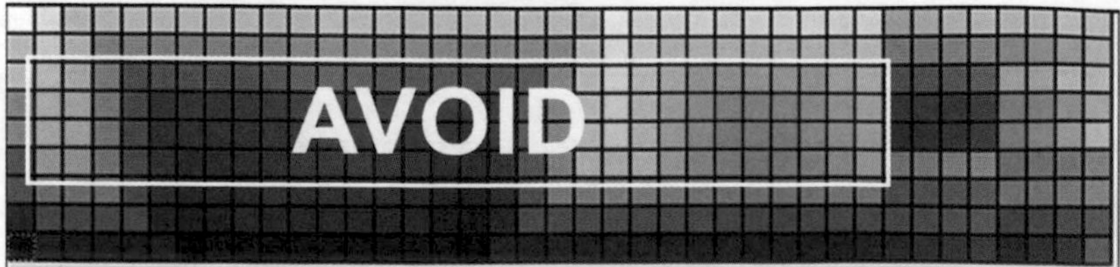

Figure 11.10 High Saturation Colors in the Web-Safe Color Palette

"like" information in an area you have sectioned off with color. This could be different types of news (e.g., financial, company, or business) or areas of navigation. By using background colors in a multicolumn layout, users will more easily be able to scan the page and determine what information is important.

The bottom part of the Web-safe palette can be used for section heads as well as section banners, or in some cases, as background colors themselves. In this example, the dark colors of the Web-safe palette are used for all three (section head, section banner, and background). Notice that only a small section has been used as a background. Here again, we see that reading white text on a dark background, while it does have significant contrast, is still more difficult to read than if it is dark text on a light background. However, this technique can be used sparingly to attract attention to an important part of the page.

How Much Color

Having too many colors on the Web page is distracting and defeats the purpose of using color to section information and call attention to important items. As we saw in the previous example, you can have a color palette of a simple light color and matching dark color. However, intranets are very large and complex and will probably require a larger color palette. In most cases, sections of similar information on your intranet should be grouped on the same color palette. While your home page and section-level navigation pages might use the same color scheme, you might want to change that color scheme when the users have navigated to the HR section of the intranet, for example. The color change helps the user understand that they are now in a different section of the intranet. Keep in mind that you will still want to maintain consistency with the location of information banners and navigation. However, the color palette for this section can be completely different. Understanding this concept can help to give individual style to parts of your intranet and allow stakeholders more flexibility for their respective areas.

Color choices for your intranet, or a section of your intranet, should usually consist of several light and dark colors for the sectioning of information. Once you have selected the main color for the site (blue, brown, green, etc.), you can then choose light and dark analogous colors (next to one another on the color wheel) or complementary colors (opposite one another on the color wheel). This is the easiest way to create the color scheme for your intranet. If you choose to use different primary colors for other sections of the intranet, you can repeat the process. Remember to stay with your chosen color palette when creating pages or individual sections of the intranet. If you change colors halfway through, the user will become disoriented. By choosing the colors first and then using them throughout the design, you will not have the difficulty that can arise from having too many colors or having colors that do not match.

Conclusion

While many of the techniques provided here will help you create a well-designed and usable intranet, it is important to keep in mind that the design is just one of the means to an end. The designer's ultimate goal is to produce Web interfaces that function as the user would intend them to if they could design their own interfaces. This is certainly not an easy task with an intranet that has a broad range of user types and needs. It is important that the visual designer continue to take a proactive approach to maintaining a well-designed and functioning Web site. Questionnaires and interviews with end-users are an essential part of understanding user needs. During the production phase, user feedback is also important. This can be accomplished through volunteer testing of prototype interface designs. Even after release, designers need to solicit feedback from users to determine if the site functions to meet their needs. Ultimately, ongoing communication is the paramount tool for creating intranet usability.

It is important to remember that the Web is not a stagnant medium. Its dynamic ability to provide up-to-the-second information makes the Web a work-in-progress. Additionally, user behaviors and needs change, browsers and tools change, and more advanced technology becomes available to enhance the Web users' tasks and make them more productive. Because of this, Web designers must constantly test and retest designs and update designs to ensure the site still accomplishes its goals and meets current standards of usability. Continue to make your intranet a better place for your users, and they will pay you back in dividends.

Afterword

Mary Lee Kennedy
TKG Consulting LLC

This book was written with the intent that each chapter can be useful on its own or, if the reader so chooses, it can be read cover to cover. Whichever path is chosen, our wish is that the reader takes away a greater understanding of the potential uses of an intranet.

Today's multitasking and continuously, partially attentive information workers experience the ubiquitous nature of information and easily exchange information and knowledge across technology platforms—in this case, between the intranet, extranet, and Internet. In fact, a user may not always be aware which one he or she is in.

From a purely technological perspective, gone are the days of flat HTML pages. Today, there is increasing overlap between content management systems and the portal. Web applications have also become the norm, with portlets or Web parts. However, the management of the intranet space is distinct, even if the technology choices are consistently the same with the Internet, since there remains both a difference in purpose and in governance between the market-led environment of the Internet and the supply-led environment of a given organization. Given this, information professionals need to understand the organizational dynamics in which their products and services will operate, including the type of governance structures that will make sense and the user behavior associated with working across potentially three interconnected spaces: the intranet, the extranet, and the Internet.

While the Internet sets the bar for user expectations of functionality, the intranet is often less developed. In fact, a 2006 study by Jane McConnell showed that many organizations suggested the intranet had yet to realize its potential strategic value. There may be significant pressure on information professionals to articulate the value and benefit of an intranet beyond its more humble dwelling. Significant pressure also exists to produce a Return on Investment (ROI) analysis. There is little to measure in terms of revenue generation or brand value. However, content management and findability efforts associated with the intranet can decrease the amount of time spent looking for meaningful content, increase the ability to complete tasks 24/7, increase the capability that can be brought to bear on problem resolution, and reduce duplicate efforts. They can also reduce the amount of time spent working with the wrong information, enable the movement of useful and usable content from inside the firewall to outside the firewall, and ensure that teams are coordinating their efforts.

With these general points in mind, this book provides several chapters for information professionals to understand what is most meaningful in their environment and a series of examples on topics that remain at the core of the design, development, implementation, and management of effective internal knowledge and information-sharing environments enabled by an intranet. Some key findings include the following:

1. Most intranets sprouted up as grassroots or top-down efforts at communication or policy sharing. Today, organizing intranets is largely about making them more predictable and assuring their intended audiences that the content is relevant, accurate, and reliable.

2. While it is difficult to prove that the intranet is driven technologically by the work on the Internet or in IT application development, there is a significant set of actual practice that indicates this is so. Information professionals need to understand the IT available in the previously mentioned areas so they can understand how best to leverage them, and they need to partner with IT professionals to create useful and usable intranet environments.

3. Designing an intranet with the required end in mind is important with the one caveat that collaboration and knowledge sharing cannot necessarily be orchestrated, but rather they are enabled. Part of the intranet needs to be left open to accommodate emerging behaviors. There continues to be a natural tension between the supply-driven world of an organization and the market-driven world of the Internet in terms of managing user expectations. Good design, though, is essential for the effective use of content inside any given organization, regardless of where the context comes from.

4. Intranets are complex environments with applications, information management, service, and products, and therefore, they require clear governance about roles and responsibilities, as well as creating the ability of the team to work well together. There are multiple disciplines involved that range from those focused on human dynamics to information dynamics to the dynamics of hardware and software. The degree to which this complexity affects what can and cannot be done should not be underestimated.

5. It is possible that portals, content management, and search will be influenced by significant changes in technology platforms. However, these critical applications are the reason why people use intranets (i.e., views into content and easy access to prior knowledge, the ability to organize information in meaningful ways, and the ability to find it). These remain core competencies of information professionals, and organizations count on them to get the work done efficiently and effectively.

The obvious question to ask next is, "Where do we go from here?" We have provided a significant set of references and additional resources for the reader. There are many ongoing studies of information professionals as well as intranets. We have highlighted some of the most recent work throughout the book. Our belief is that the information user of tomorrow will not be the same as those of today. At the simplest level of extrapolation, this is because the starting place is so different today. One can expect the starting point for the next generation of information workers will be different as well. For example, Google Desktop did not exist even two years ago, social tagging was a mere thought in someone's mind until quite recently, and the ability to download videos into a small handheld device from the Web was nonexistent, let alone pervasive. Devices have changed dramatically along with the ease with which content moves in different shapes and forms between one state and another. Content management today is nothing like it was five years ago. Information professionals will have to be very information technology savvy in order to meet user expectations. One would be naive to suggest that humans remain the same in all of this. Studies on partial cognitive attention (consider how often you interact with various content forms on any given day) and the need to multitask are perhaps changing the way we work. Early studies certainly suggest this is true. Information professionals must also study the dynamics of human behavior as they interact with each other with new technological devices. While research has begun to study efforts such as the Web Science program at MIT, there is little evidence to suggest a surge of research on internal information environments.

As information professionals, we play a critical role in enabling organizations to work within a very complex setting. Rarely do information professionals hold positions that are responsible for driving the direction of an organization. Those roles are held by functional leaders such as marketing and product development, CEOs, or heads of nongovernmental organizations (NGOs) and government bodies. However, behind the scenes, and sometimes at the same table as CIOs, CKOs, or executive directors are information professionals who play fundamental roles in ensuring that the organization can accomplish its goals. In that framework, information professionals bridge requirements and possibilities, while ushering them into a tangible reality. They are at the interface of business requirements and the dynamic information environment. As trusted advisors, architects, and those responsible for weaving the pieces together into a significant environment, there is a future to understand as well as a future to build.

Bibliography

ABC Canada Literary Foundation. www.abc-canada.org (accessed July 20, 2007).

Abell, Angela. (2005). "Skills for Knowledge Working: A Guide to Good Practice." British Standards Institution.

Abell, Angela and Hazel Hall. (2006). "New Role Realities: Avenues for Extending the Reach of Information Specialists." Paper presented at annual meeting of the American Society of Information Science and Technology, Austin, TX, November 3–9, 2006.

Abell, Angela and Val Skelton. (2003). "Knowledge and Information Management (KIM) Competency Dictionary." TFPL Ltd.

Abels, Eileen et al. (2003). "Competencies for Information Professionals of the 21st Century." Rev. ed. The Special Libraries Association Board of Directors (June 2003). www.sla.org/PDFs/Competencies2003_revised.pdf (accessed December 1, 2006).

Agile Project Management Advisory Service Web Site. (2006). Cutter Consortium. www.cutter.com/project.html (accessed December 17, 2006).

Anderson, Chris. (2004). "The Long Tail." *Wired Magazine* 12.10 (October 2004). www.wired.com/wired/12.10/tail.html.

Anderson, Janna Quitney and Lee Rainie. (2006). *The Future of the Internet II.* Washington, D.C.: Pew Internet and American Life Project.

Aon Limited. (1995). "Aon Biennial Risk Management & Risk Financing Survey 1995."

Aon Limited. (2005). "Aon Biennial Risk Management & Risk Financing Survey 2005." www.aon.com/uk/en/about/Press_Office/biennial_2005/default.jsp (accessed December 1, 2006).

Asilomar Institute for Information Architecture. (2003). "Future of Information Architecture Survey." January 2003. iainstitute.org/pg/future_of_information_architecture.php (accessed April 24, 2005).

Asilomar Institute for Information Architecture. (2003). "IA Curriculum Initiative Phase 1: Worldwide List of Information Architecture Education." October 2003. iainstitute.org/edu/2003/AIfIA_List-of-IA-Programs.2003.pdf (accessed April 24, 2005).

Australian Government Information Management Office. (2004). "Better Practice Checklist 15: Information Architecture for Websites." Version 1 2004. www.agimo.gov.au/__data/assets/file/33933/BPC15.pdf (accessed April 24, 2005).

Benkler, Yochai. (2002). "Coase's Penguin, or, Linux and the Nature of the Firm." *Yale Law Journal* 112 (Winter 2002–2003).

Boiko, Bob. (2005). *Content Management Bible.* 2nd ed. Hoboken, NJ: Wiley Publishing.

Boyle, Cailin. (2001). *Color Harmony for the Web: A Guide for Creating Great Color Schemes On-Line.* Gloucester, MA: Rockport Publishers.

Brancheau, James C., Larry Schuster, and Salvatore T. March. (1998). "Building and Implementing an Information Architecture." *ACM SIGMIS Database* 20.2 (Summer 1989): 9–17.

Bruner, C. (1991). *Thinking Collaboratively: Ten Questions and Answers to Help Policy Makers Improve Children's Services.* Washington, D.C.: Education and Human Services Consortium.

Byrne, Tony. (2004). "Enterprise Information Architecture: Don't Do ECM Without It." *EContent* 27.5 (May 2004): 22–29.

Cabinet Office: Prime Minister's Strategy Unit. (2005). "Connecting the UK: The Digital Strategy." April 2005. www.strategy.gov.uk/downloads/work_areas/digital_strategy/report/pdf/digital_strategy.pdf (accessed December 1, 2006).

Cabinet Office. (2005). "Transformational Government: Enabled by Technology." November 2005. www.cio.gov.uk/documents/pdf/transgov/transgov-strategy.pdf (accessed December 1, 2006).

Choo, Chun Wei. (1998). *The Knowing Organization: How Organizations Use Information to Construct Meanings, Create Knowledge, and Make Decisions.* New York: Oxford University Press.

Christensen, Clayton, Eric A. Roth, and Scott D. Anthony. (2004). *Seeing What's Next: Using Theories of Innovation to Predict Industry Change.* Boston: Harvard Business School Publishing.

Cognitive Edge. cognitive-edge.com (accessed December 1, 2006).

Collins, Heidi. (2001). *Corporate Portals: Revolutionizing Information Access to Increase Productivity and Drive the Bottom Line.* New York: AMACOM.

Cooper, Alan. (1999). *The Inmates Are Running the Asylum: Why High Tech Products Drive Us Crazy and How to Restore the Sanity.* Indianapolis: Sams Publishing.

Damsgaard, Jan and Rens Scheepers. (2000). "Managing the Crises in Intranet Implementation: A Stage Model." *Information Systems Journal* 10.2: 131–150.

Davenport, Thomas. (2006). "E2.0? Marginal at Best." *Optimize Magazine* 59 (September 2006). www.optimizemag.com/showArticle.jhtml?articleId=192300298 (accessed December 1, 2006).

Davenport, Thomas and Laurence Prusak. (1997). *The Information Ecology: Mastering the Information and Knowledge Environment.* New York: Oxford University Press.

Davenport, Thomas and Laurence Prusak. (1998). *Working Knowledge: How Organizations Manage What They Know.* Boston: Harvard Business School Press.

David A. Kolb on Experiential Learning. www.infed.org/biblio/b-explrn.htm (accessed December 1, 2006).

Davydov, Mark M. (2001). *Corporate Portals and eBusiness Integration.* New York: McGraw-Hill.

DeLong, David W. (2004). *Lost Knowledge: Confronting the Loss of an Aging Workforce.* New York: Oxford University Press.

Dervin, Brenda, Lois Foreman-Wernet, and Eric Lauterbach (Eds.). (2003). *Sense-Making Methodology Reader: Selected Writings of Brenda Dervin.* Cresskill, NJ: Hampton Press.

Dixon, Nancy M., Nate Allen, Tony Burgess, Pete Kilner, and Steve Schweitzer. (2005). *CompanyCommand: Unleashing the Power of the Army Profession.* West Point, NY: Center for the Advancement of Leadership Development & Organizational Learning.

Dragoon, Alice. (2004). "A Travel Guide to Collaboration." *CIO Magazine* (November 15, 2004). www.cio.com/archive/111504/guide.html (accessed July 20, 2007).

Drucker Foundation. *Meeting the Challenge Collaboration Workbook: Developing Strategic Alliances Between Nonprofit Organizations and Businesses.* San Francisco: Jossey-Bass 2002. Available at the Leader to Leader Institute site: www.pfdf.org/collaboration/challenge/download.html.

Dutra, Jayne. "NASA Taxonomy Development: Stitching Together Vocabularies for a Unified Information Architecture." PowerPoint presentation for NASA and the Jet Propulsion Laboratories, April 28, 2004. colab.cim3.net/file/work/Expedition_Workshop/2004-04-28_Multiple_Taxonomies/Dutra_20040428.ppt (accessed December 1, 2006).

Economist Intelligence Unit. (2005). *Know How: Managing Knowledge for Competitive Advantage.* New York: EIU.

Evernden, Roger and Elaine Evernden. (2003). "Third-Generation Information Architecture." *Communications of the ACM* 46.3 (March 2003): 95–98.

Fallows, Deborah. (2005). *Search Engine Users.* Washington, D.C.: Pew Internet and American Life Project.

Farnum, Chris. (2002). "Information Architecture: Five Things Information Managers Need to Know." *Information Management Journal* 36.5 (Sep/Oct 2002): 33–39.

Fiorito, David. (2005). "Thinking Navigation: Navigation on Vanguard, pt. 2." PowerPoint Presentation. March 2005. www.iasummit.org/2005/final papers/101_Presentation.ppt (accessed December 1, 2006).

Fox, Chiara and Peter Merholz. (2002). "PeopleSoft.com Case Study: Enterprise Information Architecture." PowerPoint presentation at ASIS&T Conference. March 16, 2002. www.asis.org/Conferences/Summit2002/peoplesoft_case_study_FINAL.ppt (accessed December 1, 2006).

Garrett, Jesse James. (2000). The Elements of User Experience. March 30, 2000. www.jjg.net/elements/pdf/elements.pdf (accessed April 24, 2005).

Groff, Todd R. and Thomas P. Jones. (2003). *Introduction to Knowledge Management: KM in Business*. Boston: Butterworth-Heinemann.

Hall, Tamra. (1999). *Intelligence Community Collaboration: A Baseline Study.* Washington, D.C.: CIA. Available at collaboration.mitre.org/prail/IC_Collaboration_Baseline_Study_Final_Report/toc.htm.

Hogue, Teresa. (1994). "Community Based Collaborations—Wellness Multiplied." Oregon Center for Community Leadership. crs.uvm.edu/nnco/collab/framework.html (accessed July 20, 2007).

Ignacio, Art. (2005). "Information Architect—Requirements." Developed for the STC Information Design SIG. April 15, 2005. www.info-design.com/ID/InformationArchitect.htm (accessed April 24, 2005).

"Information Assets in the Government of Alberta: A Management Framework." (2003). Sponsored by Alberta Government and the Office of the Corporate Chief Information Officer. October 2003. www.im.gov.ab.ca/imf/pdf/IMFrameworkReport.pdf (accessed December 1, 2006).

Kim, Amy Jo. (2000). *Community Building on the Web: Secret Strategies for Successful Online Communities*. Berkeley, CA: Peachpit Press.

Kouzes, James M. and Barry Z. Posner. (2002). *The Leadership Challenge.* 3rd ed. San Francisco: Jossey-Bass.

Krug, Steve. (2000). *Don't Make Me Think: A Common Sense Approach to Web Usability*. Berkeley, CA: New Riders Press.

Kurzweil Technologies. www.kurzweiltech.com (accessed July, 20, 2007).

Lave, Jean and Etienne Wenger. (1991). *Situated Learning: Legitimate Peripheral Participation*. Cambridge: Cambridge University Press.

Leise, Fred, Sarah A. Rice, and Amy J. Warner. (2006). "Building a Faceted Classification." PowerPoint Presentation for Information Architecture Summit, Montreal, Canada. March 6, 2006. www.iasummit.org/2005/finalpapers/50_Presentation.ppt (accessed December 1, 2006).

Lelic, Simon (Ed.). (2004). *Communities of Practice: Lessons from Leading Collaborative Enterprises*. London: Ark Group.

Leonard, Dorothy and Walter C. Swap. (2005). *Deep Smarts: How to Cultivate and Transfer Enduring Business Wisdom*. Boston: Harvard Business Press.

Lipnack, Jessica and Jeffrey Stamp. (2000). *Virtual Teams: People Working Across Boundaries with Technology*. 2nd ed. New York: John Wiley & Sons.

Lombardi, Victor, Scott Robinson, and Rasmi Sinha. (2004). "IAInstitute Competency Survey, 2004." iainstitute.org/documents/research/results/IA.competencies.graphs.pdf (accessed April 24, 2005).

Maloney, Krisellen, and Paul J. Bracke. (2004). "Beyond Information Architecture: A Systems Integration Approach to Web-Site Design." *Information Technology and Libraries* 23.4 (December 2004): 145–152.

Market Wire. (2006). "IBM's Intranet One of the World's Top Ten." Press Release. January 26, 2006. www.marketwire.com/mw/release_html_b1?release_id=107490 (accessed November 24, 2006).

McAfee, Andrew. (2006). "Enterprise 2.0: The Dawn of Emergent Collaboration." *MIT Sloan Management Review* 47.3 (Spring 2006): 21–28.

McConnell, Jane. (2006). "Global Internet Strategies Survey Report 2006." Net Strategy JMC. netjmc.com/engl/survey06summary.html (accessed July 20, 2007).

Meyerson, Debra, and Joanne Martin. (2001). "Cultural Change." In Warwick Organizational Behavior Staff (Ed.), *Organizational Studies* Vol. 1. Florence, Kentucky: Routledge: 330–335.

Moore, Connie and Erica Rugullies. (2005). *The Information Workplace Will Redefine the World of Work—At Last!* Cambridge: Forrester Research.

Moore, Geoffrey A. (1999). *Crossing the Chasm: Marketing and Selling High-Tech Products to Mainstream Customers*. New York: HarperCollins.

———. (2002). *Living on the Fault Line: Managing for Shareholder Value in Any Economy*. Rev. ed. New York: Harper Collins.

Morris, Meredith. (2005). *How Do Users Feel About Technology?* Cambridge: Forrester Research.

Morville, Peter and Louis Rosenfeld. (2002). *Information Architecture for the World Wide Web: Designing Large-Scale Websites*. 2nd ed. Sebastopol, CA: O'Reilly Media.

Morville, Peter. (2005). "Ambient Findability: Libraries at the Crossroads of Ubiquitous Computing and the Internet." *Information Today Online* 29.6 (Nov/Dec 2005). www.infotoday.com/online/nov05/morville.shtml (accessed December 1, 2006).

MyLifeBits Project. Microsoft Research. research.microsoft.com/barc/media presence/MyLifeBits.aspx (accessed December 1, 2006).

National Institute for Literacy. www.nifl.gov (accessed July 20, 2007).

Newell, Sue, Jacky Swan, and Harry Scarborough. (2001). "From Global Knowledge Management to Internal Electronic Fences: Contradictory Outcomes of Intranet Development." *British Journal of Management* 12.2: 97–112.

Nielsen, Jakob. (1999). *Designing Web Usability: The Practice of Simplicity.* Berkeley, CA: New Riders Press.

Nielsen, Jakob. (2006). "Usability of Intranet Portals. A Report from the Trenches: Experiences from Real-Life Portal Projects." www.nngroup.com/reports/intranet/portals (accessed July 20, 2007).

Nielsen Norman Group. "Intranet Design Annual 2006: Ten Best Intranets of the Year." nngroup.com/reports/intranet/design (accessed July 20, 2007).

Nonaka, Ikujiro and Hirotake Takeuchi. (1995). *The Knowledge Creating Company: How the Japanese Companies Create the Dynamics of Innovation.* New York: Oxford University Press.

Norman, Donald A. (1998). *The Design of Everyday Things.* Cambridge: MIT Press.

Ordman, Nancy et al. (2005). "Traversing the Corporate Web: IBM's Information Management Workflow." PowerPoint presentation for the Information Architecture Summit, Montreal, Canada. March 2005. www.iasummit.org/2005/finalpapers/106_Presentation.ppt (accessed December 1, 2006).

O'Reilly, Bill. (2005). "What Is Web 2.0?" O'Reilly Media Web Site. September 30, 2005. www.oreillynet.com/pub/a/oreilly/tim/news/2005/09/30/what-is-web-20.html (accessed December 17, 2006).

Popadiuk, Silvio and Chun Wei Choo. (2006). "Innovation and Knowledge Creation: How Are These Concepts Related?" *International Journal of Information Management* 26: 302–312.

Pring, Roger. (2000). *WWW.color.* New York: Watson-Guptil Publications.

Rajan, Amin and Penny van Eupen. (1996). *Leading People.* 2nd ed. Centre for Research and Technology in Europe.

Rand, Paul. (1985). *A Designer's Art.* New Haven: Yale University Press.

Rockley, Ann. (2005). *Managing Enterprise Content: A Unified Content Strategy.* 2nd ed. Indianapolis: New Riders Publishing.

Rosenfeld, Louis. (2003). Enterprise Information Architecture Roadmap. August 2003. www.louisrosenfeld.com/home/bloug_archive/images/EIAroadmap2.pdf (accessed April 24, 2005).

Rosenfeld, Louis. (2002). "Information Architecture: Looking Ahead." *Journal of the American Society for Information Science and Technology* 53.10 (August 2002): 874–876.

Rosenfeld, Louis and Peter Morville. (2002). *Information Architecture for the World Wide Web: Designing Large-Scale Web Sites.* 2nd ed. Cambridge: O'Reilly.

Rubenstein, Joshua, David E. Meyer, and Jeffrey E. Evans. (2001). "Executive Control of Cognitive Processes in Task Switches." *Journey of Experimental Psychology: Human Perception and Performance* 27.4: 763–797.

Rumizen, Melissie Clemmons (2002). *The Complete Idiot's Guide to Knowledge Management.* Indianapolis: Alpha.

Saint-Onge, Hubert and Charles Armstrong. (2004). *The Conductive Organization: Building Beyond Sustainability.* Boston: Elsevier.

Saint-Onge, Hubert and Debra Wallace. (2003). *Leveraging Communities of Practice for Strategic Advantage.* Boston: Butterworth-Heinemann.

Sano, Darrell. (1996). *Designing Large-Scale Websites: A Visual Design Methodology.* Hoboken, NJ: John Wiley & Sons.

Skyrme, David J. (1999). *Knowledge Networking: Creating the Collaborative Enterprise.* Boston: Butterworth-Heinemann.

Solomon, Marc. (2005). "Tune Up Your Searches: Searching for Information Can Be a Waste of Time." *Baseline* 1.42 (April 2005): Z.000

Solomon, Marc. (2005). "Under Budget, on Time, and in Sync: How to Stage Successful Rollouts." *Searcher* 13.2 (February 2005): 28–39.

Snowden, David. (2005). "Stories from the Frontier." *E:CO* 7.3,4 : 155–165.

State Records, New South Wales. (1999). "An Information Management and Technology Blueprint for NSW: A Well-Connected Future." www.records.nsw.gov.au/publicsector/erk/polerk/title.htm (accessed July 20, 2007).

Stone, Linda. "Blog on Continuous Attention." continuouspartialattention.jot.com/WikiHom (accessed July 20, 2007).

Sullivan, Dan. (2003). *Proven Portals: Best Practices for Planning, Designing, and Developing Enterprise Portals.* Boston: Addison-Wesley Information Technology.

Sullivan, John. (2006). "Implementing the Federal Enterprise Architecture at EPA." Presentation at the US EPA. cio.doe.gov/Conferences/AITC/presentations/EPA-DOE-EA.ppt (accessed December 1, 2006).

Sultan, Terrie, and Richard Shiff. (2003). *Chuck Close Prints: Process and Collaboration.* Princeton, NJ: Princeton University Press.

"Survey: Talent." (2006). *Economist.* 5 October 2006.

Terra, Jose Claudio and Cindy Gordon. (2003). *Realizing the Promise of Corporate Portals, First Edition: Leveraging Knowledge for Business Success.* Burlington, MA: Butterworth-Heinemann.

TFPL Ltd. (1999). "Skills for Knowledge Management: Building a Knowledge Economy." TFPL Ltd.

TFPL Ltd. (2001). "Scenarios for the Knowledge Economy: Strategic Information Skills." TFPL Ltd. for the ISNTO.

U.S. Army Material Command. (2007). *Partnering for Success: A Blueprint for Promoting Government-Industry Communication and Teamwork.* acc.dau.mil/CommunityBrowser.aspx?id=30351&lang=en-US (accessed July 20, 2007).

Wallis, Claudia. (2006). "The Multitasking Generation." *Time Magazine.* March 27, 2006. www.time.com/time/magazine/article/0,9171,1174696,00.html (accessed July 20, 2007).

Weill, Peter and Jeanne W. Ross. (2004). *IT Governance.* Boston: Harvard Business School Press.

Welborn, Ralph and Vince Kasten. (2003). *The Jericho Principle: How Companies Use Strategic Collaboration to Find New Sources of Value.* Hoboken, NJ: John Wiley & Sons.

Welcome to the CMMI Web Site. (2005). Carnegie Mellon Software Engineering Institute. www.sei.cmu.edu/cmmi (accessed April 24, 2005).

Wenger, Etienne. (1998). *Communities of Practice: Learning, Meaning, and Identity.* Cambridge: Cambridge University Press.

Wenger, Etienne, Richard McDermott, and William M. Snyder. (2002). *Cultivating Communities of Practice: A Guide to Managing Knowledge.* Boston: Harvard Business School Press.

White, Martin. (2004). "Information Architecture." *The Electronic Library* 22.3: 218–219.

White, Martin. (2005). *The Content Management Handbook.* London: Library Association Publishing Ltd.

Wurman, Richard Saul. (1996). *Information Architects.* New York: Graphis, Inc.

About the Contributors

Angela Abell, TFPL Ltd. (www.tfpl.com)

Angela Abell, who has held senior library and information management posts in the public, private, and academic sectors, is a visiting professor at London Metropolitan University and serves on the advisory board of the Sheffield University Department of Information Studies. In her capacity as a director with TFPL Ltd. from 1994–2006, she set up and led the consultancy division (including developing a knowledge management consultancy) and became director of business development.

Within the information and knowledge management domain, her main areas of interest are the value and impact of information, information and knowledge flows and utilization, and the development of information roles, skills, and competencies. She is an experienced consultant, trainer, and author in all of these areas. Angela can be contacted at angela.abell@btinternet.com.

Cory Costanzo, ABT Associates (www.abtassociates.com)

Cory Constanzo is a consultant who works largely with variations on user-centered research and data analysis that informs areas such as IT design specifications, organizational strategy, and corporate initiative design and implementation. She has a BA in anthropology from Harvard University and an MBA from Northeastern University. Cory can be contacted at ccostanzo@post.harvard.edu.

Mike Crandall, Senior Lecturer and Chair, Master of Science in Information Management Program, The Information School, University of Washington

Prior to coming to the University of Washington, Mike Crandall was technology manager for the U.S. library program of the Bill & Melinda Gates Foundation. He also helped develop the public access computing portal WebJunction as well as place Internet connections and computers in 14,000 public libraries throughout the U.S. Prior to joining the Gates Foundation, he worked on search technology and knowledge organization for the intranet at Microsoft (MSWeb) and on information architecture and online library services at Boeing. He has served on the Dublin Core Metadata Board of Trustees since its inception in 2001 and is active in ASIST. Mike is interested in public access computing, ICT in developing countries, metadata and knowledge organization, social dimensions of knowledge transfer, and large-scale information systems.

Eric Hards, Lockheed Martin Team Lead—Multimedia Services (www.ehards.com)

Eric Hards is the Lead Multimedia Engineer for Lockheed Martin Enterprise Information Systems in Orlando, Florida. For the past 10 years, he has been working with multimedia, streaming media, Web design, information architecture, usability, and Web technologies for Lockheed Martin's Internet and intranet. He is an award-winning designer and considered an industry expert in intranet design and usability. Eric holds a BS in design from the University of California at Davis and a master's degree in multimedia technology from San Francisco State. He has taught and lectured for the State University of New York and California State University. He has presented at many conferences including Streaming Media, Info Today, Intranets, Computers in Libraries, Intranets and Employee Communications Conference, Seybold, Comdex, Intracomm, and AfgaCon. Eric's design work covers everything from tradeshow booths to Web applications and includes work for such companies as Intel, IBM, Goldstar, Levi's, Sun Microsystems, Oral-B, and Loral. Eric can be reached at eric@ehards.com.

Ian Littlejohn, Partner, ICP Consulting (www.icpconsulting.co.za)

Ian Littlejohn has worked with a large number of organizations in a wide range of industries to assist with transformation and adaptation to changing business conditions through knowledge and innovation. He has a BComm from Rhodes University in Grahamstown, South Africa. Ian can be contacted at ian@icpconsulting.co.za.

Cynthia Ross Pedersen, President, Adeo Communications Corp. (www.adeo.com)

Adeo Communications Corp. is an e-business firm providing corporate and government clients with consulting and development services.

Adeo specializes in strategic planning, site and application development, and Internet marketing. Cynthia Ross Pederson developed the Web Writers' Workshop as a framework to provide planners, contributors, and writers of Web sites and intranets with the mind and skill sets to produce user-centric online content. She has been conducting workshops across North America since 1997. In 2005, Adeo Communications Corp. celebrated 10 years of innovative thinking and expert delivery. For more information on Adeo or the Web Writers' Workshop, visit www.adeo.com.

Avi Rappoport, Search Tools Consulting (www.searchtools.com)

Avi Rappoport is a leading authority on Enterprise Search Engines for Web sites, intranets, and topical portals. She combines her research in information retrieval with her years in the software industry to bring a practical and straightforward approach to Web search and navigation issues. She evaluates search engines for features, functionality, and usability, with an emphasis on finding the best way to meet end-user needs. Avi has been analyzing enterprise search engines and providing search consulting since 1998. She consults in every stage of search engine analysis, from problem-definition through product choice, implementation, and usability testing to long-term maintenance and log analysis. In addition to consulting, she is active in information architecture, usability, and information retrieval organizations and advises students from the Berkeley School of Information Management and Studies.

Craig St. Clair, TKG Consulting LLC (www.tkgconsult.com)

Craig St. Clair specializes in strategy and design for corporate portals, KM systems, content management systems, content strategy and modeling, and taxonomy and metadata design. Craig has more than 12 years of experience in strategic design and tactical implementation for a range of Web-based communications and KM projects. He has designed and deployed enterprise content management and KM solutions for Fortune 1000 companies in a variety of industry verticals including biotechnology, finance, and retail. Craig can be contacted at craig@tkgconsult.com.

Jose Claudio Terra, PhD, CEO, TerraForum Consulting, and Coordinator of the Executive MBA in Knowledge Management (KM) at the University of Sao Paulo, Brazil (www.terraforum.com.br)

Jose Claudio Terra is frequently invited to speak about knowledge management (KM) in North America, Europe, and Brazil. Recently, he has assisted various companies and institutions with their KM programs, corporate portals, and e-business projects. He has held management and executive positions in large business and media organizations such as Organic, Rogers, Globocabo, and Editoria Abril in Canada and Brazil. He played a fundamental role in pioneering the launch of the broadband Internet in Brazil and of the Excite@Home portal in Canada. He has also worked as a senior consultant for McKinsey & Company in a number of organizations and strategy projects. Terra has published widely (in English and Portuguese) on business strategy, KM, innovation, creativity, managing R&D, and industrial and technology policy. He has also written two books in English: *Corporate Portals: The Revolution in Knowledge Management* and *Winning at Collaboration Commerce.* He has also written three books in Portuguese: *The Great Business Challenge* (an enormous success in Brazil), *Knowledge Management in Small and Medium Enterprises,* and *Knowledge Management and E-learning in Practice.* He has also contributed chapters to several collections published in the U.S. and Portugal.

Debra Wallace, PhD, Partner, TKG Consulting LLC (www.tkgconsult.com)

As an organizational learning consultant, Debra Wallace draws upon her expertise in education, business, and information studies to design strategies and systems that enable organizations to increase capacity and use their knowledge capital. She is the co-author of *Leveraging Communities of Practice for Strategic Advantage* (Butterworth-Heinemann, 2003) and continues to research the role of collaboration and communities in building knowledge. Deb can be reached at deb@tkgconsult.com.

About the Editors

Mary Lee Kennedy, Partner, TKG Consulting LLC (www.tkgconsult.com)

Mary Lee Kennedy has global experience in multinational corporations, government, and higher education on all organizational levels. She specializes in the formulation and implementation of practical information and knowledge strategies that positively impact organizational and business performance. She achieves this through strategy development and business planning, product and service portfolio creation and alignment, organizational capability planning and alignment, business process improvement, cross-organizational engagement, information and knowledge integration, and information technology application. In addition to leading knowledge and information projects and operations in North America (Canada, the U.S., and Mexico), Mary Lee has also worked in the U.K., France, and China. She is an experienced practitioner with significant expertise in high technology, professional services, research, manufacturing, and academia. Mary Lee can be contacted at marylee@tkgconsult.com.

Jane Dysart, Principal, Dysart & Jones Associates (www.dysartjones.com)

Jane Dysart is a principal of Dysart & Jones Associates (D&J), an internationally recognized leader in library and information service consulting, which focuses on assisting libraries in the areas of information management, strategic and business planning, service design, organizational structuring and market positioning, conference planning, information audit, customized workshops, facilitation, and team and management coaching. Since 1992, D&J has developed a strong track record of working with information service providers in public and private sectors to develop plans, products, and services that are as visionary as they are tactical and responsive in a rapidly changing environment. Prior to founding D&J with Rebecca Jones, Jane spent 17 years as Manager, Information Resources, for Royal Bank of Canada. Jane is the former editor of the newsletter *Intranets*. She is Conference Program Director for Internet Librarian, Computers in Libraries, and KMWorld & Intranets, and she teaches at the University of Toronto, Faculty of Information Studies, and is faculty for their Managing Information Enterprises Certificate Program. Jane can be contacted at jane@dysartjones.com.

Index

A

ABC Canada Literacy Foundation, 149
Abell, Angela, 34
Abels, Eileen, 34
access
  to content, 173
  Open Source software, 12
  search engines and, 211–212
accountability
  in communities of practice, 112
  governance and, 79–81
action learning sets, 51
actionable information
  delivery of, 25
  on intranets, 39
ad-hoc session analysis, 224–225
Adobe Acrobat files, 157
After Action Reviews, 52
Agile Computing, 11, 12, 67
alignment, description of, 5
Allen, Nate, 97
alliances, choice of, 105*t*
allies
  characteristics of, 80*t*
  governance between, 80
  information architecture roles of, 199
American Library Association (ALA), 50
American Society for Information Science and Technology (ASIST), 52, 184–185
"An Information Management and Technology Blueprint for the NSW," 36
Anderson, Chris, 11–12
AON Biennial Survey of 1995, 37
APIs (application programmer interfaces), 211
architectural design, 189–190
"Architecture of Information" (Wurman), 184
archiving practices, 29, 44. *see also* repositories
Argus Associates, 189
Arial font, 244
Aristotle, 98
Ark Group, 117
Armstrong, Charles, 108
artificial intelligence, 28
Arugs Associates, 184
Asilomar Institute for Information Architecture (AIfIA), 185, 195. *see also* Information Architecture Institute
Ask.com, 207
asset management, 129, 139–146
audiences. *see also* customers; stakeholders; users
  analysis of, 204–205
  communication with, 63
  content management and, 135, 145
  for corporate portals, 177–178
  definition of, 57*t*
  protection of, 85
  user-centric writing, 56, 151–153
Australia
"An Information Management and Technology Blueprint for the NSW," 36
Government Information Management Office, 204, 205*f*
authoring. *see also* Web writing
  bulleted points, 156, 157, 162, 166
  collaborative, 38
  content creation and, 45
  content format choices, 157–158
  effective writing styles, 151

authoring (*cont.*)
- language issues, 149–151
- page design and, 235–238
- paragraph length, 156
- sentence length, 156
- templates, 158–159
- user-centric writing, 151–152
- "Webby" material, 157–158
- word size, 156

authors, content organization by, 135–138

B

banners, 234
Bazille, Frederic, 121
Bell, Gordon, 39
benchmarking, 52, 59
Benkler, Yochai, 24
Berners-Lee, Tim, 34, 229
Bertlesmann site, 220, 220*f*
boards, roles of, 84–85, 94, 95
Bracke, Paul J., 186, 187*f*
Brancheau, James C., 184
branding, 19, 127, 158
The Bridge on the River Kwai (Broulle), 99
British Computer Society, 51
broker pages, 153–154, 155
Bruner, C., 98
bulleted points, 156, 157, 162, 166
business cases
- core processes, 177
- functional specifications and, 147
- information architecture integration with, 197
- information strategy and, 44
- intranet initiatives and, 30

business drivers, 35–36
business process analysis
- during the control stage, 95
- feature tracking, 62*t*
- function tracking, 62*t*
- intranet design and, 61–62
- resurgence of, 16

Byrne, Tony, 193, 197

C

call centers, procedures for, 163–164
Campos, 52
Canada
- ABC Canada Literacy Foundation, 149
- "Informational Assets in the Government of Alberta," 37
- International Development Research Centre (IDRC), 103
- University of Manitoba, 100
- University of Toronto, 114
- York Region District School Board, 114

capability, focus of, 21
Capability Maturity Model Integration suite, 196
career stages, knowledge transfer and, 7
Cascading Style Sheets, 236, 243
categorization, content management and, 137–138
Caterpillar, 115
centralized repository
- benefits of, 140–141
- challenges, 141
- implementation, 139–140
- models for, 139–141, 140*f*
- successful implementations, 141

change
- business drivers of, 35–36
- challenge of, 5
- continuous improvement, 69
- informational drivers of, 37–38
- life-long learning and, 50
- management of, 74–75
- opportunities for, 61
- organizational cultures and, 89–90
- powered by context, 26
- private sector drivers of, 37
- public sector drivers of, 36–37
- speed of, 29
- technology disruption and, 24

change control, 94
Chartered Institute for Personal Development, U.K., 51
Chartered Institute of Library and Information Professionals (CILIP), U.K., 50–51
cheating. *see* collaboration, inappropriate
chocolate cake analogy, 154–156

Choo, Chun Wei, 8, 42, 43, 118
Christensen, Clayton, 24
Chuck Close Prints (Sultan and Shiff), 107
Clarica Life Insurance Co., 116
click-through analysis, 224
clients, expectations of, 20, 35–36, 230
Close, Chuck, 107
CMPros, 34–35
co-opetition, definition, 113
coaches, professional development and, 52
coalitions, choice of, 105*t*
Cognitive Edge, 12
Cognos, 12
collaboration
  50-Foot Rule, 97
  benefits of, 121–122
  common goals and, 100, 103–104
  communication and, 102
  communities of practice and, 97–123
  community linkages, 105*t*
  content creation and, 45
  during the control stage, 95
  corporate portals and, 176–177
  critical factors for success, 102–104
  critical mass, 101
  the dark side of, 115–116
  definitions of, 98–99
  elements of, 99–102
  empathy and, 104
  inappropriate, 100
  individuals in, 8
  intranet spaces for, 10
  language and, 28
  levels of, 104–105
  management support for, 101
  maturity model for, 104–105
  mutual benefit in, 101
  openness and, 104
  organizational cultures and, 36, 92*t*
  within organizations, 7
  potential of, 106–107
  process of, 100
  rules of engagement for, 101
  skills required for, 104
  social computing and, 38
  stakeholder awareness of, 103
  team rewards, 101
  trust and, 100–101, 102
  workflows and, 100
collections, information architecture and, 44
collective knowledge, as an asset, 6
color, use of, 245–249, 246*f*, 247*f*, 248*f*
column size, 234
comfort zones, stepping out of, 52
committees. *see also* steering committees
  editorial, 28
  roles of, 85, 94, 95
communication
  breakdowns, 61
  business development, 46
  categories within, 45–46
  collaboration and, 102
  in communities of practice, 120
  interdepartmental, 41
  intranet usefulness and, 22
  plain language movement, 149–151
  project management and, 68
  with stakeholders, 70
  Web writing, 156
Communispace, 117
communities
  building of, 7
  characteristics of, 108, 109–116
  collaboration and, 97–123
  the dark side of, 115–116
  linkages, 105*t*
  online, 161–162
  virtual, 109
communities of practice
  accountability within, 112
  capabilities of, 118, 120
  collaboration within, 112
  common purpose in, 110
  composition of, 110
  content, 118, 120
  dark side of, 115–116

communities of practice (*cont.*)
definition of, 107–109
function of, 110
the future of, 116
information architecture and, 183
knowledge generation by, 112
policies, 119–120
procedures, 119–120
resources, 118, 120–121
roles of, 118, 119
self-governance, 112
strategy of, 118–119
vision of, 118–119
Community Based Collaborations (Hogue), 105*t*
company news, 135
CompanyCommand, 108, 111
competencies
capability and, 21
identification of, 63
in information architecture, 199
for information professionals, 33–35
learning and, 55
organizational cultures and, 92*t*
performance and, 106
self-assessment, 199
Web writing, 160
Competencies for Information Professionals of the 21st Century (SLA), 33
competitive intelligence, 46
The Complete Idiot's Guide to Knowledge Management (Rumizen), 110
compliance content, 166
conferences, learning and, 51
"Connecting the U.K. The Digital Strategy," 36
consortium benchmarking, 52
"contagion" stage, 82, 93
content
access to, 173
acquisition, 45
analysis of, 192, 204
announcement-style, 145
audits, 134–139
consumption of, 130–131, 132, 138, 147
creation of, 45, 49, 50, 158–159
descriptions of, 135
design elements, 227
development of, 135
end-user experience, 227–250
format choices, 157–158
intellectual control over, 129–130
inventories, 134–138
layout of, 239–242
library-style, 145
life cycles, 139
migration initiatives, 141
online, 153–154
prioritization of, 65–67
production of, 130–134, 138
quality of, 211
relevancy, 160–161
resource-style, 145
scalable, 154–156
search for, 210–211
selection of, 94, 128, 135
storage of, 139, 143
structure determination, 154
tools for, 158–150
content management
categorization schemes, 137–138
centralized repository models, 139–141
CMPros on, 34–35
control over content, 129–130
during the control stage, 94
decentralized behaviors and, 39
decentralized repositories, 141–143
duplications and, 39
enterprise information architecture and, 44
history of, 129
implementation and, 63*t*
information overload and, 28–29
for intranets, 125–148
organizational change and, 147
reasons for, 126–129
redundancy and, 39
roles for, 28
tools for, 38
updating sites, 128

content management systems (CMS), 175, 176
content mapping, 139
context
  analysis of, 192
  change powered by, 26
continuous improvement, 69
continuous partial attention, 6–7
control
  establishment of, 83
  organizational cultures and, 92*t*
  over content, 129–130
control stage, 93–95
controlled vocabularies, 204–205. *see also* taxonomies
Cooper, Alan, 20, 21*f*
cooperation, choice of, 105*t*
copyright, 212
corporate portals
  adoption of, 178
  assessment of, 171–180
  case study, 178–180
  collaboration and, 176–177
  concept of, 170–171
  content management and, 176
  deployment of, 177–180
  functionality, 172–173
  future of, 181
  information broadcasts, 175
  integration of applications, 175–176
  intranets and, 169–182
  Microsoft's, 193
  origin, 171–172
  perspectives on, 171–180, 172*t*
  project management and, 176–177
  re-design, 179–180
  standardization and, 180–181
  use of, 177–180
corporate standards, 45
Courier font, 244
credibility, 59, 68. *see also* trust
cross-departmental data, 25
cultural diversity. *see also* organizational cultures
  e-learning and, 27
  forms of governance and, 84
  intranet localization and, 26–27
  organizational complexity and, 5
curation, 45
customer relationship management systems (CRMS), 37, 175
customers. *see also* audiences; stakeholders
characteristics of, 80*t*
communities of, 117
governance between, 80–81
needs analysis, 57*t*
customization. *see also* personalization
corporate portals and, 173–174
"my pages" concept, 174
template use and, 82–83

D

Damsgaard, Jan, 81
dashboards, 25
data analysis, 38, 49, 131
data collection, 45
data management
  cross-departmental, 25
  data structure and, 6
  document storage and, 6
  enterprise information architecture and, 44
  number crunching, 26
  text crunching, 26
data presentation, 44
datasets, size of, 10
Davenport, Thomas, 9, 40
David Kolb on Experiential Learning, 52
decentralized repositories
  approach to, 141–143
  benefits, 142
  challenges, 142
  requirements, 142
  successful implementations, 142–143
decision-making. *see also* governance
  collaboration and, 106
  information exploitation/use and, 46
  intranet function in, 9

decision-making (*cont.*)
organizational perspective in, 42
paths for, 63
prioritization and, 65
rights of, 63
rule-based software for, 12
transparency in, 91
DeLong, Dave, 24
departmental information, 137
dependencies, confirmation of, 65
deployment, 69, 174
Dervin, Brenda, 8
design
basic, 235–238
column size, 234
elements of, 227
fonts, 241, 243–248
graphics, 234
information architecture and, 189–190, 231–235
intranet development and, 230–231
size and, 239–242
sketches in, 238–242
type faces, 243–248
use of color, 245–249, 246*f*, 247*f*, 248*f*
use of lines, 239–242
use of shapes, 239–242
use of white space, 242–243
visual scanning and, 235*f*
desirability, definition of, 21
Desk Set (movie), analogy, 125, 146–147
digital libraries, management of, 39
disposal issues, 45
Dixon, Nancy M., 108
documents
life cycles, 37, 139
storage issues, 6
"The Downside of Communities of Practice" (Wenger), 115–116
Dr Foster Holdings LLP, 38
Dr Foster Intelligence, 38
Dragoon, Alice, 101

E

e-business support, 46
e-information job market, 33
e-learning, 27, 46
e-mail campaigns, 116
early adoption
benefits of, 197
biases related to, 40
change and, 108
learning from, 76
The Economist, on innovation, 24
Economist Intelligence Unit, 25
editing, content creation and, 45
education, 17, 95. *see also* learning; professional development
electronic document and records management systems (EDRMS), 37
electronic resources, management of, 43–44
Elements of User Experience (Garrett), 188*f*, 193
Eli Lilly, 115
Eliot, T.S., 121
empathy, collaboration and, 104
employees. *see also* human resource management
benefits, 135
expectations of, 35–36
retention of, 24
empowerment, intranets and, 19
end-users. *see* users
energy industry, 6
English language, 41
Enterprise 2.0 Technologies, 40
enterprise information architecture (EIA), 193
categories within, 43*f*, 44
checkpoints for, 204*f*
roadmap for, 194
search log analysis, 223
search needs, 223
enterprise information systems, 184
enterprise suites, 180–181
entertainment, expectations of, 234
Environmental Protection Agency (EPA), 36
environments. *see also* organizational cultures
continuous change, 69

during the control stage, 94
governance and, 73
intranet implementation and, 61
intranet integration into, 83
Eureka community of service technicians, 115
Evans, Jeffrey, E., 7
Evernden, Elaine, 185, 186*t*
Evernden, Roger, 185, 186*t*
Excite, 170
executives, senior
information overload, 25
organizational perspective of, 42
views on intranets, 3
expectation management
prioritization and, 65
stakeholder expectations, 57–58
under-promising, 68
experience gaps, 57
experiential learning, 51*f*, 52
Extended Information Architecture, 187
extranets, description of, 23

F

faceted classification, 204
Factiva, 38
Fallows, Debra, 39, 41
FAQs (Frequently Asked Questions), 135
Farnum, Chris, 189
features, prioritization of, 65–67
FedEx, 219
Feldman, Susan, 208
50-Foot Rule, 97
file formats, search issues, 128, 210
file storage, 128
financial-based assessments, 30
findability
basis of, 5
need for, 203–204
flexible creativity, 39
Flickr, 12
folksonomies, 12
format control, 39, 161
Forrester Group, 25, 39
full versions, of content, 157–158
functionality, prioritization of, 65–67
"The Future of the Internet II" (Fallows), 41

G

gap analyses
of content production, 134
process change and, 62–64
Garrett, Jesse James, 187–188, 188*f*, 193
Gilman Group, 52
globalization
diversification and, 26
as a drivers of change, 37
goals, collaboration and, 100, 103–104, 110
Go.com, 170
gold rush analogy, 126, 129
Google
change and, 12
consumer portals, 170
impact of, 190, 207
PageRank system, 216
search technologies, 27
Google Desktop, 1
Google Scholar, 97
governance
accountability and, 79–81
categories within, 45
in communities of practice, 110, 112
consistency and, 96
during the control stage, 94
definitions of, 73–74
education and, 95
forms of, 84–86
implementation of, 81–84
industry triggers, 77–78
infostructure teams and, 48
initiating a structure of, 74–78
in the integration phase, 95
internal triggers, 75–76
intranet adoption and, 84*t*
intranet usefulness and, 22, 28
ongoing, 74
organizational cultures and, 86–91
overlap, 74
Partnering Philosophy, 79

governance (*cont.*)
  redesign and, 96
  relationships and, 79–82
  roles and responsibilities, 91–95
  scope of, 78–79
  societal triggers, 78
  stakeholders and, 81
  timing and, 78–79
  triggers, 75–78, 75*f*
grammar checking, 162
graphics. *see also* visualization
  design elements, 227
  implementation and, 63*t*
  intranet design and, 234
Groff, Todd R., 102
guidelines, function of, 86, 165–166

H

H1 tags, 217
Hall, Hazel, 99
Halliburton, 115
Harvard University search page, 220, 221*f*
headlines, 155
healthcare sector, 38
Hepburn, Katharine, 125
heuristics, 216–217
Higgins, Christy Confetti, 198
Hogue, Teresa, 104, 105*t*
home pages
  headlines for, 155
  MiamiDade.gov, 241*f*, 242*f*
  moving information to, 233*f*
  outline for, 237*f*
HTML forms, 213
HTTP URL queries, 213
human dynamics, 5, 24
Human Genome Project, 121
human relations information, 135
human resource management
  information on the intranet, 233–234
  intranets and, 4
  tools for, 175
hybrid repositories
  benefits, 145–146
  challenges, 146
  requirements, 145
  successful implementations, 146

I

IBM, 26
ICT. *see* information and communication technology (ICT)
implementation
  of a centralized repository, 139–140, 140*f*
  communication roles, 63*t*
  "contagion," 82
  information design, 63*t*
  information roles, 63*t*
  of intranets, 55–71
  project management steps, 67*f*
  responsibilities in, 63*t*
  of search, 209–225
  steps in, 55–56
"Implementing the Federal Enterprise Architecture at the EPA," 36
indexes, 178, 212, 223
individuals, collaboration and, 8
industries, governance triggers, 77
informatics, 46
information
  acquisition of, 48, 49
  actionable, 39
  delivery, 50
  design, 63*t*
  exploitation/use categories, 46
  external, 45
  faceted classification, 204
  findability, 203–204
  for home pages, 233*f*
  identification of sources, 64
  internal, 45
  life cycles, 37
  need for, 208
  networked processes, 40
  organization of, 190
  overload, 6, 25, 27–29, 36
  responsibility for, 53–54
  ROT (Redundant, Outmoded and Trivial), 211
  searching for, 41
  sharing of, 99, 100–101
  software tools, 37–38
  strategy categories, 43*f*, 44
information and communication technology (ICT), 35, 36

information architects, requirements, 201*f*
Information Architects (Wurman), 184
Information Architecture for the World Wide Web (Rosenfeld and Morville), 184, 194
information architecture (IA), 183–206
 architectural design and, 189–190
 blogs, 206
 checklist for success, 204
 description of, 34, 183–184
 education for, 200, 202
 enterprise-related, 44
 framework for, 232–235
 future developments, 195–198
 history of, 184–185, 186*t*
 implementation and, 63*t*
 information organization and, 190
 Information Service Group, Microsoft, 199*f*
 infostructure teams and, 48
 intranets and, 185–189, 231–235
 job descriptions, 200
 key components of, 189–192
 labeling of elements, 191
 lessons learned, 203–205
 lists, 206
 managing for, 198–202
 measurement of results, 196
 navigation issues, 190
 organizations, 206
 people resources, 205–206
 process of, 192–193
 searches and, 190–191
 skills need by, 199
 staffing for, 198–202
 taxonomies in, 191–192
 Web 2.0 and, 11
 Web Sites, 206
 Web Sites Checklist, 205*f*
Information Architecture Institute (IAI), 34, 183. *see also* Asilomar Institute for Information Architecture (AIfIA)
Information Architecture Summit, 52, 184–185
information asset management, 129, 139–146
Information Centre for Health and Social Care, 38
information flow, 36, 147
information management
 dataset size, 10
 enterprise information architecture and, 44
 history of, 6–9
 knowledge Management and, 33–34
 nature of, 9–10
 prioritization in, 10
 stakeholders in, 47, 47*t*
Information Management Journal, 189
information management systems, 4–5
information professionals
 business drivers, 35–36
 capabilities, 53
 description of, 3–4
 early adoption bias, 40
 job titles, 31–32
 market analysis for, 32–33
 the marketplace for, 31–35
 in multi-disciplinary teams, 53
 organizational complexity and, 4–6
 responsibilities of, 41–46
 roles of, 48*f*
 team building and, 46–49
 as translators, 42*f*
Web page design b y, 227
Information Service Group, Microsoft, 198, 199*f*
Information Services National Training Organization (ISNTO), U.K., 48
Information Society, formation of, 106
information systems. *see* technology
information technology information, 136
Information Worker Productivity Council, 11

"Informational Assets in the Government of Alberta," Canada, 37
infostructure teams, 48–49
infrastructure
- changing, 29
- content management and, 29
- decentralized behaviors and, 39
- development of, 147
- gold rush analogy, 129

initiation phase roles, 92–93
The Inmates Are Running the Asylum (Cooper), 21*f*
InnoCentive community, Eli Lili, 115
innovation
- collaboration and, 121–122
- gold rush analogy, 129
- success of organizations and, 24

"Innovation and Knowledge Creation," 43*f*
integration phase
- aspects of, 83
- governance and, 95–96
- roles and responsibilities during, 95

Intelliseek, 38
interdependencies, intranet-created, 64–65
interface design, 94, 230
internal information, sourcing of, 45
International Adult Literacy Survey (IALS), 149
International Development Research Centre (IDRC), Canada, 103
Internet
- commercial sites, 228
- designing for, 228–230
- impact survey, 41
- intranet compared to, 19–20, 23
- investment priorities for, 41
- via intranet environments, 29

interviews
- narrative techniques, 131
- needs analysis and, 83
- questions used, 131
- sample size, 131
- script construction, 132
- with users, 130–134

intranet adoption curve, 81, 82*f*
"Intranet Design Annual 2006," 18
intranets
- adoption of, 81–82, 82*f*, 84*t*
- component analysis, 56, 61
- conceptual framework, 17–19, 18*f*
- content management for, 125–148
- corporate portals, 169–182
- current state of, 17–23
- customization, 137
- definition of, 2, 15–16
- design of, 227–250
- development of, 22, 126–129
- evolution of, 15–16
- as filing cabinets, 157
- future of, 23–30
- goals of, 1–3
- implementation, 55–71
- information architecture and, 185–189
- management governance, 74
- ownership of, 23
- potential of, 17
- rebuilding in portals, 179
- requirements for search, 208–209
- searches, 207–226
- trends, 38–41
- unconnected, 127–128, 127*f*
- writing for, 149–167

inventories, case study, 135–138

J

Jones, Thomas P., 102

K

keyword tags, 217
KM Europe, 52
KMWorld, 52
The Knowing Organization (Chun Wei Choo), 8, 118
knowledge
- generation of, 112
- organizational, 43*f*
- sharing of, 6–9, 24, 99, 101 (*see also* information, sharing)
- transfer of, 7, 24

Knowledge Board, 52
Knowledge Management (KM)
emergence of, 33
information management and, 33–34
information professionals in, 32
sense-making theories and, 8
Kolb, David, 52
Kouzes, James M., 106, 122
Kurzweil Technologies, 12

L

labeling
of elements, 191
navigation and, 205
taxonomies and, 205
language
barriers, 57
e-learning and, 27
English usage, 41
intranet localization and, 26–27
organizational complexity and, 5
partnerships and, 28
plain language movement, 149–151
of queries, 213
style guides and, 158
word length issues, 150
lateral transfers, 52
Lave, Jean, 107
leadership, community-level, 108–109
leadership communication, 26
learning
experiential, 117–121
forms of, 50–52, 51*f*
intranet function in, 9
legacy content, 160–161
legal content, 166
legislation, 45
Lelic, Simon, 117
Leonard, Dorothy, 10
life-long learning, 50
links, problems with, 210
Lipnack, Jessica, 97
literacy, of users, 149–151
Literacy Collaborative, 114
localization, intranet, 26–27
location-specific programs, 136
The Long Tail, impact of, 11–12
Lovitt, Steve, 82–83
Lycos, 170

M

Macworld, 2
Maloney, Krisellen, 186, 187*f*
management governance, 74
March, Salvatore T., 184
market behavior, assessment of, 21
market research, 20, 21
marketing, communication and, 46
Martin, Joanne, 87
Massachusetts Institute of Technology, 34
McAfee, Andrew, 40
McConnell, Jane, 2, 3
McDermott, Richard, 108
mentored learning, 51*f*, 52
mergers-and-acquisitions, 77
metadata, 10, 27, 28, 173, 204, 212, 226
Meyer, David E., 7
Meyerson, Debra, 87
MiamiDade.gov, 241, 241*f*, 242*f*
Microsoft
MSN, 170
MSWeb, 193, 197, 198–199
organizational structure, 197
Word tools, 159
Modernists, methods used by, 8
Monet, Claude, 121
monitoring, control stage, 94
Monster.com, 31–32
Moore, Geoffrey, 24, 91, 92*t*
Morville, Peter, 184, 189, 193, 194, 203–204, 211
motivation, 92*t*
MSN, 170
MSWeb, 193, 197, 198–199
multimedia formats, 10, 50. *see also* visualization
multitasking, environment of, 6–7
"My Pages" concept, 174
MyLifeBits Project Web site (Bell), 39

N

naming. *see* labeling
narrative techniques, 131, 132–133
National Cancer Institute site, 204
National Institute for Literacy, 149
National Network for Collaboration, 104
native files, 157
Naturalizers, methods used by, 8
navigation
  buttons, 239
  information architecture and, 190, 194, 204
  labeling and, 205
  menus, 239
  sketches in design of, 239
  tabs, 239
needs analysis
  business-related, 76
  customer, 57*t*
  interviews and, 83
  search requirements, 208–209
networking, 51, 105*t*
New South Wales, Australia, 36
Newell, Sue, 27
Newton, Isaac, 8
Nielsen Norman Group, 18
Nonaka, Ikujiro, 10
number crunching, 26

O

objectives, organizational complexity and, 5
online communities, 51, 161–162. *see also* communities; communities of practice
online content, 153–154, 162–166
Open Source software, 12
openness, collaboration and, 104
operating system obsolescence, 222–223
operational planning, 44
opportunities for improvement, 94. *see also* quality management
organizational cultures. *see also* cultural diversity; environments
  case studies, 88–91
  collaboration and, 98
  governance and, 86–91
  motivators within, 92*t*
  paradigms of, 87–88
  sharing and, 99
organizational dynamics, 40
organizational knowledge, 43*f*
Organizational Studies (Meyerson and Martin), 87, 87*t*
organizations
  collective knowledge, 6
  complexity of, 4–6
  environment within, 61
  flattening of, 7
  impact of hierarchies within, 40
  networking of, 36
  policies of, 85
  varying cultures within, 16
out-of-date content, migration of, 141
outsourcing, 36
over-delivering, 68
ownership, 23, 85, 95, 199

P

packaging, communication and, 46. *see also* presentation
PageRank system, 216
paragraphs, length of, 156
Partnering for Success Guide (U.S. Army Material Command), 79
Partnering Philosophy, 79
partners, 79, 80*t*, 105*t*
PDF files, 157, 158
PeopleSoft, 205
perception, integration and, 83
performance measures
  cross-unit, 25
  governance and, 74
  information architecture and, 196
  productivity and, 30, 228–229
  project management and, 69
  search log metrics, 223–224
  search query analysis, 224
personalization. *see also* customization
  of content, 17, 26

of corporate portals, 169
corporate portals and, 173–174
members-only areas, 176–177
tag creation and, 26
personas, building of, 20–21
Pew Internet and American Life project, 39, 41
pilot projects, 119
Plain Language Action and Information Network (PLAIN), 150
Plain Language Association International, 150
plain language movement, 149–151
policies
as content, 159–162
creation of, 85
sponsors and, 92
Popadiuk, Silvio, 42, 43
Popper, Karl, 8
port 80, 213
portal infrastructure, 147
portals. *see also* corporate portals
concept of, 170–171
design of, 232
focus areas for, 174
presentation layers, 140*f*, 144*f*
rebuilding intranets in, 179
software vendors, 171–172
Posner, Barry Z., 106, 122
Post-Modernist, methods used by, 8
practice, integration and, 83
presentation
of data, 44
end-user experience, 227–250
infostructure teams and, 49
results pages, 218
user-modified, 173
prioritization
during the "contagion" stage, 93
during the control stage, 94
project management and, 65–67
sponsors and, 92
privacy, loss of, 41
problem statements, 60
procedures
at-a-glance, 165–166
for a call center, 163–164
as content, 159–161
intranet placement of, 166
online, 162–166
process design, 44
procurement, of external information, 45
product design, components of, 20–22, 21*f*
product requirements, 21*f*
product support, 46
productivity measures, 30, 228–229
professional associations, 50–51
professional development, 44, 49–52
professional learning communities, 114
project governance, 73–74
project management
during the "contagion" stage, 93
corporate portals and, 176–177
governance and, 73–74
high-level steps in, 67*f*
iterative processes, 68
objectives and, 60
outcomes measures, 69
prioritization, 65–67
problem statements, 60
resource management and, 67–68
role of communication in, 68
team support, 41
vision statements and, 59
protocols, collaboration and, 101
Prusak, Laurence, 9
publication categories, 45–46
publishing, 10, 19. *see also* authoring; editing, content creation and; presentation

Q

quality management, 61, 94, 161
queries
case of, 213
frequency distribution, 225*f*
no matches for, 215–216
script, 213
search log analysis, 224
stemming, 214
quotation marks, 215

R

RAIDs, 222
Rajan, Amin, 50, 52
Rand, Paul, 229
ranking algorithms, 191
re-purposing, communication and, 46
readability, page design and, 235–238
records, content creation and, 45
regulatory controls
  collaboration and, 101
  compliance content, 166
  content management and, 29
  globalization and, 37
  information governance and, 45
  legal content, 166
relationships
  in communities of practice, 119–120
  matrix of levels for, 104
relevancy
  algorithms, 216
  ranking, 216
  trust in, 59
repositories. *see also* archiving practices
  centralized, 139–141
  centralized models, 139–141, 140*f*
  decentralized, 142–143
  hybrid approach to, 143–146, 144*f*
  unconnected, 128
reputation management, 37
resource management
  collaboration and, 101
  during the "contagion" stage, 93
  project management and, 67–68
  sponsors and, 92
results pages
  dates, 222
  font sizes, 222
  interactive interfaces, 219
  items on, 219–222
  lists, 219
  presentation, 218
  URLs on, 221
retrieval, of search results, 215
return on investment (ROI), 30, 161, 207–208
risk analysis, 45
risk management, 37
robot crawlers, 210
Rosenfeld, Louis, 184, 189, 192, 194, 195, 211
ROT (Redundant, Outmoded and Trivial), 211
Rubenstein, Joshua, 7
Rumizen, Melissie Clemmons, 110

S

Saint-Onge, Hubert, 108, 109, 110, 113
Sarbanes-Oxley ruling, 78
Scarborough, Harry, 27
Scheepers, Rens, 81
schemas, 204–205
Schuster, Larry, 184
screen configurations, 26
search engines
  access control and, 211–212
  HTTP server on port 80, 213
  information architecture and, 190–191
  information overload and, 27–28
  maintenance of, 222
  ranking algorithms, 191
  research-oriented, 212
  security and, 211–212
  server updates, 222–223
  software updates, 222–223
  test, 210
search functions
  ad-hoc session analysis, 224–225
  click-through analysis, 224
  content quality and, 211
  enterprise information needs, 223
  finding content, 210–211
  footers, 218–219
  handling queries, 213
  headers, 218–219
  implementation, 209–225
  indexes, 178, 212, 223
  interactive results interfaces, 219
  interfaces, 213

intranet, 207–226
matching, 215
metrics, 223–224
no matches for, 215–216
page design, 218
process of, 209*f*
query frequency distribution, 225*f*
query languages, 213
quote marks, 215
relevance algorithms, 216
relevance heuristics, 216–217
relevance ranking, 216
requirements for, 208–209
results pages, 218, 219–222
retrieval, 215
return-on-investment, 207–208
ROT information, 211
spell checking, 214
stemming, 212–213
stop words, 212
suggestions, 217–218
synonym expansion, 214
tags, 217
traffic, 223–224
usability, 213
search log analysis, 223
search research, 46
security
information governance and, 45
intranet issues, 20
members-only areas, 176–177
search engines and, 211–212
self-directed learning, 51–52, 51*f*, 52–52
self-governance, 108, 112
self-management, 110, 112
semantic Web debate, 28
sense-making, 8
sentences, length of, 156
serendipity, managing for, 9
servers, updates, 222–223
service-based organizations, 6
Service Oriented Architecture Protocol (SOAP), 25–26
Simple Object Access Protocol (SOAP), 25–26
situation-gap-use" triangle, 8–9
Six Sigma, 8
sketches, use of, 238–242, 240*f*
skills, intranet success and, 22
Skype, costs of, 1
Skyrme, David J., 106
snippets, 157, 162
Snowden, Dave, 9
Snyder, William M., 108
SOAP (Simple Object Access Protocol, Service Oriented Architecture Protocol), 25–26
social computing, 38
Society for Technical Communications (STC), 202, 203*f*
software
collaborative tools, 38
as information drivers, 37–38
updates, 222–223
Software Engineering Institute, 196
Solomon, Marc, 197, 198, 204, 204*f*
sourcing, 45, 135
Special Libraries Association (SLA), 33, 50
spell checking, 162, 214
sponsors
during the control stage, 94
governance and, 81–82
during the integration phase, 95
roles and responsibilities, 92–93
stakeholders. *see also* audiences; users
collaborative success and, 103
communication with, 63
in communities, 113
engagement of, 68–69
governance structure and, 81
governance triggers, 76
information architecture roles of, 199
intranet design and, 231
in intranet implementation, 56
language of, 70
scope of governance and, 79
Stamp, Jeffrey, 97
standardization. *see also* guidelines, function of
corporate portals and, 180–181
page design and, 230

standards. *see also* quality management
corporate, 45
creation of, 85–86
external, 85
quality and, 61
sponsors and, 92
Stanford University Search Page, 219*f*
steering committees, 94, 95
stemming, 212–213, 214
Stone, Linda, 7
stop words, 212
storage
of content, 139, 143
document, 6
of files, 128
storytelling, 120. *see also* narrative techniques
strategic linkages, inter-unit, 26
strategic planning
boards of directors and, 84–85
information architecture integration with, 197
information strategy and, 44
stretch assignments, 52
style guides, 158–159
success, 58. *see also* expectation management
summaries, 157
Sun Microsystems Sun Library, 198
surveys, of users, 130–134
Swan, Jacky, 27
Swap, Walter C., 10
synonym expansion, 214
syntax, 215. *see also* language

T

tabs, navigation, 239
tags, 26, 217
Takeuchi, Hirotake, 10
task forces, 85, 94
taught learning, 50–51, 51*f*
taxonomies. *see also* controlled vocabularies
case study, 135–138
construction of, 94, 135, 205
faceted labeling and, 205
information architecture and, 191–192
integration of, 205
intranet design and, 39
for policy content, 161
team building, 46–49, 68, 93
team development, 44
teamwork, 41, 159
technology
as an information driver, 37–38
collaboration and, 101
corporate portals and, 171–172
desktop applications and, 29
disruption by, 24
human control of, 41
implementation and, 63*t*
integration and, 83
intranet development and, 20, 39–40
nature of, 11–12
opportunities for change, 61
organizational function and, 23–24
roles of, 125
Web design and, 232
technology plans, 23
templates, 82–83, 157, 158–159
text crunching, 26
TF-IDF (Term Frequency—Inverse Document Frequency), 216
TFPL, Ltd., 32–33, 34, 47, 48*f*
Times font, 244
title tags, 217
TKG Consulting, 20
tools for content, 158–150
topic-at-a-glance content, 157
Tracy, Spencer, 125
training, 69, 101. *see also* education; professional development
"Transformational Government: Enabled by Technology," UK, 36
trust, 100–101, 102, 117
type faces, 243–248

U

U.S. Army, 111
under-promising, 68

University of Manitoba, Canada, 100
University of Southampton, 34
University of Toronto, Canada, 114
upcoming events, 136
URLs, 221
usability standards, 39
usability studies
in building of personas, 20
for the Internet, 229
intranet design and, 27
for procedure content, 166
usage, measures of, 59
user assessments, 132–134
user-centric content, 169
user-centric writing, 151–152, 162–163
User Experience, 187
user testing, 162
users. *see also* stakeholders
behavior of, 42
demographics, 131
desirability and, 21
education of, 17
elements of experience of, 188*f*, 193
expectations of, 20, 230
interaction with content, 17
interviews with, 130–134
literacy issues, 149–151
personalization for, 26
product requirements, 21*f*
requirements of, 76
satisfaction of, 229
skills needed, 63
surveys of, 130–134
synthesized profiles of, 131
ultimate experience for, 227–250

V

Vanguard, 205
viability, focus of, 21
virtual working, content creation and, 45
vision, governance triggers, 77
vision statements
definitions of success and, 59
governance triggers, 76
team inputs, 64
visual scanning, 235*f*
visualization
design and, 237–242
graphics and, 234
of information, 32
intranet delivery of, 25
tools for, 25–26
use of color, 245–249
VoIP-enabled communication, 1

W

w3 On Demand Workplace (IBM), 26
Wall Street Journal, 243
Wallace, Debra, 109, 110, 113
Web. *see* World Wide Web
Web 2.0, 4, 11, 37
Web crawling, 178
Web Science programs, 34
Web Sites Checklist, 205*f*
Web Writer's Workshop, 150
Web writing. *see also* authoring
content format choices, 157–158
size and tone, 156
skills for, 160
style guides, 158
templates, 158–159
user-centric, 162–163
Webby Award for Government sites, 204
"Webby" material, 157–158, 163–166
Wenger, Etienne, 107, 108, 109, 113, 115–116
White, Martin, 188–189
white space, use of, 242–243
Wikipedia, 12
wikis, 40
Williams, Barbara, 76
Wired Magazine, 11
words, choice of, 156
work design, 4, 41
workflow
collaboration and, 100
in content production, 134
embedded information and, 4
sharing and, 5
workflow analysis
intranet design and, 28, 61–62
prioritization of work and, 65–67

workforce diversity, 26–27
workplace of the future, 25
World Summit on the Information Society, 106
World Wide Web
  broker pages, 153–154, 155
  design sketches, 238–242
  fonts used, 241, 243–248, 245*f*
  home pages, 155, 233*f*, 237*f*, 241*f*, 242*f*
  intranet complexity *versus*, 152–153
  page content, 151–154
  page redesign, 241
  research for design, 237–238
  searching, 207
  technology and, 232
  type faces used on, 243–248
  use of color on pages, 245–249, 245*f*, 246*f*, 247*f*
  use of white space on pages, 242–243
  writing for, 157–160
Wurman, Richard Saul, 184

X

Xerox, 115

Y

Yahoo!, 170, 207
York Region District School Board, Ontario, Canada, 114

Z

Zachmann Framework, 205
"zipf" distribution, 224

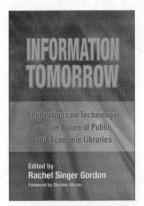

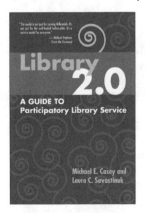

Computerization Movements and Technology Diffusion

From Mainframes to Ubiquitous Computing

Edited by Margaret S. Elliott and Kenneth L. Kraemer

"Computerization movement" (CM), as first articulated by Rob Kling, refers to a special kind of social and technological movement that promotes the adoption of computing within organizations and society. Here, editors Margaret S. Elliott and Kenneth L. Kraemer and more than two dozen noted scholars trace the successes and failures of CMs from the mainframe and PC eras to the emerging era of ubiquitous computing. The empirical studies presented here show the need for designers, users, and the media to be aware that CM rhetoric can propose grand visions that never become part of a reality and reinforce the need for critical and scholarly review of promising new technologies.

608 pp/hardbound/ISBN 978-1-57387-311-6 $59.50

Making Search Work

Implementing Web, Intranet and Enterprise Search

By Martin White

This important book is designed to help organizations understand, evaluate, and implement desktop, Web site, intranet, and enterprise search applications. Martin White explains search technology in clear, nontechnical language and describes the benefits and issues for a range of solutions—from high-end to affordable plug-and-play software products. In addition to providing critical guidance, the book features a glossary, suggestions for further reading, and an annotated listing of firms providing Web, intranet, and enterprise search solutions.

200 pp/hardbound/ISBN 978-1-57387-305-5 $69.50

Laughing at the CIO

A Parable and Prescription for IT Leadership

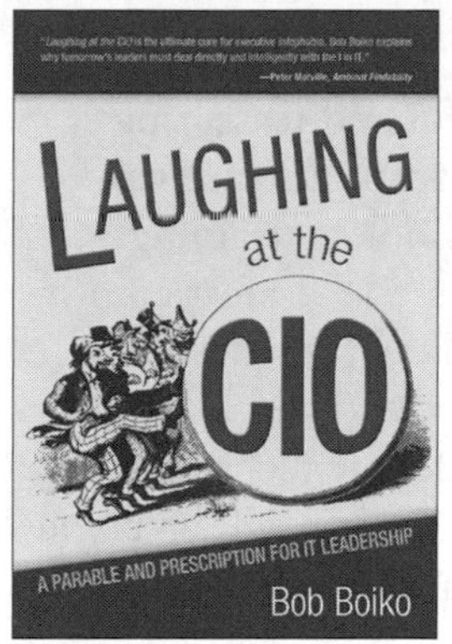

By Bob Boiko

Here is a prescription for IT executives and professionals who are sick of suffering through a never-ending stream of technology "solutions" that never really solve anything. Through his modern-day fable of information technology gone awry, Bob Boiko shows execs and tech staff alike how to harness the "I" in "IT" to become leaders by making measurable movement toward strategic goals. Boiko's business parable leads to a set of concrete methods you can use to create IT strategy and action in your organization. Whether or not you are a CIO, if you recognize the power of information and have the desire to be an information leader, this book and Web-based ebook will show you the way.

224 pp/softbound/ISBN 978-0-910965-78-1 $29.95

The Librarian's Internet Survival Guide, 2nd Edition

Strategies for the High-Tech Reference Desk

By Irene E. McDermott
Edited by Barbara Quint

In this updated and expanded second edition of her popular guidebook, *Searcher* columnist Irene McDermott once again exhorts her fellow reference librarians to don their pith helmets and follow her fearlessly into the Web jungle. She presents new and improved troubleshooting tips and advice, Web resources for answering reference questions, and strategies for managing information and keeping current. In addition to helping librarians make the most of Web tools and resources, the book offers practical advice on privacy and child safety, assisting patrons with special needs, Internet training, building library Web pages, and more.

328 pp/softbound/ISBN 978-1-57387-235-5 $29.50

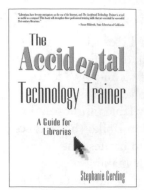

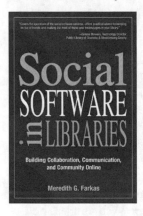